RACING POST
ANNUAL 2014

Racing Post One Canada Square, London E14 5AP.
020 7293 2001

Irish Racing Post Suite 413,
The Capel Building, Mary's Abbey,
Dublin 7. 01 872 7250

Editor Nick Pulford

Art editor David Dew

Cover design Jay Vincent

Chief photographers Edward Whitaker,
Patrick McCann

Other photography Caroline Norris, Martin Lynch,
Getty, Mark Cranham, John Grossick

Picture editor David Cramphorn

Graphics Samantha Creedon, David Cramphorn

Picture artworking Stefan Searle, Nigel Jones

Illustrator Samantha Creedon

Feature writers Scott Burton, Graham Dench,
Steve Dennis, Alastair Down, Nicholas Godfrey, David
Jennings, Tom Kerr, Jessica Lamb, Rodney Masters, Lee
Mottershead, Jonathan Mullin, Lewis Porteous, John
Randall, Stuart Riley, Peter Scargill, Mark Storey, Peter
Thomas

Advertisement Sales

Racing Post: One Canada Square, London
E14 5AP. 0208 263 0226

Cheryl Gunn, cheryl.gunn@racingpost.com

Archant Dialogue Prospect House, Rouen Road,
Norwich, NR1 1RE. 01603 772554

Andy Grant, andy.grant@archantdialogue.co.uk

Kay Brown, kay.brown@archantdialogue.co.uk

Dean Brown, dean.brown@archantdialogue.co.uk

Distribution/availability 01933 304858

help@racingpost.com

Published by Racing Post Books in 2013
Axis House, Compton, Newbury, Berkshire, RG20
6NL. Copyright © Racing Post 2013

A catalogue record for this book is available from the
British Library.

ISBN 978-1-908216-88-5 [UK]

ISBN 978-1-909471-00-9 [Ireland]

Printed in Great Britain by Buxton Press

Every effort has been made to fulfil requirements with
regard to copyright material. The author and publisher
will be glad to rectify any omissions at the earliest
opportunity.

www.racingpost.com/shop

The best a worst of ti

FRANKEL was gone, never to be forgotten, but 2013 had virtually everything else a racing fan could wish for, and we hope the Racing Post Annual 2014 captures the spirit of a remarkable year.

After Frankel's departure, everybody looked towards Sprinter Sacre as the next big thing and he didn't disappoint. He was the first since Istabraq to win at all three major spring jumping festivals and his status as the new 'people's horse' was confirmed by a triumphant end-of-season appearance at Punchestown.

Stars lit up the entire jump racing season. Hurricane Fly and Quevega, the king and queen of Irish hurdling, had landmark victories at the Cheltenham Festival, Bobs Worth was dogged and determined in a vintage Cheltenham Gold Cup and the crop of novice hurdlers was perhaps the best ever.

When winter turned to summer, the racing was as glorious as the weather. Royal Ascot, as ever, set the tone and Gold Cup day was one of the most memorable racing occasions in many years as the Queen and Lady Cecil enjoyed spine-tingling triumphs.

Some of the best performers were predictable at the start of the season. But many others were not, and the discovery of new stars made for an exciting Flat season.

Ruler Of The World was the first Derby winner in 20 years to have been unraced as a juvenile, Al Kazeem came back from serious injury to score a Group 1 hat-trick in six weeks, Novellist arrived from Germany and left with the King George, Lethal Force made enormous strides in pre-season and on the racecourse, while along came Treve to top them all with her stunning Arc triumph.

The year held great sadness too. The death of Sir Henry Cecil, Frankel's trainer, had long been dreaded but was no less numbing when it came, and the outpouring of emotion showed the racing community at its best. So, too, did the response to the profoundly shocking fate of JT McNamara when he fell at Cheltenham in March.

But racing was scarred by scandal, too, most shamefully by the revelation that 22 Godolphin horses had been given steroids by trainer Mahmood Al Zarooni. It was a doping case with far-reaching implications and the fallout did not clear all year.

With so many negative headlines, perhaps the best result of the year was that all the runners in the Grand National came home safe and sound. Racing needed some good news and Auroras Encore – with his debutant jockey, husband-and-wife training team, big odds and lucky owners – had all the ingredients of an old-fashioned National tale.

In the end, for many racing fans, the good will have outweighed the bad.

Nick Pulford
Editor

BIG STORIES

5   **Sprinter Sacre** Jump racing's hottest property wows Cheltenham, Aintree and Punchestown

10   **Perfect day** Gold Cup day at Royal Ascot produces the most highly charged atmosphere of the year

20   **Treve** Criquette Head-Maarek's wonder filly has the world at her feet after her brilliant Arc triumph

28   **Frankie Dettori** Comeback year ends in agony as broken ankle denies him Arc glory on Treve

40   **Novellist** Andreas Wohler's colt produces another stunning German triumph in the King George

42   **Al Kazeem** The middle-distance star of early summer makes a remarkable comeback from serious injury

46   **Champions Day** Farhh takes top honours with a thrilling and hard-fought victory in the Champion Stakes

50   **Toronado v Dawn Approach** Europe's top milers go head to head in three thrilling contests

Bobs Worth
Page 66

52   **Willie Mullins** The record-breaking trainer conquers Ireland, Cheltenham and even Japan

56   **Hurricane Fly** Back to his best to regain the Champion Hurdle crown and complete a perfect season

61   **The Young Ones** Our Conor shines in a novice hurdle crop of enormous potential

66   **Bobs Worth** Another star for Nicky Henderson as he takes the Cheltenham Gold Cup

74   **Scandal** Racing finds itself mired in negative publicity with a series of shocking cases

76   **Godolphin** The Mahmood Al Zarooni doping case sends shockwaves through the sport

Solwhit
Page 128

88   **Ruler Of The World** In the space of two months the Ballydoyle colt goes from unraced to Derby winner

94   **Grey wonders** Greys enjoy a spectacular year with big-race victories from Cheltenham to Royal Ascot

96   **Lethal Force** The European sprint scene is set alight by Clive Cox's front-running grey

102   **Moonlight Cloud** The darling of Deauville completes a remarkable Group 1 double

106   **Black Caviar** The great Australian mare is as dominant as ever on her brief return to the track

108   **Johnny Murtagh** The trainer and jockey enjoys a glorious year in his dual role

114   **Grand National** Hard work and several twists of fate combine to produce a deserved win for Auroras Encore

120   **The other Nationals** Grand designs for the winners of the Welsh, Scottish and Irish versions

124   **Bryan Cooper** Ireland's rising star comes of age with a string of big-race successes

126   **Davy Russell** Two-time Irish champion jump jockey is not going to give up his title easily

128   **Solwhit** The rebranded hurdler steps into the hole left by Big Buck's to take two major staying prizes

132   **JT McNamara** The amateur rider's catastrophic fall casts a shadow over the entire year

136   **Richard Hughes** The British champion finally wins his first British Classic . . . and then his second

140   **Sir Henry Cecil** Genius remembered in excerpts from the Racing Post's special tribute edition

150   **Arab racing** Growing branch of the sport takes a more prominent role

154   **The Annual 20** Our pick of the people and horses to watch in 2014

FINAL FURLONG

166 **Joseph O'Brien and Patrick Mullins**
Prodigious sons set new records

167 **Lucy Alexander** Britain's champion
conditional takes her place in history

168 **The Annual Awards** Our choice of
the best of the year – plus the alternative
awards

170 **Numbers crunched** A different view of
the 'recalibration' of past greats

172 **Steve Drowne** Nunthorpe victory marks a
dream comeback from his nightmare

174 **Busted Tycoon** Tony Martin's remarkable
filly scores a historic hat-trick at Galway

176 **Martin Dwyer** Jockey achieves landmark
victory in battle over Indian ban

180 **A-Z of the year**

182 **Soul Magic** Cartmel course specialist
claims track record

184 **Jane Mangan** Unlucky Cheltenham loser
bounces back with Grade 1 win

STATISTICS

188 **Flat statistics** The top performers of 2013

200 **Jumps statistics** The champions of the
2012-13 season

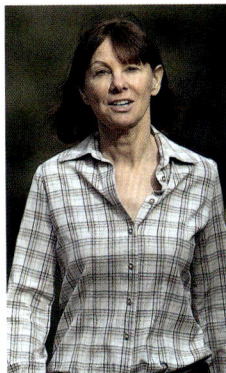

Lady Cecil
Page 10

Ryan Mania
Page 114

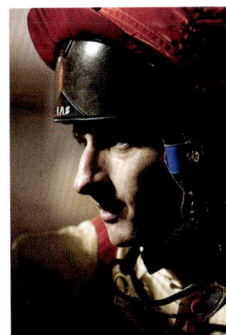

Adam Kirby
Page 96

Lethal Force
Page 96

'He's like Pele, who used to do it all so easily because his speed and power and skill gave him the time to do it. Sprinter Sacre has all the time in the world and he has such grace too'

Barry Geraghty Page 5

'I thought, "Bloody hell, I'm at Becher's second time and I'm still travelling. Oh God, I never really planned for this." I couldn't believe my luck'

Ryan Mania Page 114

'My sister Sally said to me: "So dreams really do come true." I couldn't stop smiling. It was just a perfect day, although it felt a bit unreal'

Lady Cecil Page 10

'In the string you'd never know he's there. He's much the same in a race, buried in the mid-division just mooching along and then, all of a sudden two fences from home, up he pops. He's the most remarkable horse'

Nicky Henderson Page 66

'I thought, "If he's ever going to get beat, this will be it." But he found another gear and went again. That's why he's special; he doesn't just pick up once, he picks up twice'

Adam Kirby Page 96

'At the start of the year so many people were telling me that I couldn't be a trainer and be a jockey, that it wasn't possible. Those people who were saying it, maybe they couldn't do it – but I can'

Johnny Murtagh Page 108

4 WAYS TO SAVE*

Receive a £40 Gift Voucher
When you Buy £400

Receive a £30 Gift Voucher
When you Buy £300

Receive a £20 Gift Voucher
When you Buy £200

Receive a £10 Gift Voucher
When you Buy £100

* While Vouchers Last

TOGGI · **HORSEWARE** · **L/G** · **176** · **MUSTO**

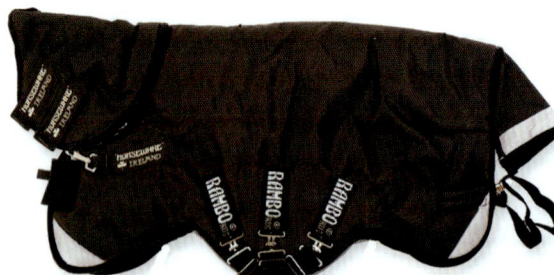

SUPERSTAR

Sprinter Sacre was expected to go to the top in the 2012-13 season.
How he got there, impeccably guided by Nicky Henderson, was spectacular

By Graham Dench

IF Nicky Henderson put a single foot wrong as he charted Sprinter Sacre's course from outstanding novice to chasing superstar, then most of us missed it. Every target was met, even when the weather did its best to intervene, in a season that put Sprinter Sacre in a class of his own. By the end Henderson knew he wasn't just training the best horse of his 35-year career. This was a phenomenon.

A flawless display in the Queen Mother Champion Chase was followed by a superb defeat of Cue Card and Flemenstar over uncharted territory in Aintree's Melling Chase and a bold trip to Punchestown for the Champion Chase, where he became the first horse since Istabraq in 1999 to win at all three major spring jumping festivals. Excitement was at fever pitch by the time he went to Punchestown, where he drew a record first-day crowd, and throughout the season British and Irish racegoers alike revelled in his rare brilliance.

If that final success, which took Sprinter Sacre's unbeaten run over fences to ten races, was less spectacular than the others it is no wonder, for three festivals in six weeks would tax even the strongest of constitutions, and the rain-softened ground was never going to show such an exuberant and spring-heeled chaser to best advantage.

Conventional handicapping methods suggest he was probably 10lb or more below his brilliant best that day, but it did not matter in the slightest. Punchestown was all about showing Irish racegoers first hand what all the fuss was about and he had already done enough at Cheltenham and Aintree to see his Racing Post Rating elevated to a giddy 190 – just 1lb short of the best ever registered, by Kauto Star in the 2009 King George – and to 188 by the BHA, again second only to Kauto Star.

Henderson insists training horses as talented as Sprinter Sacre is "quite straightforward really. The good horses train themselves, as you know where they are going

»Continues page 6

and they are so naturally talented." The campaign went like clockwork, he says, although Aintree and Punchestown were a step or two further than he ever expected to go.

"I think we quite rightly treated the Queen Mother Champion Chase at Cheltenham as his principal target and on that day he was 100 per cent. We then asked him only three weeks later to go and do it again at Aintree, and just over two weeks after that at Punchestown, and you cannot expect a horse to be 100 per cent for three Grade 1 races in six weeks.

"He was probably only 90-something per cent at Aintree, and a bit less than that at Punchestown, where the ground didn't help. I know he gets easy races, but those festival races take it out of them, and especially him, because he puts so much into it and he's such a show-off. Although it looks as if he's getting easy races, the tension, the pressure and the atmosphere all have an effect."

◆◆◆◆

SPRINTER SACRE had just two races on the way to Cheltenham and won them both in such devastating fashion that few could countenance defeat in the Queen Mother. In Sandown's Tingle Creek Chase there was just a chance he might be unsettled by being taken on at his own game by Sanctuaire, but he sauntered clear under Barry Geraghty to win as he liked by

THE SPECIAL ONE
WHAT THEY SAY

Rivals, fans and handicappers were united in awe of Sprinter Sacre

"Sprinter Sacre is some horse. It was worth taking a shot at him to find out how good he is, and it just shows you he is a proper horse" *Sizing Europe's jockey Andrew Lynch at Cheltenham*

"What a horse. Three out it looked like it might be a race. Then it was over. Sizing Europe is no muppet and he was dismissed in a canter" *Racing Post reader Gary McKenzie after Cheltenham*

"He's the best I've seen and I don't think I'd be in a hurry to take him on again. Once a year is enough" *Cue Card's trainer Colin Tizzard at Aintree*

"It was exceptionally impressive because it was an end-of-season run and he still had the gears to pull away in the end. I came here especially to see him and I'm glad I did" *Punchestown racegoer Seamus Brophy*

"He was the highest-rated novice last year on 169, a record, and is now the highest-rated chaser at two miles in the history of the classifications. He is only seven and how good can he be?" *BHA handicapper John de Moraville*

15 lengths from Kumbeshwar, prompting Nick Luck on Racing UK to wonder "what kind of ridiculous, unthinkable monster is this?"

Henderson had been "petrified" of Sanctuaire but any worries proved unfounded, even on ground that did not have 'good' in the description for the first time in Sprinter Sacre's chasing career.

"He has so much pace and is such a good jumper that my only concern at the start of the season was how he would handle really soft or heavy ground," Geraghty recalls. "It was soft enough in the Tingle Creek, but he coped well apart from getting in a bit tight at the first down the back."

The ground was the worst he had encountered next time in a postponed Victor Chandler Chase, run at Cheltenham after Ascot was frozen off, but he had coped with only slightly better ground in a stronger race at Sandown and Geraghty no longer had any worries. Sprinter Sacre won easily again, this time by 14 lengths from Mad Moose.

Henderson was grateful everybody had pulled together to stage the race, not least because the timing – six and a half weeks before Cheltenham – allowed him to "switch the engine off the aeroplane for a week". That short break may well have been crucial not just in getting Sprinter Sacre to an absolute peak for his return to Cheltenham for the Queen Mother, but ultimately in keeping

him going through an extended spring campaign.

In his first two races of the season Sprinter Sacre had achieved a new career-best RPR of 178, but the likes of Kumbeshwar, Mad Moose and Sanctuaire were never going to push him to the levels of the other recent greats of two-mile chasing – Moscow Flyer, also Geraghty's ride, Well Chief, Azertyuiop and of course Master Minded.

Master Minded set a new gold standard in the category as a mere five-year-old in the 2008 Queen Mother with what was then an almost unthinkable RPR of 186, when he had former Queen Mother and Arkle winner Voy Por Ustedes, plus good yardstick Fair Along, to push him to new heights in a display that had to be seen to be believed.

Although Sprinter Sacre's opponents in the Queen Mother did not include the previous year's winner Finian's Rainbow, who was missing on account of the ground, or old novice rival Cue Card, who was sent instead for the Ryanair, he too had a Queen Mother and Arkle winner to beat in Sizing Europe, plus another good yardstick in Wishfull Thinking.

Sent off at 1-4 and trained to the minute, he moved upsides Sizing Europe at the third-last and then eased away in a manner that betrayed the high quality of the opposition. The winning margin was identical to that by which Master Minded had

scored five years earlier, but it could have been extended considerably as Sprinter Sacre barely came off the bridle in a sensational display.

"It's easy to say now, but I never had any worries," Geraghty says. "Sizing Europe was no back number, but we just needed a clear round and in a race run at a good gallop he was faultless and coasted in. He's like Pele, who used to do it all so easily because his speed and power and skill gave him the time to do it. Sprinter Sacre has all the time in the world, and he has such grace too."

Cheltenham brought a quantum leap in his RPR to 190, 4lb ahead of Master Minded's peak performance and a stone better than he had started the season. Just as significantly, the racing public wanted to see more and the wider media picked up on the fact that Sprinter Sacre was something out of the ordinary. Suddenly there was heightened interest in Henderson's next move.

◆◆◆◆

AINTREE was not initially on the agenda after Cheltenham, and when asked after the Queen Mother about the two and a half miles of the Melling, and the three miles of Kempton's King George, Henderson's immediate response was to say: "I'm sure he'll get further, but would you ever dare ask him?"

However, reflecting at the end of
▸ **Continues page 8**

▸ Approaching the home straight at Punchestown (right) and (above, from left) taking the final fence in the Champion Chase, the centre of attention at Punchestown and leaving the parade ring at Aintree

HIGHLY RATED
THE RPR VIEW

Sprinter Sacre recorded a Racing Post Rating of 190 twice in the 2012-13 season, at the Cheltenham and Aintree festivals. He is the best two-mile and two-and-a-half-mile chaser since Racing Post Ratings began and is a close second to Kauto Star in the overall list of RPRs over jumps

Kauto Star 191

Sprinter Sacre 190

Desert Orchid 189

Carvill's Hill 187

Master Minded 186

Denman 184

Moscow Flyer 182

Imperial Commander 182

Istabraq 181

Long Run 181

Bobs Worth 181

the season on the change of heart, he said: "At the start of the season we weren't necessarily going to try him at two and a half miles, but if you don't try different things you are stuck in a groove, albeit a pretty good groove."

Henderson's initial caution was in contrast to Geraghty's growing confidence in Sprinter Sacre. The trainer evidently had sleepless nights worrying about the longer trip at Aintree before finally receiving reassurance when his stable jockey returned from a short break in Tenerife. "I just told him he should have called me sooner as it wouldn't be a problem," Geraghty says. "I knew he'd get it, as two miles on that bad ground in the Victor Chandler was probably a tougher test than two and a half around Aintree on good ground."

Cue Card, who Sprinter Sacre had not met since beating him in the Arkle, and Flemenstar, who had notched seven straight wins before suffering two three-mile defeats, threatened to give Sprinter Sacre more problems at Aintree than Sizing Europe had at Cheltenham. Whereas Sizing Europe was now 11 and two years past his peak on Racing Post Ratings, Cue Card was from the same generation as Sprinter Sacre and Flemenstar only a year older. What's more, Cue Card was

THE PERFECT TEN
THE FACTS AND FIGURES

Sprinter Sacre had a perfect season in 2012-13, adding to his remarkable figures as he stretched his unbeaten run over fences to ten

Age 7

Born April 23, 2006

Height 17 hands 1½ inches

Weight 540kg

Trainer Nicky Henderson

Jockey Barry Geraghty

Owner Caroline Mould

Cost Bought in a batch of 21 horses for £260,000 (£12,381 per horse)

Total prize-money £724,886

Chase wins Ten out of ten

Grade 1 wins 7

Average winning distance over fences 12.4 lengths

Longest winning odds over fences 11-10

Shortest winning odds over fences 1-9

Profit to a £1 stake on all ten chase wins £3.84

Official rating 188

Racing Post Rating 190

coming off a career-best win in the Ryanair and Flemenstar had recorded his best RPR the last time he had run over the Melling distance.

The winning margin at Aintree was much reduced from Cheltenham, but Sprinter Sacre coasted home from Cue Card without being remotely extended, despite Geraghty finding it harder to let his jumping flow at the steadier pace. Cue Card was beaten four and a half lengths, with Flemenstar another 19 lengths behind in third. One by one, allcomers were being beaten.

Taking in the Melling Chase as an unscheduled 'extra' might have put the trip to Punchestown in jeopardy, but Geraghty says he conserved Sprinter Sacre at Aintree, rather than "let rip", and so long as the signs were good at home – and here the counsel of work rider Nico de Boinville was crucial – Henderson was always keen to show him off to jumps fans in Ireland. "This fellow loves what he's doing and I'm conscious he's something to be enjoyed," Henderson said at Aintree. "I'm the custodian, and lucky to be the custodian of a spectacular horse. I must try to bring him back to the racecourse as often as I can."

Punchestown would show just how much the racing public appreciated Henderson's response

to their wish for more. "I've never seen a crowd like it," Geraghty says. "Unlike the crowds at Cheltenham or Aintree, nearly everyone was there to see one horse." The jockey relished the occasion in his homeland, although he was conscious that the hectic schedule rendered Sprinter Sacre more vulnerable than odds of 1-9 might imply. "The ground from the winning post to five out was fine and he jumped beautifully, but going to four out we hit really heavy ground and had to work harder. He didn't have the reserves to boss the race like he had in the earlier ones, but he still showed real quality and was brave at the last."

◆◆◆◆

LOOKING ahead, Henderson does not think there is any question of stepping Sprinter Sacre up to three miles. "There's no need to, and I don't think he'd get it," he says. "If you've got that much natural speed it would be madness to risk breaking it." Geraghty's view is that it "might be considered in time, when he is more laid back, but not yet".

Sprinter Sacre will be only eight in 2014 and it is quite conceivable there is even better to come. It is hard to imagine a scenario that might push him to a higher RPR, which would put him level with Kauto Star or even take him to a

▶▶(From left) Nico de Boinville leads Sprinter Sacre from the covered gallop during a snowstorm at Seven Barrows in January, Nicky Henderson shows off his pride and joy during an open morning in February, Barry Geraghty celebrates Cheltenham victory, flying towards home at Aintree and (below) in the winner's enclosure at Punchestown with Henderson, Geraghty and Corky Browne, the trainer's long-serving right-hand man

new high, but Geraghty comes up with two.

"He broke Barnbrook Again's course record at Newbury on only his third start over fences, winning the Game Spirit by six lengths pulling up," he says. "That was a hell of a performance at such an early stage and, with a better winter and a good spring, who knows? Then there's Simonsig. He wasn't at his best in the Arkle, but in the Wayward Lad he was top drawer and there's not an awful lot between them at home. Fortunately, or perhaps unfortunately, Simonsig is probably the main threat to Sprinter Sacre, and if they were ever to meet I'd face a massive dilemma."

That might be Geraghty's worst nightmare, but what a prospect for the rest of us.

UP CLOSE AND PERSONAL
WHAT HE'S LIKE AT HOME

Nicky Henderson describes Sprinter Sacre as "the perfect article to look at" and adds: "This is one of those rare occasions when the best-looking horse is actually the best horse." But what is he like at home?

"He's a grumpy old sod in his box and puts his ears back and growls at you, but that's the only bad thing I could say about him," Henderson says. "He's a funny old horse. He lives at the far end of one of the barns and if you took your biggest owner round and showed him where you had put him he wouldn't be very impressed, but when we tried him in the front yard he just didn't like it. He likes his corner up there and that's him."

Corky Browne, the trainer's long-serving right-hand man, reckons it was just too busy for him in the main yard. "He was too inquisitive and didn't want to miss anything. He was always on the go, rushing about, and he wouldn't settle, and so we decided to try him up in the barn and he's been there almost ever since. We did try him again in the yard last season, but not for long. He didn't like it."

Browne admits Sprinter Sacre is "a character, no doubt about that" but insists there is no malice in him. "He doesn't enjoy being groomed and you have to watch him

or he'll have a good bite at you, or try to kick you, but it's playful."

While Sarwar Mohammed takes care of Sprinter Sacre on the ground, it is Nico de Boinville, the successful amateur turned conditional, who enjoys the privilege of riding him almost every morning.

De Boinville also partners King George and Gold Cup winner Long Run at home and says: "They are two smashing horses – both really big and with so much presence. Sprinter Sacre is everything a good horse should be, very professional in his attitude and the way he goes about his work. He answers every question that could be asked of him. He's quite fantastic.

"He's always been a big, scopey horse – much more in the shape of a chaser than a hurdler – and you know you are on a big horse when you ride him as he's big up front and big behind."

De Boinville, who has ridden Sprinter Sacre since the day he arrived, adds: "He's a very easy ride really, but you always know there's a lot of horse there. I school him when Barry's not about and he's very impressive.

"I've been with him all of the way and I don't think we've ever had a worry with him."

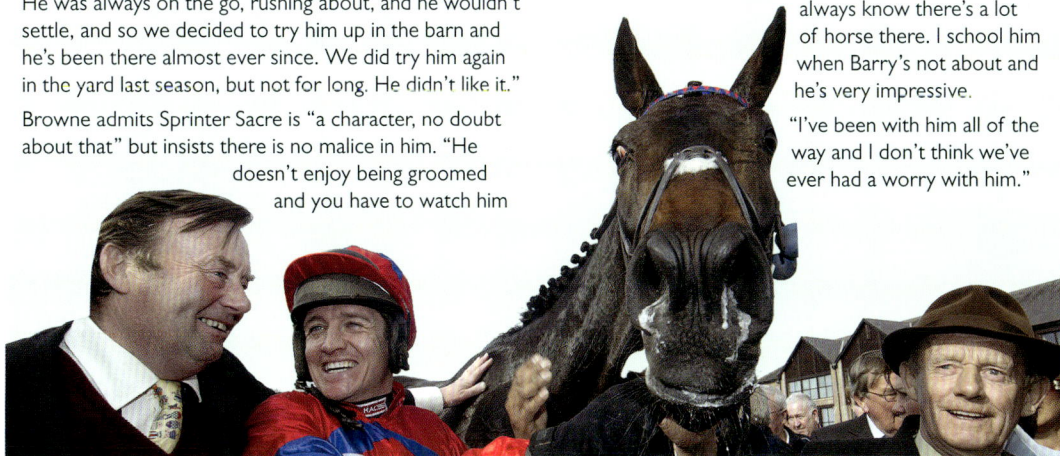

PERFECT DAY

Gold Cup day at Royal Ascot produced the most highly charged atmosphere of the year as the crowd willed the Queen and Lady Cecil to emotional and unforgettable victories

▶▶Golden moment: the Queen, flanked by Sir Michael Stoute and jockey Ryan Moore, after Estimate had made her the first reigning monarch to win the Gold Cup

By Steve Dennis

THURSDAY JUNE 20 was not the longest day of the year – that was the following day – but it managed to pack in more action, emotion and celebration than any other in 2013. When the sun rose over Newmarket, over London, over Ascot, it dawned on a day rich with possibilities and by the time it sank below the horizon in the west those possibilities had been exhausted in the most delightful and rewarding fashion.

On one side of Newmarket, a subdued Warren Place was beginning the usual daily duties. If Warren Place was subdued, then so, to a slightly lesser extent, was the racing fraternity after the death, just nine days earlier, of the great trainer Sir Henry Cecil, whose battle with cancer had been fought so nobly yet so heartbreakingly in vain.

The obituaries had been read through a veil of tears, the old stories recounted with a catch in the throat, yet in a racing yard life must go on even when death intrudes and Cecil's widow Lady Jane was determined that business would continue as usual.

"I don't really know how to describe it," she says, the clarity she seeks undefined by the passing of time, even from the vantage point of autumn. "It was so important to the staff that we carried on all the good work that had been done. I would go out on the gallops for first lot and that was for my own benefit, to keep up the routine so there was less time to think about what had happened.

"Henry always so looked forward to Royal Ascot, he loved those five days, and he knew we had a very promising team of horses this year. He thought he'd be there as usual, we thought he'd be there as usual. But it didn't happen as

we thought it would. My main thought was simply to get through the week as best I could, to try to have a winner for Henry."

On the other side of Newmarket, along the Bury Road, a bay filly named Estimate stood in her box at Sir Michael Stoute's yard. In a few minutes a horsebox would pull out of the yard and begin the journey to Ascot, and Estimate would be standing in the back as mile by mile her destiny drew nearer.

The Queen, Estimate's owner, may well have been up and about at the same time as her horse, poring over the Racing Post as usual as the breakfast things were laid out. But perhaps, instead, she was still asleep – and what do monarchs dream of? They dream of the same things as their subjects. The Queen had a horse running that afternoon, in the Gold Cup no less; of course she dreamed that it might win.

▶▶Continues page 12

At midday, this day of days half gone already, Estimate was standing in the racecourse stables at Ascot. A few boxes away was another filly, a three-year-old named Riposte who was ready to represent Lady Cecil in the Group 2 Ribblesdale Stakes, the race before the Gold Cup. The Ribblesdale – although not as historic a contest as the Gold Cup – is one of the royal meeting's more traditional races, having first been run in 1919. Cecil himself had won the race five times, most recently with Yashmak, who carried the same pink, green and white silks of Prince Khalid Abdullah that would shortly be borne along by Riposte.

"Riposte is a sweet filly – well, she looks sweet, but she can certainly have her moments – and she'd been working really well," Cecil says. "We were optimistic but we'd had a couple of disappointments earlier that week. Tiger Cliff ran a great race to be second in the Ascot Stakes and I was thrilled, but it was a case of so near yet so far, and Chigun hadn't liked the ground the previous day, so I didn't dare to dream that Riposte might win."

The Queen had still to arrive at Ascot, her time-honoured daily procession down the straight mile in the royal carriages yet to begin. One of the last of the traditional owner-breeders, she was coming to Ascot to watch a horse whose genetics had little to do with the normal output of the royal breeding operation.

Estimate is a product of a gift horse, a gift made by the Aga Khan to the Queen on the occasion of her 80th birthday seven years earlier. In an interview with Greg Wood in The Guardian on the day of the Gold Cup, the Queen's racing manager John Warren outlined the nature of the gift that has kept on giving.

"This has been quite a journey," he said. "It started when the Aga Khan, for the Queen's 80th birthday present, very kindly suggested that she might like to use a couple of his mares. The mating was designed and the filly was born. You could never design a mating around a Gold Cup. It's fair to say the mare [Estimate's dam, Ebaziya] had produced a Gold Cup winner [Enzeli] but then she had also produced a Group 1-winning two-year-old [Edabiya]."

When the Queen chose Monsun as a mate for Ebaziya, she would have envisaged a middle-distance horse as a result, perhaps a Derby or an Oaks prospect. What she got was a filly with boundless stamina. The Queen had never won the Gold Cup, the most royal of races at this most royal of meetings.

In fact, no reigning monarch had won the race in its 207-year history. Estimate was the favourite, with the evidence available to both heart and head making her the market choice. She stood in her box in the racecourse stables as her owner made her way down the racecourse, and waited for her moment.

◆◆◆◆

THE DAY started in spectacular style, almost as soon as the Queen had climbed down from her carriage and taken her place in the royal box. The first race on the card was the Group 2 Norfolk Stakes and that went to the
▸▸Continues page 14

▸▸ The royal box (top) and happy scenes in the winner's enclosure after Estimate's neck victory over Simenon

COUNTDOWN TO HISTORY

How Gold Cup day unfolded with a series of firsts

2.00 The Queen, wearing purple and accompanied by Prince Andrew, her grandson Peter Phillips and Peter's wife Autumn, leads the traditional procession

2.33 No Nay Never blasts down the track in the Norfolk to set a five-furlong juvenile course record

3.08 Riposte wins the Ribblesdale for Lady Cecil, nine days after the death of her husband Sir Henry

3.50 Estimate lands the Gold Cup, making the Queen the first reigning monarch to win the race

4.27 The Britannia goes to Roca Tumu, the first Royal Ascot winner for trainer Joanna Morgan and jockey Billy Lee

5.03 The John Gosden-trained Remote wins the Tercentenary in the Riposte colours of Khalid Abdullah

5.38 Martin Harley rides his first Royal Ascot winner on Elidor in the King George V Handicap

ROYAL LANDMARKS

Estimate's Gold Cup was the pinnacle for the Queen in her long and successful association with Royal Ascot

Estimate became her 22nd winner at Royal Ascot and was the first of them to win twice at the meeting, following victory in the 2012 Queen's Vase

In 1953, Coronation year, she celebrated her first winner at the meeting when Choir Boy won the Royal Hunt Cup

Above Suspicion's win in the 1959 St James's Palace Stakes was her first in one of the races that now carry Group 1 status. Her second was Aiming High in the 1961 Coronation Stakes and her third was Estimate

Estimate was her first Group 1 winner in Europe since Dunfermline added the St Leger to Oaks victory in 1977, Silver Jubilee year

And Estimate was her first Group/Grade 1 winner anywhere since Unknown Quantity in the Arlington Handicap in Chicago in 1989

Wesley Ward-trained No Nay Never, ridden by Joel Rosario, who produced an electrifying display of brute speed to lead early, lead late and set a new two-year-old course record into the bargain.

The big, bonny American colt – who would go on to embellish the form by winning the Group 1 Prix Morny at Deauville in August – gave the vast ladies' day crowd an instant lift. There was a potent buzz about the draughty Ascot grandstand that accelerated as the fillies for the Ribblesdale began to circle the parade ring, with Lady Cecil standing on the greensward observing Riposte from beneath the brim of an elegant black hat.

There couldn't have been a man or woman within the bounds of the racecourse – save maybe a few of the hardiest 'hoorays' in the darkest recesses of the royal enclosure – who was not praying for a victory for Riposte in tribute to her great former trainer. Few men attain the widespread popularity and devotion that the whole spectrum of racegoers accorded Cecil; any of those who backed any of the other eight runners would certainly have accepted defeat at the hands of Riposte with a smile and an internal word of thanks that the racing gods had been so just.

And today, this day of all days, the racing gods were sticking to the script. When Riposte ranged up under faithful Tom Queally to challenge early in the straight, a wail, a wall of sound, went up from the enclosures. In a famous commentary it was said that the crowd at Aintree were willing Red Rum home; in similar vein, Riposte rolled to the line on a great tide of rapture. It was one for Henry, dear old Henry.

"She was slow to break, and I just sighed," Lady Cecil says. "I thought 'oh God, here we go again'. When she began to make her challenge she looked good but I didn't allow myself to imagine that she might win. Yet she was travelling so well . . . and then it got a bit scary because it was clear it was going to happen."

Riposte drew away to win by two and a quarter lengths. And then there were tears rolling down cheeks to meet the corners of smiles coming up. For Lady Cecil the day became a blur, a whirl of emotion that she cannot describe with any clarity. She was there but she was somewhere else as well, ably going through the motions of interviews and presentations on autopilot.

"I shy away from cameras, microphones, journalists anyway," she says. "Then suddenly Clare Balding just appeared and everything was a

complete blur. I can't remember what she said, I can't remember what I said. My children recorded it for me but I've never watched it.

"I do remember saying that the victory was for Henry, the Prince and all the staff, but that's all I can recall of what was said. The atmosphere of the day, though, I remember the feel of that, it felt as though everyone was on our side, was so pleased for us. It was very emotional."

The world discreetly blew its nose, wiped its eyes, cleared its throat. As Lady Cecil received the trainer's prize for the Ribblesdale Stakes, the runners for the Gold Cup began to enter the parade ring.

◆◆◆◆

THE QUEEN stood with her racing manager John Warren and trainer Sir Michael Stoute as jockey Ryan Moore tipped his black velvet cap and the small knot of hopeful people began to talk about what was to come. The Queen had enjoyed 21 winners at Royal Ascot during 60 years of ownership, yet never before had there been a strongly fancied runner in the showpiece event. The formalities took little time, Moore was

▸▸Continues page 16

▸▸(Clockwise from top left) No Nay Never sets a juvenile course record in the Norfolk Stakes; Riposte takes the Ribblesdale Stakes under Tom Queally; emotional scenes in the winner's enclosure as Lady Cecil greets Riposte

WHAT THEY SAID

"Some of the greatest scenes ever seen in the long history of the royal meeting" *Ascot chief executive Charles Barnett*

"This win is very high on my list, because it's been done for a lady who, never mind being the Queen, loves racing and is so good for British racing" *Estimate's trainer Sir Michael Stoute*

"It's amazing. This is her passion and her life and to win the big one at Royal Ascot means so much to her. Everyone is just thrilled. It's very close to her heart and today is very special" *Peter Phillips, the Queen's grandson*

"I wasn't disappointed to be second, maybe for the first time in my life. This is a fantastic result for racing. The stands just erupted from about the furlong marker and then everyone rushed to the back of the stands to see the winner. A fantastic day and atmosphere" *Willie Mullins, trainer of Gold Cup runner-up Simenon*

"I really don't have the words for what I'm feeling but I'm sure you can imagine" *Lady Cecil*

"This is a seriously historic day in our world" *Newmarket trainer John Gosden*

مهرجان سُمُو الشيخ
منصور بن زايد آل نهيان
العالمي للخيول العربية
الأصيلة

HH Sheikh Mansoor
Bin Zayed Al Nahyan
Global Arabian Horse
Flat Racing Festival

Presents

جائزة دارلي
Darley Award

سمو الشيخة فاطمة بنت مبارك
HH Sheikha Fatima Bint Mubarak
Darley Award
HOLLYWOOD 2014

April 4 - 5 , 2014

Organised by:

ABU DHABI TOURISM & CULTURE AUTHORITY

Coordinated by:

Abu Dhabi Sports Council

In association:

ERA

IFAHR

Supported by:

General Authority of Youth & Sports Welfare

Official Carrier:

Emirates

Sponsored by:

INVEST AD
Abu Dhabi Investment Company

arabtec

TDIC

al rashid investments

SAS
Investment Co. LLC

Dr Nader Saab
SWITZERLAND

Ladies Sports Academy

EASTERN MANGROVES HOTEL & SPA, ABU DHABI

AD SPORTS

EASTERN MANGROVES SUITES, ABU DHABI

Kabale

RACING POST
Truly the Market Leaders

AL ANANI

AL WATHBA
CENTRE

ABU DHABI 2013
INTERNATIONAL HUNTING & EQUESTRIAN EXHIBITION

www.sheikhmansoorfestival.com

lifted aloft and Estimate went one way out to the racecourse and the Queen another, back to the royal box.

Racing in general and this crowd in particular had already had the result they wanted thanks to Riposte, but there was, suddenly, a terrific possibility about the day, a feeling that something truly special was on the cards. The previous year the narrow victory of Black Caviar had sent everyone into paroxysms of delight, and as Estimate broke from the stalls and Saddler's Rock led them down the straight for the first time at a dawdle the stage was set for something similar.

A couple of minutes later, as the field turned into the straight, the bell rang and the real fight began, the be-braided Moore could be seen in the ideal position just adrift of the front rank. The leaders fanned out as they faced the straight, Colour Vision on the rail, Estimate in the centre with Moore rowing away, Simenon coming fast and late down the outside with Top Trip at his heels. The noise from the stands grew into a rolling, boiling Babel of encouragement for the brown filly just nosing into the lead. Moore clamped himself aerodynamically low as Simenon threw down one last unavailing challenge and drove Estimate over the line, the winning margin a neck.

Everyone's Gold Cup runneth over. And that meant absolutely everyone, as those watching on television were shortly to discover. A camera was trained on the royal box and, as Estimate sustained her stretch drive, viewers were rewarded with the sight of a wholly animated Queen, behaving just like any other owner with a winner in the offing.

Everyone in the royal box was on their feet apart from the Queen and Warren, who was punching the air like a shadow boxer as the race played out. The Queen banged on the arms of her chair in unison with all the five-pound punters across the land, clapped her hands and wore the widest, most unguarded smile at surely any time during those past 60 years. If anyone doubted what such a victory meant to her, this footage provided the answer. She had a winner and loved every second of it.

◆◆◆◆

EMOTION lifted away from Ascot like steam, but there were no tears this time. The great feelgood double had come up and the huge crowd revelled in it. One problem immediately manifested itself: who would present the trophy to the winning owner? The Queen was down for that duty, but obviously a substitute was required, and her son

▶▶ (Clockwise from left) Roca Tumu (yellow colours with green cap) charges home in the Britannia Handicap; Remote wins the Tercentenary; Martin Harley celebrates his first Royal Ascot winner in the King George V Handicap on Elidor

Prince Andrew stepped forward to do the honours. He passed his mother a small, slender, elegant gold trophy, and anything they may have said to each other in this rare moment of public triumph was drowned out by a tidal wave of applause and cheering.

The earth exhaled. No doubt champagne sales increased. It might have been apposite to have had an hour's break so that the prevailing mood could gently return from somewhere north of cloud nine. The whole emotional rollercoaster ride had taken around 50 minutes, an hour at the outside. One hour so fierce and sweet that no-one who experienced it will ever forget.

The remaining races absorbed in comparison a quotidian hue, despite an individual newsworthiness that on another afternoon would surely have lent them a greater prominence. The Britannia Handicap was won by Roca Tumu, trained by Joanna Morgan and ridden by Billy Lee and a first winner at the royal meeting for both parties. Martin Harley also put his name on the roll of honour for the first time when victorious aboard the Mick Channon-trained Elidor in the King George V Handicap, while in between times the Riposte colours were carried to victory in the Tercentenary Stakes for the powerful John Gosden-William Buick axis.

SIX OF THE BEST

'I was there moments'

Gold Cup day at Royal Ascot It was emotional

Day one of Cheltenham Hurricane Fly and Quevega rewrite history

Sprinter Sacre winning the Champion Chase Greatness confirmed

Toronado edges Dawn Approach in the Sussex Stakes A real duel on the Downs

Treve runs away with the Arc Frankie winced; everybody else applauded

The day Sprinter Sacre wowed Punchestown Yes, him again

Yet these could only be anti-climactic when set against what had gone before on a day that vastly exceeded expectations but matched all hopes – and how rarely does that happen? The evening news bulletins and the following day's front-page stories were safely taken care of.

In recounting her memories of the afternoon, Lady Cecil more than once reaches for the phrase "it's so hard to convey what it was really like", yet in doing so illuminates the experiences of all those at Ascot and all those watching from afar.

"It was emotionally quite draining," she says. "By the time we got home and put the horses to bed I was ready for a cup of tea and an early night. While it was all happening I just went along with everything because there was no time to stand back and take it all in. It wasn't until I was in the car, on the way home, that the events of the day began to sink in.

"My sister Sally said to me, 'so dreams really do come true'. I couldn't stop smiling. It was just a perfect day, although it felt a bit unreal, as though it were happening in a dream."

Everyone who shared in the afternoon of Thursday June 20, from punters to pundits, from racegoers to armchair TV viewers, will know precisely what she is talking about.

مهرجان سُمّو الشيخ
منصور بن زايد آل نهيان
العالمي للخيول العربية
الأصيلة

HH Sheikh Mansoor
Bin Zayed Al Nahyan
Global Arabian Horse
Flat Racing Festival

Presents

المؤتمر العالمي لخيول السباق العربية
WORLD ARABIAN HORSE RACING CONFERENCE

لنـــدن 2014
LONDON

كأس الشيخ زايد بن سلطان آل نهيــان
SHEIKH ZAYED BIN SULTAN AL NAHYAN CUP

كأس سمّو الشيخة
فاطمة بنت مبارك لفرق سيدات القدرة
HH Sheikha Fatima Bint Mubarak Ladies
Endurance CEIO Cup

بطولة العالم لسمو الشيخة فاطمة بنت مبارك للسيدات (إفهار)
H.H. Sheikha Fatima Bint Mubarak Ladies World Championship (IFAHR)

May 27 to 30, 2014, St James Theatre London

May 31, 2014, HH Sheikh Zayed Bin Sultan Al Nahyan Cup &
HH Sheikha Fatima Bint Mubarak Ladies World Championship IFAHR at Newbury Racecourse

---

1st June HH Sheikha Fatima Bint Mubarak Ladies endurance CEIO Cup 2 ** at Newbury Racecourse

---

Organised by:

هيئة أبوظبي للسياحة والثقافة
ABU DHABI TOURISM & CULTURE AUTHORITY

Coordinated by:

مجلس ابو ظبي الرياضي
Abu Dhabi Sports Council

In association:

ERA

IFAHR
ifahr.net

Supported by:

الهيئة العامة لرعاية الشباب والرياضة
General Authority of Youth & Sports Welfare

Official Carrier:

Emirates

Sponsored by:

INVEST AD
شركة أبوظبي للاستثمار
Abu Dhabi Investment Company

arabtec

شركة التطوير والاستثمار السياحي
TDIC

al rashid investments
الراشد للاستثمار

SAS
Investment Co LLC
شركة أس أي أس للاستثمار

N S
Dr Nader Saab
SWITZERLAND

أكاديمية الرياضة النسائية
LADIES SPORTS ACADEMY

فندق وسبا القرم الشرقي، أبوظبي
EASTERN MANGROVES HOTEL & SPA, ABU DHABI
BY ANANTARA

الرياضية
AD SPORTS

أجنحة القرم الشرقي للفنادق، أبوظبي
EASTERN MANGROVES SUITES, ABU DHABI
BY JANNAH

Kabale

RACING POST

AL AWANI
Truly the Market Leaders

AL WATHBA
CENTRE

ABU DHABI 2013
المعرض الدولي للصيد والفروسية
INTERNATIONAL HUNTING & EQUESTRIAN EXHIBITION

---

www.sheikhmansoorfestival.com

ROYAL ASCOT
in pictures

1 Johnny Murtagh celebrates King's Stand victory on Sole Power, the first of the four winners that gave him the leading rider title for a fifth time

2 The silver ring on ladies' day

3 Well Sharp, ridden by Fran Berry and trained by Jonjo O'Neill, wins the Ascot Stakes

4 Racegoers arrive on day one

5 Runners in the Duke of Cambridge Stakes, won by Duntle (left, white cap), come over the brow of the hill

6 Seamie Heffernan and the Aidan O'Brien-trained War Command win the Coventry Stakes by six lengths

7 Extortionist, ridden by Johnny Murtagh, wins the Windsor Castle Stakes by a neck, a short head and a neck. The 16-1 shot

was a first Royal Ascot winner for first-season trainer Olly Stevens

8 Princess Eugenie (left) and Princess Beatrice arrive on day one

9 Roca Tumu (left) takes the Britannia Handicap, a first Royal Ascot winner for trainer Joanna Morgan and jockey Billy Lee

10 Racegoers study the card on ladies' day

11 Alice Clapham, travelling head groom for trainer Graham Motion, prepares to walk Animal Kingdom in the pre-parade ring before the Queen Anne Stakes

12 The Sir Michael Stoute-trained Hillstar (Ryan Moore) beats Battle Of Marengo in the King Edward VII Stakes

13 The crowds around the bandstand on day two

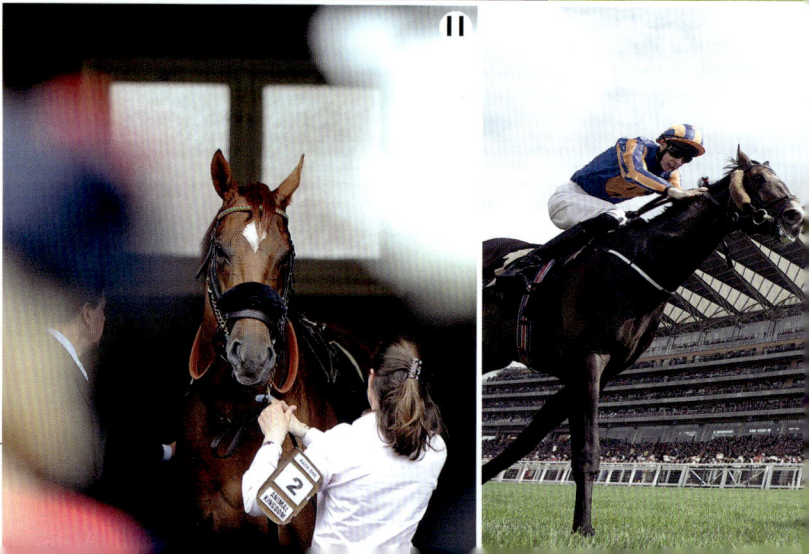

TERRIFIC TREVE

Criquette Head-Maarek's wonder filly has the world at her feet after her brilliant Arc triumph

By Scott Burton

TREVE might have ended up in any number of hands but, such was the indifference of potential owners at Arqana's exclusive August yearling sale in 2011, the Head family chose to buy back the daughter of Motivator they had bred rather than let her go for just €22,000. Nobody then thought she was a potential superstar and even Criquette Head-Maarek, stymied by a series of small setbacks with the filly early in her Classic season, wasn't exactly sure what she had on her hands. By the end of the season, however, everyone knew Treve was a rare gem.

Treve had made a fine impression when scoring on her only run at two, but she was out of sight and out of mind in the early part of 2013 as a series of niggling problems meant the main events passed by with her still in her Chantilly stable. "They were silly things," Head-Maarek recalls. "One day she had a nail in her foot and she had to be stopped. And she wouldn't come in her coat, so she wasn't ready to run. I waited and waited."

In Treve's two year-old days the trainer had told her father Alec Head, the filly's breeder, that she would be their one for the Prix de Diane, the French Oaks. By now, however, time was running short. "I wanted to run her in the Prix de Diane and I needed to have a prep race, so I decided to run her in May even though she wasn't ready. She didn't have a nice coat and she was a bit light. But from that day on, with each race, she improved physically quite a lot."

The race chosen for Treve's reappearance was a conditions event over a mile at Saint-Cloud on May 15. Just a couple of hours before she lined up under Thierry Jarnet along with four other fillies, entries for the Prix de l'Arc de Triomphe had closed. After telling her secretary to put Treve in and then take her back out several times, Head-Maarek eventually decided not to enter.

▸▸Continues page 22

Those at Saint-Cloud that afternoon, while impressed by Treve's fluent success, wouldn't necessarily have felt it was a terrible omission on the trainer's part. But a month later, when Treve routed a high-class field by four lengths to win the Prix de Diane in a clock-shattering record time, it began to look a costly error.

For the man who subsequently purchased Treve, however, the supplementary fee of €100,000 for a late entry wouldn't be a huge concern. Qatar's Sheikh Joaan Al Thani wanted to see his grey and maroon silks win the Arc, with newly appointed first jockey Frankie Dettori wearing them. Now it would be up to Head-Maarek to fulfil the sheikh's dream.

◆◆◆◆

THREE weeks before the Arc, Longchamp hosted its traditional trials card. Following a morning press conference, selected members of the fourth estate were invited to tour the

mile-and-a-half course, which would not only witness the three warm-up contests that afternoon but, of course, the main event on October 6.

Accompanying the journalists were a trio of distinguished jockeys past and present, who offered commentary on how to ride the Grande Piste and where the Arc would be won and lost. As the fleet of golf buggies headed from the top of the hill towards the finish line, the most eminent of them insisted on halting the caravan in the false straight, half a mile from the winning post.

"The false straight is a crucial part of the race and many of the English jockeys used to get over-excited here," explained Yves Saint-Martin, whose four Arc winners included arguably his country's greatest filly of the post-war era, Allez France. "The Arc can be lost here if you use up too much energy, it's still a long way to the line." One can only imagine what Saint-Martin was thinking three weeks later as Jarnet let Treve slide up the outside of the field at

▶ Treve (left) storms home along the rail to win the Arc by five lengths from Orfevre (right)

that very point, making ground rapidly on the toiling leaders.

But that was all to come. First, on the trials card, Treve and Dettori had their dress rehearsal in the Prix Vermeille, a race that threatened not to play to the filly's strengths. On the softest ground she had yet tackled and over a furlong and a half beyond anything she had previously encountered, Treve found herself imprisoned on the rail behind a typically unhurried pace.

With Head-Maarek's entreaties to remember the Arc was only three weeks away still fresh in his mind, Dettori dared not give his partner a hard race. But years of Longchamp experience, allied to the absolute trust he had already gained in Treve after just two spins on the Chantilly gallops, ensured Dettori was not about to panic. A fractional gap appeared ahead and to their left and Treve accelerated to take the opportunity, following the classic inside-to-outside route that had brought Dettori countless big-race successes at

venues like Ascot and Goodwood, as well as mirroring the manoeuvres of recent top-class Arc winners such as Zarkava and Sea The Stars.

Head-Maarek was frank in her post-race debrief. "My heart was beating because she found herself badly positioned and she pulled, but she has a lot of speed and a lot of class," she said.

For his part Dettori was now convinced Treve would need cover and to be drawn near the rail in the Arc. He, and we, had become conditioned by witnessing the filly's whirlwind turn of pace deployed from a hold-up position, as well as by the experience of watching numerous Arcs down the years. It seemed impossible to dispute Saint-Martin's analysis, even if waiting on the inner always runs the risk of traffic problems.

◆◆◆◆

THE Tuesday before the great race is traditionally the day that even the most dawn-averse Paris-based hacks make

their way up the A1 to Les Aigles, the broad grassy plain nestled within the Forest of Chantilly that plays host to the final wargames before the real battle the following Sunday.

This year Treve was the centre of attention for the assembled group of reporters, photographers, bloodstock agents and old family friends of the Heads. While Head-Maarek chatted amiably with all, father Alec was a study of concentration, perched on a shooting stick. It was a familiar scene for the four-time Arc-winning trainer and on this occasion he saw Treve inflict the usual humiliation on her mercifully anonymous galloping companion.

Head-Maarek briefed the assembled press, concluding with the hope that her charge would say "sayonara" to heavyweight Japanese challengers Orfevre and Kizuna on Sunday, and then the inner circle closed in around Treve for a private discussion of the work, conducted between Criquette,

▶▶Continues page 24

HEADS OF STATE

Treve's victory was the latest chapter in the remarkable Arc success story of the Head family

1947 Willie Head trains the winner, Le Paillon

1952 Alec Head, Willie's son, trains Nuccio to win the race

1959 Alec wins again with Saint Crespin, who dead-heats with Midnight Sun but takes outright victory after that rival is demoted to second for interference

1966 Willie wins again with Bon Mot, ridden by Alec's son Freddy. At 19, Freddy remains the youngest jockey to win the race

1972 Freddy rides his second winner, the Angel Penna-trained San San

1976 Alec and Freddy combine with Ivanjica, a third Arc winner for both

1979 Criquette Head, granddaughter of Willie, daughter of Alec and sister of Freddy, trains her first winner, Three Troikas. The filly is ridden by Freddy and carries the colours of Alec's wife, Ghislaine

1980 Detroit, jointly bred by Alec, wins for Robert Sangster, who bought her privately as a yearling

1981 Alec trains his fourth winner, Gold River

2013 Criquette, now under her married name of Head-Maarek, wins her second Arc with Treve, bred by her father. She is still the only female trainer to win the race

Alec and work rider and assistant Pascale Galoche.

All that remained now, it seemed, was for Treve to avoid any last-minute hitches and for Wimbledon champion Marion Bartoli to grasp a single-figure number when she made the draw on Friday.

Head-Maarek spent much of Wednesday afternoon at Chantilly racecourse in a meeting, fulfilling her role as president of the French trainers' association. As the formal session concluded, she shared a joke outside the sandstone weighing room with Thierry Gillet, a former jockeys' representative and Arc winner.

Across the English Channel, however, Head-Maarek's plans for Sunday's Arc had just hit a significant bump in the road. Even if she was aware of Dettori's spill from Eland Ally on the way to the start of a five-furlong handicap at Nottingham, little more than an hour earlier, she couldn't have known the extent of his injuries.

By eight o'clock in the evening she was fielding calls from the press, having been told that Dettori's Arc dream had been shattered along with his ankle, and had already been on the phone to Sheikh Joaan to ask if Jarnet was an acceptable replacement.

While the 46-year-old knew Treve "by heart", in the parlance of French horsemen, the loss of Dettori at the eleventh hour was a disruption Head-Maarek could have done without. For those of a more superstitious bent it might have been seen as a bad portent of what the race might bring, a feeling surely only reinforced when Bartoli drew number 15 for Treve on Friday morning.

Among the potential winners only Roger Charlton's Al Kazeem had been posted wider and France's number one hope would have to wreck a mountain of statistics to claim the prize. Francois Boulard, France Galop's master of ceremonies, offered some encouragement by pointing out that three past winners, including Allez France, broke from stall 15 but nobody was buying it – not even the unwittingly treasonous Bartoli.

Treve approached the Arc as a filly we thought we knew plenty about, even with only the scant evidence of just four racecourse starts (two of which were run in front of a crowd that wouldn't have made four figures). But that Friday afternoon, as he walked out to the parade ring at Saint-Cloud, Jarnet cast Treve in a different light to the one we had chosen for her.

"I don't view her as a horse who must be held up, I just need to ride her for herself," he said, while repeatedly underlining his hope that there was some pace on. In 48 hours' time, with preconceptions of the 'perfect trip' scattered to the four corners of Longchamp, we would all learn exactly what that entailed.

◆◆◆◆

SUNDAY October 6, Arc day. It is 34 years since Criquette Head, as she was then, joined her father and grandfather, Willie, as an Arc-winning trainer when she saddled the filly Three Troikas to win for her parents while brother Freddy did the steering. Although she has not won the race since, a lifetime's experience of going to Longchamp's biggest day has given Head-Maarek the advantage of habits and routines with which to shield herself from what threatens to be an overwhelming day.

"The day is a little different because it's the Arc de Triomphe but I never change my routine on the day or in the run-up

▶▶ A delighted Thierry Jarnet (above) after crossing the line and (below) arriving in the winner's enclosure

to it," she says later that week, when all the clamour surrounding Treve's breathtaking victory has begun to subside. "I knew I had a good horse and I trained her exactly as I usually do. I didn't feel under pressure, I never feel pressure. The filly was well and was ready to run her race."

To those who don't know Treve intimately, the sight of her dark coat yielding to white sweat stains before the Arc is not an encouraging sign. Japanese Derby winner Kizuna, meanwhile, is in danger of falling asleep, while his frequently excitable compatriot Orfevre is a model of calm once down at the start, aided by the constant reassurance of Christophe Soumillon. Le Parisien's racing correspondent Gilles Maarek stands on the steppings of a packed press balcony. He casts a smiling glance up to the box above and to his left, and exchanges a wave with his wife, who is about to become a two-time Arc-winning trainer.

The roar that accompanies the opening of the stalls would do the Cheltenham Festival proud and it soon becomes clear that the

▶▶ Continues page 26

next two and a half minutes hold more than a few surprises in store. Jarnet has decided not to forfeit the many lengths required to get across to the rail from stall 15 and is aiming to tuck in as best he can on the outside of the peloton. As the field begins to swing right-handed and downhill, Jarnet and James Doyle have eyes for the same hole in which to hide away. Doyle's mount, the physically imposing five-year-old Al Kazeem, is always going to win that particular argument and now Treve is bumped to the wide outer, her 'nose to the wind' to quote another Gallic racing term – not one that usually heralds a positive outcome.

"I didn't feel so confident during the race because Al Kazeem pushed her wide and she was on the flanks of the pack," Head-Maarek reflects later. "But she didn't pull. She always gallops with her head slightly in the air, which gives the impression she's pulling, but I could see she was very relaxed."

As the field thunders into the false straight, Jarnet lets out a notch of rein and Treve sweeps to the shoulders of the leader – just at the very spot where Saint-Martin had warned against getting over-excited. In the stands Gilles Maarek is half whispering, half screaming: "Wait for it, wait for it!"

But there is no holding Treve and as she rounds the turn into the home straight it is rapidly becoming clear that nothing can live with her. Head-Maarek senses it too. "Thierry knew exactly what he had underneath him. When she made the move in the false straight I started to say to myself: 'She's coming through and she's going to do it.'"

For all that every Arc is special, the images which follow must be among the happiest in recent memory at Longchamp. Head-Maarek's clenched fists of triumph are swiftly followed by tears of relief and joy. Father Alec is fighting his way to the unsaddling enclosure under siege from three camera crews. "What a filly, what a filly," is all he can keep repeating, his eyes red and his cheeks streamed with pride. Then there is the beaming delight of Sheikh Joaan, accompanied by his young sons Hamad and Tamin on the carriage ride in front of the stands on their way to the presentation.

What also emerges, both from the main actors and from numerous pundits, is just what a performance it has been from Treve to beat Orfevre by five lengths, when so much went wrong during the race. But Jarnet's observations hark back to that brief interview at Saint-Cloud 48 hours

earlier. In the intervening time he had come to the conclusion that this was an Arc without an obvious pacemaker.

"They say you win the Arc next to the rail but that's only true if there's a good tempo to the race and I felt there was little chance of that being the case this time. If I'd chosen to rein her back and slide over to the rail after the start, we would have been dead. If I'd made my challenge on the rail, I would never have got the gaps. And everyone would have said: 'Jarnet massacred Treve!'"

◆◆◆◆

ALREADY the tale of Treve is the recipe for a cracking book: the story of the filly that the bloodstock world judged to be worth only €22,000, who disappeared from view and missed both the early Classics and the obvious trials, but who blossomed into a record-breaking winner of the Diane, the Vermeille and the Arc. Add in the rich history and sheer willingness to communicate of the Head family, not to mention the drama of her sale to Sheikh Joaan and the last-minute heartbreak for Frankie Dettori. Then top it off with a race plan that couldn't be executed and a thrilling burst of speed to settle the matter. We would be greedy to ask for more.

Head-Maarek knows that racing brings its fair share of disappointments along with the fairytales. But when we speak at Saint-Cloud a few days after the

▶▶ (Clockwise from top left) Treve arrives in the winner's enclosure; Thierry Jarnet after winning his third Arc at the age of 46; owner Sheikh Joaan Al Thani with his family

'If I'd made my challenge on the rail, I would never have got the gaps. And everyone would have said: "Jarnet massacred Treve!"'

Arc, she is already planning what could be an even more exciting journey back to Longchamp in 2014, when a second triumph would put Treve among the sport's immortals.

"The next day is another day," she says simply. "You enjoy it and you live the day and there's a lot of excitement but then racing goes on. You can't stay in that past moment. You have to get your feet back on the ground very quickly. The immediate future for the filly is that she won't have any more racing this year. Next year the Sheikh wants to go back to the Arc, so I'll make a nice programme through the spring and summer through to September and the Arc. There are a lot of races she could run in. We might come here for the Grand Prix de Saint-Cloud or we could go to Ascot in June. There's plenty to look forward to next year."

Only time will tell what fresh challengers will arise next season, both from Europe and perhaps Japan. But if all goes well, Head-Maarek doesn't expect Treve to be giving up her title lightly. "For me, quality-wise, it's there now," she says. "But physically there is a lot of improvement still to come. Since the race she looks stronger."

An unbeaten five-length Arc winner with the promise of more power, more potential, to go with her proven grace and athleticism. With Treve, we can dare to dream.

BROKEN DREAM

Just when it seemed Frankie Dettori's comeback from his cocaine ban would end in glorious redemption, the opportunity was snatched away from him

By Peter Thomas

REASONS to be cheerful, one, two, three. As recently as May, Frankie Dettori was an unemployed exile, banished to endure six months of soul-searching on a desert island without horseracing. La dolce vita had disappeared.

"I'm ashamed and embarrassed," he said in the aftermath of the positive test for cocaine that led to a worldwide six-month ban from horseracing. "I dropped my guard when I was at my weakest. I was in a dark place. I was very low. I will regret it for the rest of my life."

As the British Flat season neared a close in October, however, Dettori had landed what was probably the best job he could have hoped for, as retained jockey for the increasingly successful Sheikh Joaan Al Thani. He had been afforded the opportunity to proffer two dismissive fingers to his former employers Godolphin (should he have been so minded) and was heading into the winter break comforted by the knowledge that, come next spring, he would be warming the saddle of Treve,

possibly the most gifted and exciting horse in training.

Reasons to be cheerful. So, why the long face, Frankie?

While it's true that the troubled Milanese had endured a foreshortened season that yielded roughly a tenth of the number of winners he had enjoyed in his considerable pomp, the future looked far brighter than he could possibly have imagined during the days of his exclusion at the hands of the French authorities.

He was, however, at the back of

▶▶**Continues page 30**

his own mind and in the eyes of those who write the sports headlines, no longer a major player. He had been gifted the ride on Treve, a brilliant and mercurial filly sitting high in the betting for the biggest race of the European campaign, and then had it snatched away from him when he was jettisoned at a trot by a mediocre horse on a quiet Wednesday at Nottingham.

The gods of the Turf giveth, and then they taketh away, and Dettori had seen redemption snatched from his grasp.

◆◆◆◆

DETTORI'S world came crashing around his ears when he failed a drugs test at Longchamp on September 16, 2012. While he was waiting for the test results, he was informed that, after 18 often glorious years, his services were no longer required by Godolphin. Both Mickael Barzalona and Silvestre de Sousa had been added to the Godolphin jockeys' payroll, relations within the team had deteriorated beyond repair and Dettori confessed: "My head was wrecked, absolutely wrecked."

In his youth, after being cautioned by police for possession of narcotics, Dettori travelled to Morocco to find himself. With a wife, five children and three dogs, however, a man's ability to trot off to North Africa in search of the meaning of life is severely lessened, and the family man had to look elsewhere for his rehabilitation.

So, he did what any of us would have done in the circumstances: he went on Celebrity Big Brother. What better way to lie low, slip under the media radar and lick one's wounds? Frankie isn't like the rest of us, of course. He's a celebrity jockey, the legendary rider of a Magnificent Seven winners, a Question of Sport captain, a restaurateur and the face on jars of pasta sauce, so time out of the limelight is an unsound business proposition – and the one thing he had in abundance was time.

Racing held its breath, but needlessly. Dettori acquitted himself as well as a middle-aged man can on reality television. He wore a flat cap, behaved with tactical nobility, avoided picking his nose, dressed up like Colonel Gaddafi, lasted for three weeks, was evicted fifth, picked up his cheque, donated part of it to racing charities and emerged, blinking, into flashlight that showed him he had less than four months of his ban to serve.

If there was a surprise for the viewing public, it was that the perpetually effusive Mediterranean was capable

▶▶Continues page 32

▶▶(Clockwise from top left) Dettori on Celebrity Big Brother; riding work on Zain Eagle for Gerard Butler after racing at Newmarket in April; in a press conference at Epsom on Oaks day, where he made his comeback; after finishing last on Beatrice Aurore in his first race back; coming home in fifth on Fattsota, the best placing of his comeback day; and walking back in

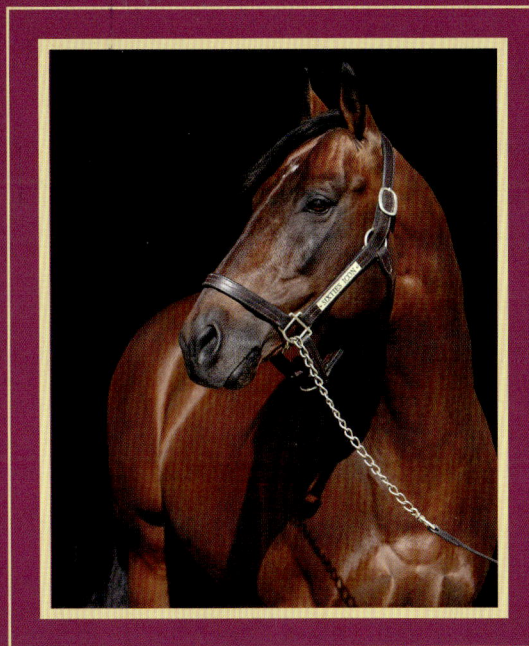

of lasting for long spells with not the faintest trace of effusiveness. He turned out to be remarkably unafflicted by a constant need to chatter or leap into the air, just as, in private, he is capable of being as grumpy as he is grinning, thoroughly cheesed off while still smiling.

What we probably gleaned from all this was that when a man has been in the adoring gaze of the public for two decades, he finds it a hard place not to be; when a man has been at the top of his profession for the same length of time and suddenly isn't, he craves the attention it brings.

If Frankie were minded to misquote Oscar Wilde, he might have said: "The only thing worse than being called an irresponsible oaf who let his sport down is not being called anything at all."

◆◆◆◆

"THE issue with Frankie was always trying to keep him between the high and low water marks," is how former employer John Gosden described the challenge of getting the best out of the mercurial rider.

Few would dispute the talent that propelled him to more than 900 winners in the Godolphin blue, but more would testify to having tried and failed to plumb the depths of those abilities on the days in between the big days, and Dettori wouldn't be human if he didn't doubt, in his darker moments, how he would be received on his return and who would give him work.

"He did his time at Wolverhampton in the nineties for me and you won't excite him with that anymore," said Gosden, "but he's a super chap and pound for pound the best rider I've ever put up on a horse. He could ride anywhere in the world, and he's still as good as ever on the big occasion or a nice two-year-old."

But Gosden has William Buick and what Dettori needed was situations vacant and prospective employers who kept the faith. If he needed a reference from an objective source he could have done worse than go to John Whitley, author of the influential and long-standing Computer Racing Form annual, which contains a numerical assessment of riding talent.

According to Whitley, despite not reaching the threshold level of data for inclusion in four of the past five tables, Dettori has earned a ratings figure for the past year of around 11.5, which equates to a place in the current top six. This may not compare with his average

▸ Continues page 34

FRANKIE'S YEAR

JANUARY 3 Enters the Celebrity Big Brother house, one of 11 participants in the Channel 5 reality show

JANUARY 23 Becomes the fifth celebrity to be evicted from the Big Brother house. "I don't think I made too much of a fool of myself," he says

MAY 16 In a Channel 4 News interview with Clare Balding, he admits for the first time taking cocaine. "A moment of weakness," he says

MAY 20 Long set as his return date but comeback is delayed after the French authorities refuse to give clearance, for reasons never fully explained

MAY 31 Finally returns at Epsom on Oaks day, finishing last, fifth and last on his three rides

JUNE 6 First winner when Asian Trader (above), trained by William Haggas, takes a Class 4 handicap at Sandown

JUNE 22 Loses by a head in final race of Royal Ascot, leaving him winless for the meeting after 20 rides

JULY 1 Racing Post reveals agreement to ride for Sheikh Joaan Al Thani

AUGUST 11 Finishes second on Sheikh Joaan's Olympic Glory in the Group 1 Prix Jacques le Marois, losing by a short head to Moonlight Cloud

AUGUST 17 Sandiva, owned by Sheikh Joaan and trained by Richard Fahey, becomes the first Group winner since his comeback when she takes the Group 3 Prix du Calvados at Deauville

AUGUST 23 Another narrow defeat in a Group 1 as Shea Shea, 3-1 favourite for the Nunthorpe at York, is beaten half a length by Jwala

SEPTEMBER 15 Teams up with Treve to land the Prix Vermeille, the first Group 1 victory of his comeback

OCTOBER 2 Breaks right ankle in a fall from Eland Ally going to the start at Nottingham and is ruled out for the rest of the year

OCTOBER 6 Treve, with Thierry Jarnet back in the saddle in place of Dettori, wins the Arc by five lengths

MAWATHEEQ

NAYEF

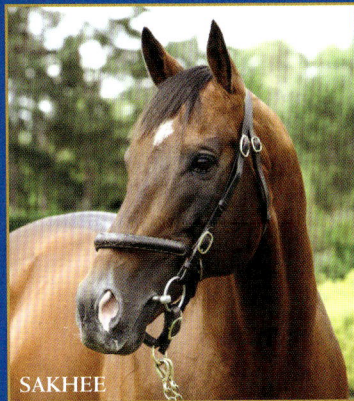

SAKHEE

HAAFHD

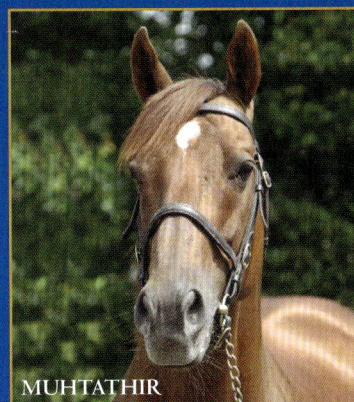

MUHTATHIR

NAAQOOS

MUJAHID

SHADWELL
STALLIONS 2014

Standing at Nunnery Stud, England

NAYEF Gulch - Height Of Fashion

A leading sire of 3YOS in Europe in 2013 including Stakes winners TASADAY, VALIRANN and SPARKLING BEAM.*

MAWATHEEQ Danzig - Sarayir

A Group winning last son of DANZIG with his first 2YO runners in 2014.

Also standing in England

SAKHEE Bahri - Thawakib
(Standing at Yorton Farm)

HAAFHD Alhaarth - Al Bahathri
(Standing at Beechwood Grange Stud, Yorkshire)

Standing in France: Haras du Mezeray

MUHTATHIR Elmaamul - Majmu

In 2013: 5th leading sire in France (prize money) & sire of Gr.I winning 2YO (Prix Marcel Boussac) INDONESIENNE.*

NAAQOOS Oasis Dream - Straight Lass

A Gr.I winner and sire of a winning first crop of 2YOS in 2013.

Standing in Italy: Allevamento di Besnate

MUJAHID Danzig - Elrafa Ah
Leading Italian based sire in 2013 for the second year running.*

SHADWELL
ADVANTAGES

- 1st January Special Live Foal terms: fees are due after the sales season
- Nominations can be charged in Euros on application
- Shadwell operate a limited books policy with all their stallions

*All statistics courtesy of Racing Post 01-10-13

Discover more about the Shadwell Stallions at www.shadwellstud.co.uk
Or call Richard, Johnny or Rachael on

01842 755913
Email us at: nominations@shadwellstud.co.uk

SHADWELL
STANDING FOR SUCCESS

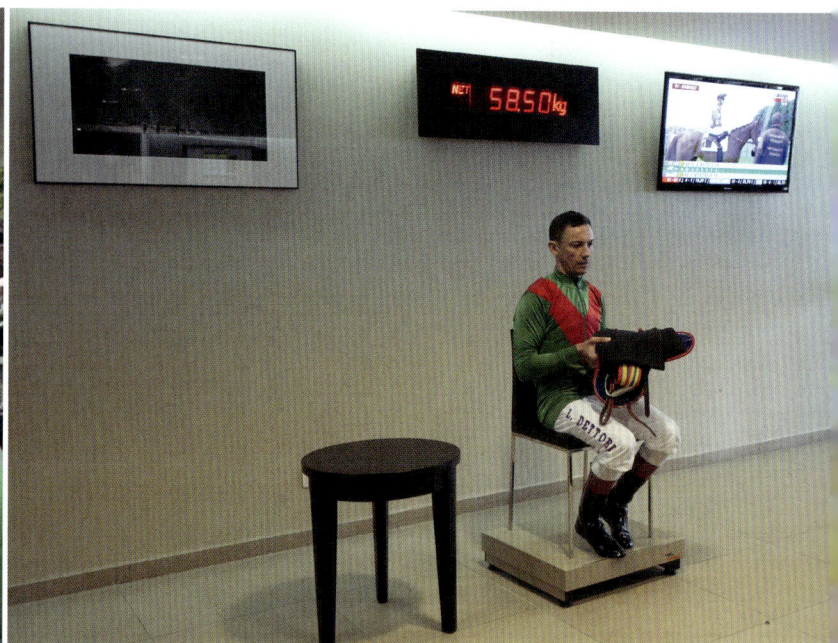

mark of 12.3 between 1991 and 2000 – when he was ranked second only to Ray Cochrane – but it was surely enough to make him a man with good job prospects.

So Dettori whirled around Newmarket like a dervish, appearing in more than two places at once as he prepared for his return, "too hungry, too excited, like a child," as another trainer put it. There was a delay to his comeback and a cloud of mystery hanging over it all, but one thing the impatient jockey would not let impede his renewed progress: lack of effort.

Before his return to the saddle, however, there was one more thing to do: the confessional interview. Talking to Clare Balding on Channel 4 News on May 16, he admitted for the first time he had taken cocaine and spoke frankly about the split with Godolphin. The two issues were linked. "Things were going bad, I was depressed and I guess [it was] a moment of weakness and I fell for it," he said of the cocaine use that led to his ban.

With that out of the way and his sentence served, Dettori was like a bull at a gate, eager to return to the arena he had missed so badly, ready to come back with a bang. There was, however, a very long fuse attached to this particular firework and the pyrotechnics began to develop into a damp squib as every news outlet under the sun waited for the prodigal son's first winner.

He made his comeback at Epsom on Oaks day, the lateness of his clearance to ride meaning that three booked jockeys had to be unbooked to accommodate him. He was at the centre of a Twitter storm involving Neil Callan, one of the jockeys who lost out, but was probably more bothered by the lack of winners, and by the lack of a Derby ride the following day.

Finally, on June 6, after 11 straight losers and plenty of what became unwelcome attention, Asian Trader won the second race at Sandown and the monkey was off Dettori's back at last. "I've won 3,000 races and everybody is waiting for this one," he said afterwards, combining a manifest streak of irritation with an unwitting degree of accuracy.

With the wind back in his sails, he allowed himself a flying dismount – once the hallmark stamped on only the most exalted of triumphs – and a hint of characteristic boldness when he added, "I know I'm aiming high, but I'd like to win 100 races this year." It was a lofty ambition that would come back to bite him on the statistical bottom.

◆◆◆◆

BY the time Dettori was unseated by Eland Ally on his way to the start at Nottingham on October 2 – fracturing his ankle, breaking his talus bone and needing to have a plate and five screws inserted by way of remedy – he had managed 16 wins from 205 rides, at a strike-rate of eight per cent that was his weakest since his career began.

Talk of centuries had long since been brushed under the carpet when the injury extinguished the one ray of sunshine that had managed to penetrate the gloom.

As he began the uphill struggle to rebuild a glittering career from ashes, Dettori had been summoned to

▶Dettori in the weighing room and paddock at Chantilly before the Prix du Jockey Club, in which he finished 15th on the Andrew Oliver-trained First Cornerstone

Chantilly to meet Sheikh Joaan, brother of the Emir of Qatar and one of the big-spending rising forces in the bloodstock world. It was perhaps the only job that could have compensated Dettori for the humiliation of being 'let go' by Godolphin. There was the cash, the kudos and the sense that he was coupled to the coming force in Middle Eastern racing, rather than a stable that in recent years had been at full stretch trying to revisit its glory days.

Put simply, while the changeable Italian likes a fat pay cheque as much of the rest of us, what he and his ego crave is adulation, appreciation, the roar of the greasepaint and the smell of the crowd. He has always been a big-top performer and the prospect of a return to that life appealed to his sense of theatre.

◆◆◆◆

FOR most of the summer, as the weather and the Flat racing season grew hotter and more intense, Dettori's comeback went poorly numerically, and in terms of raw quality it was even worse. The first sign of his reduced standing in the sport came at Royal Ascot, just over a fortnight into his return. At an occasion where he has ridden 47 winners and was used to being treated with star-struck reverence, he endured a week of frustration and being inconsequential.

One winner, in any race, would have catapulted him into the headlines in a positive way but it was not to be. After 18 losing rides, he was on board the favourite in both of the final two races

▶▶Continues page 36

of the meeting. He was beaten two lengths into second on the first of them and then, most agonisingly of all, by a head in the last.

For years quantity of winners has not bothered him, but quality always has and, having been forced to watch from the wings at Royal Ascot, he would have seen precious little to convince him that a Group 1 success was about to light up his sky. Until, that is, Sheikh Joaan hoved into view and the stars came out.

Dettori's first big ride for his new employer came in the Prix Jacques le Marois at Deauville on board the Richard Hannon-trained Olympic Glory. Odds of 18-1 suggested only an outside chance but Dettori came so close, losing by a short head to Moonlight Cloud after a desperate late run. Twelve days later, he had an even better chance in a Group 1 when he rode 3-1 Nunthorpe favourite Shea Shea for Mike de Kock but again he lost narrowly, this time by half a length to 40-1 shot Jwala. The winner was ridden by Steve Drowne, a year younger than Dettori and on a comeback of his own.

Dettori's wait for a return to the big time went on, but not for too much longer. Whenever he cast a glance across the Channel he would have been delighted to see the unbeaten Prix de Diane heroine Treve waiting for him. Here was the one bright spark that might ignite the Italian's season, but he had to be patient while she had her mid-season break.

Finally, on Longchamp's Arc trials day in September – the same card where he had given his fateful positive test 12 months earlier – he partnered her in competitive action for the first time. It was a good feeling. As he gave her a tender yet thrilling ride to victory in the Prix Vermeille, he would have felt the years rolling back to a time when such creatures lined up with soothing regularity, to carry the royal blue rather than the grey with maroon epaulettes.

This was Dettori's first Group 1 victory of the season, at the 13th attempt, but it was so much more than that. It was the passport to Europe's day of days, at Longchamp on the first Sunday in October, where he had already won three Prix de l'Arc de Triomphes. Victory there would be more than a second Group 1 of the year, it would be proof positive that Frankie was back, still a player and still the man to thrill the big top.

◆◆◆◆

WHEN Treve won the Arc in spectacular fashion under Thierry Jarnet,

▶▶ Dettori roars back into the spotlight with Group 1 victory on Treve in the Prix Vermeille and (right) with Sheikh Joaan after the win

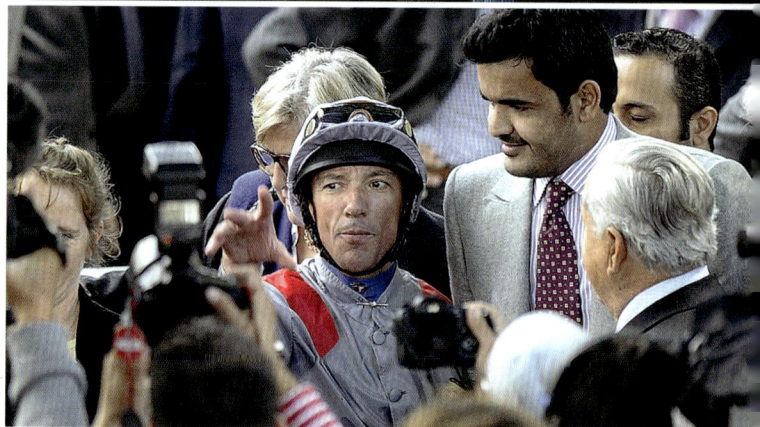

she became Dettori's brightest hope for the future and the most crushing blow he could have imagined.

All things remaining equal – which is at best an even-money chance in the topsy-turvy world of Dettori – she will stay in training next year, by which time his gently creaking body will be restored to full working order and he will have banished the psychological demons that invaded his living room on the Sunday of the Arc.

"One side of me was delighted that she won," he said, "but it would have been my 200th Group 1 winner, my fourth Arc and back on the big stage again. I was taking painkillers, not because of my leg but because I had a broken heart."

Frankie, with his sense of drama still magically intact and his ankle on the mend, will be contemplating no other future than one in which he plays the leading man in a production both scripted and directed by himself.

THE ONE AND ONLY

Treve's Prix Vermeille was Dettori's sole Group 1 win in 2013, his lowest tally in the past decade and a long way from the double-figure totals that were once the norm

Year	G1 wins	Rides	%
2013	1	14	7
2012	2	41	5
2011	11	45	24
2010	7	54	13
2009	2	58	3
2008	3	47	6
2007	11	50	22
2006	10	43	23
2005	7	29	24
2004	10	49	20

Group 1s worldwide

A horse is washed off after a race at Thurles in April. The jumps-only track in County Tipperary, run by the Molony family for four generations, remains a treasured part of the winter game in Ireland

PATRICK McCANN
(RACINGPOST.COM/PHOTOS)

SUCCESS STORY

Novellist emulated Danedream with another stunning German triumph in the King George

By Nick Pulford

GERMANY'S love affair with the King George VI and Queen Elizabeth Stakes has developed only recently and may prove fleeting, but Andreas Wohler's feeling for the race goes back to childhood and is all the stronger after Novellist became the second German-trained winner of the race, just 12 months after Danedream had broken the ice.

Wohler managed to stay cool before the race, even though he was sure Novellist had improved enough from his previous run to have a real shot at emulating Danedream, but as he watched his colt streak away to smash the course record he could contain himself no longer. By the time he greeted Novellist in the winner's enclosure, he was shaking like a leaf.

"I can't believe it," he said. "I used to come here and watch the King George when I was on holiday as a kid. To win it is unbelievable. I knew he had improved since his last race, but to improve so much is unbelievable." At that point, amid the emotion and the celebration, seeing was not quite believing.

◆◆◆◆

WOHLER, 51, was no ordinary kid when it came to racing. His father, Adolf, was one of the top German trainers and his son would work at the stable in Bremen for pocket money. From the age of 13 Andreas rode out every day and he developed into a leading amateur rider before temporarily taking over the training licence at the age of 23 after his father fell ill. The next year, following Adolf's death, the young Wohler took charge for good.

Since moving in 1994 to his current base at Gutersloh, between Dortmund and Hanover, Wohler has taken major prizes around the globe, notably with Arlington Million winner Silvano, and in Novellist he quickly spotted the potential to be a big-race contender.

"I always liked him," he said. "He wasn't a big horse, only medium-sized, but everything about him seemed to fit together in the right way. He looked like an athlete and after only a few pieces of work it was clear he had plenty of ability. On his first outing he proved it."

Novellist, in fact, proved so good that he won his first four races and in his fifth, the 2012 German Derby, he was hot favourite at 4-6. His half-length defeat by Pastorius was a shock and, when he was a lacklustre fourth to Danedream on his next run in the Grosser Preis von Baden, it seemed he had been overhyped. But there was another explanation and, once that was fully understood, there would be no stopping Novellist.

"It turned out he had an allergy to various grasses," Christoph Berglar, his owner-breeder, said. "We thought he simply had a cold, a fever, after the Derby, but when he ran below par at Baden-Baden there was obviously something else going on. The vets discovered that his lungs were full of mucus, that he couldn't breathe properly, and they found a remedy."

From that point until his retirement to stud in October

this year, Novellist never lost again. He ended 2012 with a Group 1 win in Italy and came back with a Group 2 victory at Baden-Baden in May, followed by another Group 1 success in the Grand Prix de Saint-Cloud, but still the form book said he had been beaten on the two biggest days of his career.

In those circumstances self-doubt often got the better of German trainers in the past but Wohler believed, especially after Novellist had completed a brisk seven-furlong workout seven days before the King George. There was only one problem: who would ride him?

Ryan Moore, who had been on board at Saint-Cloud, was claimed to ride Hillstar for Sir Michael Stoute, while William Buick, another familiar with Novellist, could not guarantee his availability. Keen to remove any uncertainty, Wohler booked Johnny Murtagh early in King George week and, by the time he boxed Novellist for the Thursday-night road trip to Ascot, the trainer was confident everything was in place for a big run.

◆◆◆◆

MURTAGH could not resist a wisecrack after Novellist had given him a fourth King George victory, to go with those

achieved by Sinndar, Dylan Thomas and Duke Of Marmalade. "I was third choice but I was probably worth waiting for," he smiled. It was true: Murtagh, at the age of 43, was setting the summer ablaze with a string of first-class rides and his win on Novellist was no exception.

The pace was fierce, with Universal and Ektihaam going hammer and tongs at the front, and Murtagh did not hold too far back, settling his mount in fourth place just behind Irish Derby winner Trading Leather. From three-quarters of a mile out to the four-furlong pole, Murtagh

'I loved the way he got down, he really wanted it. It was very impressive, up there with all the King Georges I've won. He feels like a very good horse'

could feel Novellist coming off the bridle slightly but, with all his big-race experience, he knew that was a good sign. Ektihaam was first to give way starting round the home turn and, before Trading Leather could collar Universal, Murtagh pounced at the two-furlong marker.

"When I asked him, I loved the way he got down, he really wanted it," he said. "He stretched well and pulling him up was the hardest part. It was very impressive, up there with all the King Georges I've won. He feels like a very good horse, very high class with a good engine."

The engine powered Novellist five lengths clear of Trading Leather and lowered the course record by more than two seconds to 2min 24.6sec. "The way he gallops it doesn't feel like he's doing a lot," Murtagh said. "It certainly didn't feel like he was breaking the course record by two seconds." Maybe that was just a sign of how easy it was.

Novellist was a top-priced 6-1 for the Arc

after the King George but, like Danedream the previous year, a fever ruled him out of Longchamp only days before the race. He wasn't as unlucky as Danedream, who didn't have a fever herself but was prevented from travelling by quarantine restrictions, but it was a cruel blow both for Novellist and his connections, and for the Arc.

"It was just bad timing," Wohler reflected a few days later. "It's hard to say whether Novellist would have given Treve a good race. It was a funny race – there was no pace – but the thing was the filly had the worst run all the way round, always keen, always on the outside, and still won very easily. That was unbelievable."

That word again – unbelievable. But with Treve and Novellist, the winners of Europe's two biggest all-age middle-distance races, seeing really was believing.

BETTER LATE THAN NEVER

By Nick Pulford

Al Kazeem was the middle-distance star of early summer as he rewarded the patience of his connections with a remarkable comeback from serious injury

AL KAZEEM, his trainer Roger Charlton and jockey James Doyle have all been through rough times, the kind of days when success at the top level seemed so far out of reach as to be an illusion. In the end, however, talent and perseverance had their reward and in 2013 the three went on a journey that had once seemed improbable.

For Doyle, the odyssey eventually led to a retainer for Khalid Abdullah, one of the most coveted jobs in the sport. Abdullah's team knew he had the temperament and the skill for the big stage after his victory aboard the Charlton-trained Cityscape on Dubai World Cup night in 2012 but Al Kazeem, racing in the colours of owner-breeder John Deer, gave Doyle the opportunity to prove it in Britain too. Every jockey needs that breakthrough horse and Al Kazeem – first British Group 1 winner, first Royal Ascot winner – will always be special for Doyle.

He knew Al Kazeem might be something special as soon as he rode his first proper piece of work on the five-year-old in the spring. "I thought 'Christ, he's come back an absolute monster,'" Doyle recalled. The road had been long and hard for Al Kazeem after he suffered a hairline fracture of the pelvis the previous May, when he landed the Jockey Club Stakes at Newmarket in highly promising fashion ahead of three Group 1 winners. He spent six weeks in a sling, suspended from the ceiling of his box, and the rest of the summer recuperating. In that time the chance to step up from his Group 2 win at Newmarket to Group 1 level passed him by, and nobody knew if he would come back as good as he had been the day he was injured.

Any anxiety to know the answer, or to make up for lost time, was resisted by Charlton and Deer. After discussing a return in the autumn or a winter trip to Dubai, they agreed to wait for the new British season. "Why rush a horse as good as this?" was Charlton's view. Doyle said it was "like having a Ferrari in the garage and waiting months and months for parts to arrive from Italy" but that first proper piece of work of 2013 told him Charlton had made the right call.

◆◆◆◆

AL KAZEEM'S season started with a Group 3 win at Sandown and then it was off to Ireland for the long-awaited first crack at a Group 1. Waiting for him in the Tattersalls Gold Cup was Camelot, but Charlton wasn't worried. "I'll never forget the feeling walking around the paddock," he said. "I may have been looking through rose-tinted spectacles but in my opinion our horse outshone Camelot in terms of physique, presence and class."

He outshone Camelot in the race too, with Doyle riding an excellent stalking race to score decisively by a length and a half. That was a sign of how far Doyle had come since he lost his way after riding out his claim in double-quick time when he was barely out of his teens. For a while, he had considered quitting the sport.

The link with Charlton, which developed slowly before accelerating after his Dubai win on Cityscape, was crucial. Charlton himself had known thin pickings in the past and admitted: "There was a time when it was a struggle and it's a worry because you are responsible for so many people's lives. But good owners stuck by me and the Group horses came back."

Al Kazeem was proving to be the best of them and his trainer and jockey shared great faith in him, as well as in each other. In the paddock before the Prince of Wales's Stakes at Royal Ascot, Charlton was confident of beating Camelot again but he was mindful it was going to be different to the cosy win at the Curragh and had one simple instruction for Doyle: "When you go for him, make sure you really go for him." The jockey was so confident that when Deer turned to him and asked how many Royal Ascot winners he had ridden, the answer was: "None. But don't worry because this is going to be my first."

What Doyle did not know was that Paul Hanagan had a plan on Mukhadram, a brilliant plan that almost came off. Hanagan set a strong pace, then gave Mukhadram a breather and kicked again off the home turn, opening a lead of three or four lengths. Doyle was alert to the move and he went for Al Kazeem, as instructed. Step by step, they closed on Mukhadram and finally got on top in the final 50 yards to win by a neck.

Both jockeys had ridden brilliantly but history records the winners and for Doyle it was that landmark first in a British Group 1 and at Royal Ascot. He finished the day with a treble after taking

▶▶Continues page 44

the Hunt Cup on Belgian Bill and the Queen Mary Stakes on Rizeena, who would give him another Group 1 success later in the year in the Moyglare Stud Stakes. Just like Al Kazeem, he had arrived in the big time.

The best was yet to come from Al Kazeem and it was just around the corner. The next stop was Sandown for the Eclipse, where he faced Queen Anne Stakes winner Declaration Of War as well as Mukhadram and The Fugue, the second and third from the Prince of Wales's. He won decisively, by two lengths from Declaration Of War, despite hanging right and hampering third-placed Mukhadram just after taking the lead. "I thought it was a better field than at Ascot but, if it was, he certainly won more easily," Charlton said. That completed a run of four victories in ten weeks and, as the three Group 1 successes had come on good to firm ground, faster than he was thought to prefer, Charlton decided it was time to give him a break.

◆◆◆◆

AL KAZEEM was rated the best middle-distance performer in Europe after the Eclipse but in the end it turned out he was only the best of the first half of the summer. By the

time he reappeared in the Juddmonte International at York, Novellist had surpassed him with his course-record win in the King George and further down the line Treve would do better still to take top spot in Europe. Al Kazeem, meanwhile, would not win again.

Charlton had long feared that a series of races on fast ground would take their toll and, with no respite during the long hot summer, those fears were realised at York. The field was strong, with Al Kazeem and Declaration Of War joined by Sussex Stakes winner Toronado, stepping up from a mile, and King George second and third Trading Leather and Hillstar.

Victory went to Declaration Of War, the new 'iron horse' of Ballydoyle, who was thriving on hard races and fast ground. "He is amazing," Aidan O'Brien, his trainer, said. "Racing is the thing that is bringing him on. He has an unbelievable constitution and is always in full work." Al Kazeem, by contrast, did not enjoy the conditions and Doyle was never happy as he was beaten two and three-quarter lengths into third. "You are always hoping he will keep doing it, but he doesn't really like the firmer ground," Charlton said.

When the middle-distance bandwagon rolled on to Leopardstown in early September, for the Irish Champion Stakes, Al Kazeem was there again and this time conditions were

▶▶ Al Kazeem wins the Eclipse, rated the best performance of his career on Racing Post Ratings and the culmination of a Group 1 hat-trick in the space of 41 days

more favourable. As at York, however, he lost to a rival he had beaten earlier in the summer. The Fugue, who finished behind him in the Eclipse and Prince of Wales's, this time won by a length and a quarter, but there were no excuses from Doyle. "He ran his race. The Fugue just had a better turn of foot," he said.

The final curtain came down with Al Kazeem only a bit-part player in sixth place as Treve stole the show in the Arc. Again, there were no excuses and Charlton felt only delight, not disappointment, at the end of a campaign that had once seemed so unlikely. "He ran a great race. It has been a great journey and he has been a great horse to train. It's rather like the end of a party. Not many horses win five Group races in a row or three Group 1 races in a row. He was very tough."

The next journey was to Sandringham Stud to begin a stallion career, with Deer taking great pleasure in a colt he had bred going to the Royal Studs. For Al Kazeem, it was a fitting end to a season that had taken his team to the Royal Ascot winner's enclosure in thrilling fashion. After the Prince of Wales's success, Deer said: "I truly believe that if you let horses develop in their own time and don't push them, they will pay you back. I think Al Kazeem has proved that to be true."

After all the difficulties, Al Kazeem was worth waiting for.

'It has been a great journey and he has been a great horse to train. Not many horses win five Group races in a row or three Group 1 races in a row'

BRAVEHEART

Farhh, so fragile off the track but so tough on it, produced a career-best performance to take top honours on British Champions Day

By Tom Kerr

WITH no Frankel to headline the show, the 2013 British Champions Day desperately needed a winner of the highest order. The organisers' ambitions for the day, its grandiose name and £3.4 million in prize-money demanded nothing less. Fortunately, the talented but fragile Farhh came to the rescue as he ran the greatest race of his life to record a brilliant and hard-fought Champion Stakes victory over Cirrus Des Aigles and Ruler Of The World.

His was a victory with just a whiff of redemption about it. Redemption for the fixture, precariously perched as it is at the blustery and damp frontier of the Flat season, and also for his owner, Godolphin, whose unhappy season began mired in scandal and ended in glory. But more than anything else the victory was redemption for a richly talented colt whose injury-plagued four-year career had yielded not even a dozen opportunities to demonstrate his ability.

"He's a great fighter – every year he has had problems," said his trainer Saeed Bin Suroor, beaming with delight in the winner's enclosure at Ascot. "He's a great horse and I'm so happy for him. I know him well and knew he had the class."

Farhh's problems have haunted him all his career. He made just one start in each of his first two seasons, although the fact that he won both hinted that his fragility off the track was contrasted by a steely resolve on it. He therefore began the third season of his career with just two starts to show for his efforts, yet victory in the 2012 Thirsk Hunt Cup heralded the beginning of the most productive season of Farhh's career, a unique complete campaign free of lameness or serious injury. It was pure bad fortune that his only full season happened to coincide with Frankel's finest.

In 2012 Farhh twice ran into the marauding Frankel, who thrashed him by six lengths in the Sussex Stakes at Goodwood and seven in the Juddmonte International at York. An ultimately fruitless tour of duty in five Group 1 races was completed by second place in the Prix du Moulin at Longchamp and inevitably followed by a trip to the vets, where Farhh was treated for the bone chips that had blighted his career.

With Frankel retired to the breeding barn, the 2013 season promised great things for Farhh – if only he could stay sound. He began the season in the Lockinge with a great shadow hanging over Godolphin, which had been rocked by the Mahmood Al Zarooni doping scandal. "To win this race is very important to us, to start this year with a big winner," admitted Bin Suroor before the race. Farhh dutifully obliged.

It was a richly deserved first Group 1 win for Farhh, who stood poised to establish himself as Britain's leading middle-distance competitor. But once again unsoundness struck. Farhh was found to be lame in early June, dashing hopes of a trip to Royal Ascot. "It is not possible to make plans for him at the moment," said Godolphin racing manager Simon Crisford, hinting at the uncertainty and frustration that surrounded everything Farhh did.

◆◆◆◆

FARHH therefore arrived at Ascot on Champions Day without a run since the Lockinge and, as connections revealed, he had hardly done any work either. "We've always had problems with him and he has to have a different programme of training from all the other horses in the stable. You have to look after him really well just to keep him sound," Bin Suroor said.

Ridden with gusto by Silvestre de Sousa, Farhh was always prominent and by the time the field turned for home and set sail for the sweeping Ascot grandstand he was virtually in the lead. Behind, however, Christophe Soumillon was stock-still on Cirrus Des Aigles and travelling with purpose. Ruler Of The World, forced wide by a poor draw, was also making ground.

De Sousa went for home with two furlongs to go and grabbed a vital two-length lead over the chasing field, but Soumillon and Moore had sent their mounts in hot pursuit. The three finest horses in the race then drew away from the rest, nostrils flaring, necks lowered, riders a-flurry. Farhh's lead diminished almost imperceptibly, but as the post approached and Cirrus Des Aigles inched up Farhh's flank the leader summoned his resolve one last time, dug deep and held off the French challenger. Again Farhh had demonstrated that he lacked nothing for toughness when at last he made it to the track.

While there was no Frankelesque reception for Farhh in the winner's enclosure, there was delight among connections and widespread goodwill

▶Continues page 48

'He's a great fighter – every year he has had problems. I'm so happy for him. I know him well and knew he had the class'

for Saeed Bin Suroor, whose understated dignity and long years of dedicated service contrasted so favourably with the rapacious behaviour of his erstwhile colleague Al Zarooni. By bringing Farhh to the track in peak condition he had executed the training feat of the meeting and, arguably, the season. "It was a great performance and Saeed has done a brilliant job in getting the horse back," Crisford said.

◆◆◆◆

THERE was disappointment for Godolphin when the 2,000 Guineas winner Dawn Approach finished fourth in the Queen Elizabeth II Stakes, his final race before retirement. It was an underwhelming performance, on ground softer than preferred, and summed up a season that began with ambitious comparisons to Frankel and went downhill from midsummer.

The QEII instead went to Richard Hannon's Olympic Glory, securing the veteran trainer a fourth' championship in what was widely speculated to be his final season before handing over the keys to son and assistant Richard jnr. Olympic Glory's astonishing victory, as he squeezed through a tiny gap and blasted more than three lengths clear under Richard Hughes, was a fitting way to seal the deal.

Frankie Dettori, hobbling excitedly about the winner's enclosure on crutches, is retained rider for Sheikh

Joaan, Olympic Glory's owner, and could barely contain his enthusiasm about the riches awaiting him when he recovers from injury. "He deserves to be the best miler in Europe, maybe the world," he said of Olympic Glory. Racing Post Ratings said otherwise, but Olympic Glory wasn't far behind his stablemate Toronado.

In second place was Top Notch Tonto, supplemented for the race at a cost to connections of £70,000. His four long white socks make him look the unlikeliest of racehorses, but he vindicated his owners' belief in him with a huge run. "I've never been so happy at finishing second," trainer Brian Ellison said.

Not everyone was pleased with second, of course. George Baker was entitled to be distraught after his mount Harris Tweed was caught on the line by Johnny Murtagh and Royal Diamond in the Long Distance Cup. Despair turned to delight for Baker, however, on Seal Of Approval, the 16-1 outsider in the Fillies & Mares Stakes. While rivals including Oaks winner Talent and Prix de l'Opera winner Dalkala laboured on the churned-up track, Seal Of Approval relished the conditions and dashed clear to deliver Baker a first Group 1 success.

"I've been waiting a long time. I'm 31 years of age, I hope I don't have to wait as long for the next one," said Baker, one of the tallest jockeys in the weighing

▶▶ (Clockwise from top left) Farhh holds off Cirrus Des Aigles in the Champion Stakes; Olympic Glory takes the Queen Elizabeth II Stakes; Saeed Bin Suroor (second right) with Farhh; and Silvestre de Sousa celebrates victory

'I've been waiting a long time. I'm 31 years of age and I hope I don't have to wait as long for the next one'

room and a man whose gaunt features betray the effort he must expend to keep his weight down.

◆◆◆◆

CHAMPIONS DAY drew a crowd of 24,290, down about 25 per cent on the previous year's attendance. Organisers pointed out that the fixture was only in its third year and that Frankel had provided a significant boost in each of the previous years. The timing of the meeting in mid-October remains controversial, however, and this year heavy rain in the days leading up to Champions Day created slow ground not generally conducive to top-class racing. Despite that, a relatively strong cast arrived at Ascot, with 20 individual Group 1 winners contesting the five championship races, compared with 21 in the comparable five all-age races at Longchamp's Arc meeting.

While Frankel casts a long shadow over the fixture – the popularity of an exhibition celebrating his career was proof of that – racing is as much about celebrating history as current stars and his association with the meeting in the years to come will do it far more good than harm.

The absence of a superstar like Frankel was naturally felt most keenly on the track, but it did at least allow others to shine. Few would begrudge Farhh the crowning moment of a short, frustrating but ultimately brilliant career.

STOKED!

TRANSLATION

IT'S AUSSIE FOR WINNING

Start brushing up on your lingo (translation: Aussie slang) because no other racing destination has as much to celebrate as Australia. With multi-million dollar stakes, exceptional returns on investment and a dream run of international champions, we've got plenty to get excited about. Come and visit us Down Under and let us share our winning streak with you.

Find out more at aushorse.com.au

AUS HORSE
The Spirit of Winning

Follow us on

By Lee Mottershead

T RUTH be told, it is nigh on impossible to say which of the two was best. A two-to-one verdict gives it to Dawn Approach but the ratings edged Toronado narrowly ahead. Some will say one, some will say the other. All, however, can agree that the rivalry between two hugely talented milers provided one of the Flat season's most enjoyable narratives.

As juveniles, their paths never crossed. Dawn Approach went through six starts unbeaten, three more than Toronado, and while Richard Hannon was able to reflect on an impressive Group 2 success for his great hope, Jim Bolger could point to Group 1 victories in the flagship contests in Britain and Ireland. After Toronado had begun his season with a dashing all-the-way win in the Craven Stakes, they came together in the 2,000 Guineas with ten triumphs between them and unbeaten records to defend. Come the first Classic of 2013, something had to give.

Anyone who spoke to Richard Hughes, listened to his words or read his thoughts would have found it hard to resist backing Toronado. The champion jockey was infectiously confident about a colt whose spring surge of improvement had coincided with his purchase by Qatar's rising racing force, Sheikh Joaan Al Thani. While the son of High Chaparral had once been viewed at home principally as a Derby candidate, now he was seen as being blessed with more than enough speed to conquer a Guineas.

And yet, despite a market move for Toronado in the days leading up to the Rowley Mile showdown, punters ultimately placed their faith in Dawn Approach. He was regarded as the safe option and as the stalls crashed open bookmakers had him as the race's 11-8 favourite. When push had come to shove, Toronado had been deserted. Odds of 11-4 about the second favourite suggested a clear-cut conclusion was expected. That was what we got.

For all his great qualities, Dawn Approach had not necessarily looked brilliant prior to Newmarket. He was ruthless and relentless, he ground others into submission and got the job done. He boasted wins but he lacked the wow factor. His first run of 2013 changed that. In a race conducted at a furious gallop they

SECONDS OUT . . .

Toronado and Dawn Approach went toe to toe in three thrilling rounds that decided the European milers' title

came together with two furlongs to run. Toronado's buttons were pressed first but, while Hughes's pressing yielded no response, Dawn Approach gave Kevin Manning the sort of exhilarating response few jockeys will ever know.

In terms of a pure match, a referee would have stopped the contest before the final furlong pole was passed. Dawn Approach, devastating in his dominance, was a Guineas hero by five lengths. Toronado, seemingly legless up the final hill, was a lacklustre fourth.

"Hughesie said he felt out on his feet going into the stalls," was the reaction of a deflated Richard Hannon jnr. One day later the Hannon-Hughes combo gained compensation when Sky Lantern took the 1,000 Guineas

and further solace of sorts came with the revelation that Toronado had suffered a displaced palate. It provided some, if not total, explanation for the performance, but on the day it would have taken a rare beast indeed to have coped with Dawn Approach.

"He was very impressive," Bolger said. Connections would "sleep on" a decision about the winner's Derby

▸▸ (From left) Dawn Approach (blue) and Toronado (grey) do battle at Newmarket, Ascot and Goodwood

participation, he added. They duly slept and decided to run. What followed the sleep-induced decision was a nightmare.

At Epsom Dawn Approach was a lunatic on hooves, an uncontrollable beast who masterminded his own Derby downfall by refusing to settle. Having spent his whole life finishing first, this time he came last. Bolger put all plans on hold, save for saying: "He definitely won't be going to Royal Ascot."

That was then, though. Bolger has never been averse to changing his mind and in the days that followed Epsom he changed it quite dramatically. Toronado, who had looked likely to headline his road to redemption at Royal Ascot, suddenly found himself up against an unexpected but familiar foe.

On the eve of the five-day confirmation stage for the St James's Palace Stakes, Bolger sent Godolphin racing manager Simon Crisford a short text message. "That's my modus operandi," he explained subsequently, doing so from the Royal Ascot's winner's enclosure after Dawn Approach had narrowly denied Toronado in a thrilling conclusion to the meeting's opening-day highlight.

Toronado, this time sporting a spoon bit, was ridden with more restraint than at Newmarket, but a little early interference left him with four lengths to bridge on the Irish star. He duly bridged almost all of it, but then halfway down the straight Hughes's ploy to come widest in search of safety backfired as a chain reaction of bumps knocked Toronado sideways. Momentum was lost and so, too, was the race, albeit only by a short head.

"I would have won," said a rueful Hughes, while Bolger, whose text to Crisford had said merely, "be prepared for a surprise", was once again the sport's canniest man.

"We are piggy-backing on the brilliance and expertise of Jim Bolger," Crisford said. "When he told me he wanted to run here, I said: 'Hang on a minute, let me talk to Sheikh Mohammed first.' Sheikh Mohammed said: 'Jim bred the horse, he owns half the horse and he trains the horse. He knows every single hair on that horse's body. Whatever direction he wants to go, we go with him.'"

The next direction was Goodwood, as it was for Toronado. "We'll take the winner on again," had been Hannon's vow at Ascot. He was true to his word.

Dawn Approach, who had been sent off 5-4 favourite at the royal meeting, was once again deemed the one to beat at 10-11. But this time, the third time, would be the lucky time for Toronado.

Everything Hughes had learned from the previous setbacks was put into place. In the Sussex Stakes he challenged wide, he challenged late and he won, quite brilliantly. Dawn Approach was given no time to answer, but even with the luxury of time it is doubtful he could have denied a colt who justified his rider's belief that he had never ridden a better thoroughbred.

For Hughes, there was a massive release of pressure. After Royal Ascot, Frankie Dettori had been appointed Sheikh Joaan's retained rider but at Goodwood Hughes was allowed to keep his seat on Toronado. "For me, personally, there was a lot of riding on the race," he wrote in his Racing Post column. "I knew if I messed up I wouldn't have been able to ride him again. That would have broken my heart."

But his heart was not broken. It might even have swelled when the BHA upped Toronado to a rating of 126, bettering Dawn Approach's high of 125. Racing Post Ratings also agreed Toronado was tops, deeming the Sussex victory to be worthy of a 129 mark. To put the performance in context, Dawn Approach was adjudged to have posted his personal-best effort at 128.

Both horses raced again in Europe, without success but with excuses. After Goodwood their seasons were not over but their rivalry had come to an end.

"I'd say they were two top-class horses," was Richard Hannon's assessment after the Sussex. That pretty much sums it up.

CLOSE CONTEST

How the title fight played out and how it was assessed by Racing Post Ratings

ROUND ONE 2,000 Guineas, Newmarket, May 4

Dawn Approach punches to a five-length win, while Toronado is left legless in fourth place **Racing Post Ratings** Dawn Approach 127 Toronado 109

ROUND TWO St James's Palace Stakes, Ascot, June 18

Toronado, roughed up at one point, finishes strongly but is repelled by Dawn Approach, who holds on by a short head
Racing Post Ratings Dawn Approach 126 Toronado 126

ROUND THREE Sussex Stakes, Goodwood, July 31

Toronado finally lands a telling blow, wearing down Dawn Approach for a half-length win that gives him the overall verdict on points
Racing Post Ratings Toronado 129 Dawn Approach 128

COMMANDER IN CHIEF

Willie Mullins enjoyed a memorable year at home, at Cheltenham, even in Japan. With fresh investment in his team and Ruby Walsh back in Ireland full time, the next one could be even better

By Jonathan Mullin

IN Willie Mullins' war room it is easy to imagine the maps spread across the table, targets identified in Ireland, Britain and France, and longer-range sights set on east and west. Yes, even towards the west, meaning America. As Ireland's most successful jumps trainer looks for new territory to conquer, everywhere is under consideration.

"We have looked at running horses in America all right and it will happen, though I don't know when," he says. But a new front was opened this year when Mullins looked east to Japan and eyed up the Nakayama Grand Jump, one of the world's richest jumps races. The result was an audacious victory with Blackstairmountain that summed up Mullins' incredible season.

At home he was more dominant than ever, breaking Aidan O'Brien's record of 155 jumps winners by February and finishing the season with 193, a mammoth 139 ahead of Gordon Elliott. He also set a new mark for prize-money – €3,908,059, beating his own record by almost €1m – and was leading trainer at the Cheltenham and Punchestown festivals.

Japan was a new frontier, but it wasn't an afterthought for Mullins. Florida Pearl and Alexander Banquet had been invited in the early days of the Grand Jump, first run in 1999, but Mullins had been afraid to take them over without knowing the lie of the land. "So I went over and got a look at the track and did a little recce one year," he says. "I decided then on the type of horse I would need and I put it in the back of my mind that if I had one good enough we would go. Hoping, of course, that we might get invited with the right horse."

Eventually that horse came along. "The moment it went from the back of my mind to the front of it was when Blackstairmountain won his Grade 1 novice over fences at Leopardstown in 2012," Mullins says. "I thought then that would qualify him for going to Japan. After that it was about trying to find out what we needed to do to get to Japan."

It wasn't as easy as it had been in the early years of the Grand Jump, when an invite came with travel allowances and expenses. "The next step is even more difficult because you need an owner who is a big enough sportsman to sign up for it because it isn't a cheap trip," Mullins says. The costs –

frontloaded as they were – were severe, but the rewards were great: nearly £500,000 in first-place prize-money.

Rich Ricci, Blackstairmountain's owner, was willing to roll the dice and the plans were put in place. Willie's nephew Emmett Mullins and young staffman Dermot Keeling were sent to Japan with the horse. An unexpected bonus, discovered at the last moment, was that Dermot spoke some Japanese.

"I sent the horse over early to go into quarantine," Mullins says. "We thought it might be a good idea to take in a prep race in the Grand Jump trial [the Pegasus], which worked out beautifully. With Emmett and Dermot being out there, it was good to have our own team members giving us great feedback. That meant we could adjust things rather than just sending a man off the plane hoping and trusting that he would do everything right. It was great to get that feedback."

Well, it worked out beautifully – and it didn't. On March 23, eight days after the end of the Cheltenham Festival, Blackstairmountain went into the trial race as one of the big fancies for the Grand Jump three weeks

▶▶**Continues page 54**

▶▶(From left) Mullins with Quevega at Punchestown, Blackstairmountain in Japan and Hurricane Fly celebrations at Punchestown

later but, after trailing in ninth, he came out of it as one of the big-race outsiders. The Nakayama track takes some getting used to, however, with its stalls start, twists, uneven gradients and bewildering array of obstacles, and there were signs in Blackstairmountain's display that all was not lost.

"We learned a lot from that and the horse did too," Mullins says. Was he worried or disheartened by the performance? "Oh, I was, yes. The only thing that kept me going was that in the last mile of the Pegasus he ran well and didn't drop away, which indicated to me that he was getting used to the track and the jumps.

"When Ruby came in after the race he was happier than I was because he could obviously feel what was underneath him. He thought Blackstairmountain was beginning to like it. That gave me enough hope that we might at least get into the money and pay the expenses for the trip.

"We started favourite for the prep race and they obviously thought afterwards that this type of racing didn't suit us, but what they didn't realise is that we were just getting used to the conditions there, not least jumping out of stalls, going down to the first fence from there, the second being a water fence – things like that."

The Grand Jump was over an extra half-mile, which helped, and Blackstairmountain was much more comfortable on his return to the track. Rikiai Kurofune, the Pegasus winner, was best of the home team again but this time Blackstairmountain came out on top by half a length – a huge turnaround from the 22 lengths he was beaten in the Pegasus, albeit on 7lb better terms.

"It was all new and it was understandable maybe that the Japanese couldn't see the scope for improvement," Mullins says. "I think about 25,000 people were there and nobody really saw past our trial run. So there was huge satisfaction in winning because after that prep run the best I was hoping for was to scrape something out of it to justify going over and to cover expenses. To see him winning was huge."

East is conquered, the west should watch out.

◆◆◆◆

SPIN the clock back to the Friday evening of Cheltenham 2012. The Foxhunter has just drawn to a close and Willie and Jackie Mullins wait at the unsaddling enclosure for son Patrick and his mount Boxer Georg to come back in. It's the unsaddling enclosure you don't want to be in, the one accommodating those who didn't finish in the first four.

Mullins is reflecting on a Cheltenham Festival that saw him train three winners, a tally beaten only by Nicky Henderson. Sir Des Champs, Champagne Fever and Quevega had all collected, but there is no mistaking the dolefulness in Mullins' gait, an observation he acknowledges even now.

"Yes, I was disappointed with myself for being disappointed. I was sort of feeling that way, yet knowing myself how hard it is to get a winner, never mind three. To be competitive you probably have to look at everything like that. Sometimes it is disappointing that you don't enjoy the winners because you're thinking about the ones you thought would win. I suppose that's just being competitive."

Maybe it was the disappointment of having some of the 'bankers' turned over, of Hurricane Fly finding a couple too good in the 2012 Champion Hurdle, or of Boston Bob failing to reel in the ill-fated Brindisi Breeze in the Albert Bartlett. But even before the 2012-2013 season kicked into gear, Mullins was already talking about his string being his best ever – "this is the greatest quantity of quality we have had" – and he was right.

As if to leave no room for disappointment, Mullins cut a swathe across the season. He amassed 22 Grade 1 winners in Britain and Ireland and three of them came at Cheltenham, followed by another six at Punchestown.

In all there were five Cheltenham winners, with the tone set on the opening day when Hurricane Fly became the first horse since Comedy Of Errors in 1975 to regain the Champion Hurdle and Quevega equalled Golden Miller's record of winning at five consecutive Cheltenham Festivals.

"It was fantastic to get Hurricane Fly back to his best but to get Quevega into the position she is in now gave me huge satisfaction," Mullins says, although that victory in the David Nicholson Mares' Hurdle wasn't without a hiccup.

"I thought her run was coming to an end," he admits. "Heading up the hill along the back, I happened to take down my binoculars when she tripped and I didn't see it until the replay. When I put back my binoculars I couldn't figure out why she had dropped about five places crossing the top. I thought, 'wow, what's wrong here, this doesn't look good'. But once they opened up going to the last and she saw daylight, she put it to bed fairly quickly and that gave me huge satisfaction."

By the time she turned up at Punchestown for the World Series Hurdle, she was even better. "She was, wasn't she? She seemed better for the race. We've always decided against giving her a prep run for Cheltenham but you'd think with the way she improved from Cheltenham to Punchestown that maybe we should rethink things this season. I don't know, I hate saying that we might because we've always just done what we've done. I'd be sick if I ran her and she got injured. We'll see."

What Mullins has now is a team of horses and a team of owners ready to take on the best and, like a top-flight football manager, the off season was used to sign up the stars of the future. "You have to have the resources to renew, that is very important, and we're lucky that we have clients who have those resources at the moment. It wasn't always that way and I'm sure somewhere down the road it won't be like that either.

"You buy ten or 15 and hope one of them does the trick. Maybe once every three or four years you get a Kauto Star or a Sprinter Sacre. Those horses are hard to come by no matter how much money you have. But that's what you're in this game for, to find that 'one'."

Mullins made another important summer signing – the permanent transfer back to Ireland of Ruby Walsh – and that has opened the door to having more runners in Britain throughout the season, not just at the big festivals.

"I have quite a few owners based there and they would enjoy seeing their horses run in England more often," Mullins says. "I will be going over much more regularly with our better horses. It makes sense, especially now I have Ruby around all the time. His knowledge of British courses and horses will be a huge help."

Mullins, more than ever, is ready to fight on all fronts.

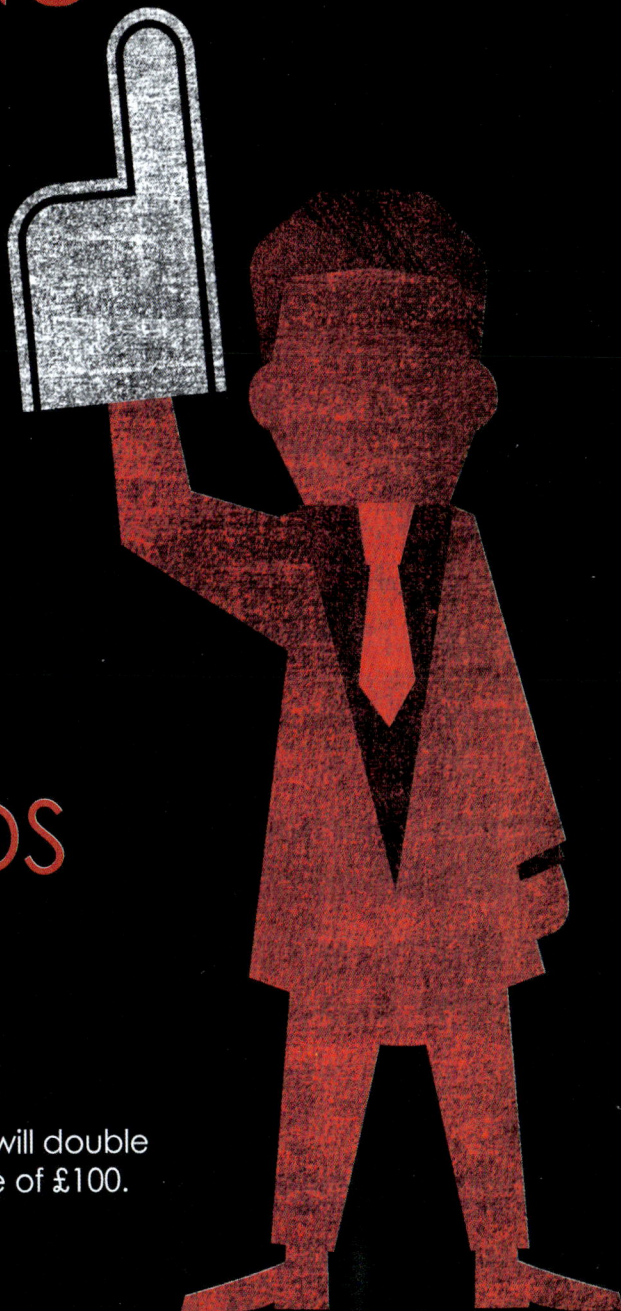

BACK WITH A BANG

Hurricane Fly returned to his best to regain his Champion Hurdle crown and complete a perfect season

By Jonathan Mullin

LIKE plenty of happy stories, this one begins on a sorry note. Not that Hurricane Fly can ever be regarded as a rags-to-riches tale – he was, after all, a Listed winner on the Flat in France. But when he walked out of the parade ring at Cheltenham after a 2012 Champion Hurdle that saw him bloodied and bowed, many presumed this was a prizefighter handing over his title belt for good.

After his success the previous year, the market had seen little chance of defeat, punters making him their Tuesday banker, their festival banker, and the 4-6 favourite. But sometimes the market can only capture the superficial.

Inside, where it matters, Hurricane Fly was not the pocket-sized force he was in 2011. And although Cheltenham defeat was followed by a Grade 1 win at Punchestown, the bar had been set so high by his Irish Champion Hurdle win at Leopardstown the previous January that it was difficult not to be underwhelmed by the Punchestown success. Loose plans to go to Auteuil in June were shelved and Willie Mullins saw enough to prescribe the medicine: a summer surrounded by grass, peace and tranquillity.

◆◆◆◆

IN County Carlow, the support team waited patiently on his autumn return, none more so than his groom. Meet Gail Carlisle: Mrs Hurricane Fly. Carlisle, from Ballynahinch in County Down, knew from an early age that horses were the life she yearned for. Her school was so close to Downpatrick that she could literally walk to the races and, upon leaving, she started out with Colm McBratney. Then, five years ago, she joined the Mullins team and soon she inherited a lively son of Montjeu.

She couldn't say she came into the 2012-13 season full of trepidation, but there was more than a little anxiety. Minding Hurricane Fly requires a special set of skills: great patience, great strength and a wary attention to detail.

"He's a handful because he never stands still for a second. He loves having a nip at you but he doesn't mean it in a malicious way, he's just all go. I've never been bitten by him but I've lost count of the amount of times he has stood on my toes while I've been brushing him down.

"Of course we were worried [when he came back] because he wasn't himself the previous season and you're thinking, 'right, let's see, will you return to the horse you were? Are you going to be as good

▶Continues page 58

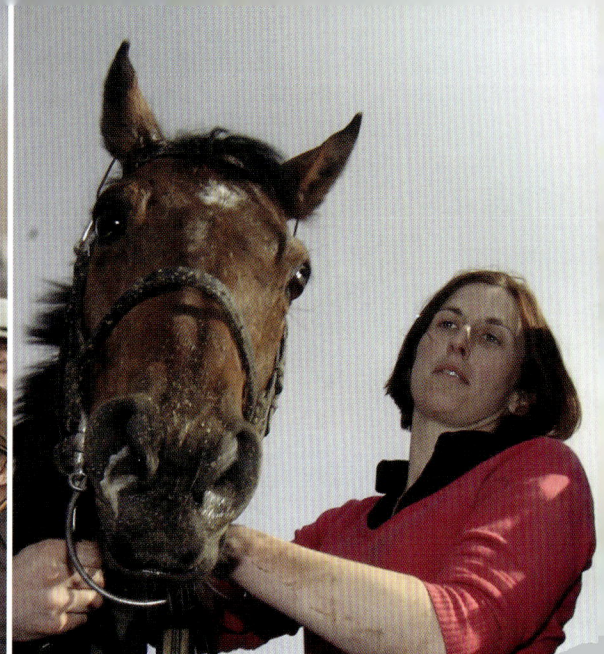

again?' For a while we had to wait and see how it would play out and let the horse tell us."

Mullins doesn't rush his horses, taking things steady in September and October before picking up the pace in mid-November. The policy has reaped rich dividends and enables his team to keep their winter form right into Punchestown in late spring and early summer. And, according to Mullins, the summer holiday worked wonders. "Hurricane Fly came back really well and had got much stronger."

But still Carlisle and her colleagues were waiting to see whether their stable star was back in the form of 2011. Finally, in the early days of November, a glimmer, and then, weeks later, an unmistakable glint in his eye. "In the days before he ran in the Morgiana we could see he was coming back," Carlisle says. "He was not making it easy for Paul [Townend, his regular work rider] and up the gallops he was taking Paul on the whole time. Personally I could see that he was charging his stable door. He could hear the other horses getting tacked up and he wasn't happy that he wasn't one of them.

"If I go in to put his head collar on, I have to bolt the door behind me or he'll be gone. I come back from my lunch at two o'clock and he is hopping off the door. 'Me, me, me.' He has a clock in his head, this fella, and knows when it's his turn to go to the paddock."

That impatience, the impetuousness, told Mullins, Carlisle and the rest of the team that Hurricane Fly was back. "When Fly's on tune he's a little bugger," Carlisle says. "He's hard work and the lads would say 'he's a bit hyper'. But when's he quiet he's not right. If he was standing in his box with his four feet in the four corners you would be worried. But the whole winter went so well, you couldn't have asked for better. Having

three races before Cheltenham, the Morgiana at Punchestown, the Istabraq Festival and Irish Champion Hurdles at Leopardstown – the programme that Willie has set out for him – just seems to work."

Hurricane Fly was imperious in Ireland, stretching his winning run on home ground to ten – all Group 1s – as he took those three races with ease. The question now was whether he could put 2012 behind him at Cheltenham. As the tipster Mark Winstanley quipped at a Cheltenham preview night: "Regaining a Champion Hurdle is so difficult Shakespeare wrote a play about it." Comedy Of Errors, in 1975, was the only Champion Hurdle winner to have lost the crown and claimed it back again, and the weight of history hung heavy on Hurricane Fly.

"It was a nervous time," Carlisle says, "because so many said he couldn't do it and so many said it couldn't be done. Paul and I were trying to convince each other he could do it."

And, as Mullins always suspected and then found out to his cost in 2012 was true, the danger with talking one of your horses up before a race like the Champion Hurdle is that it will come back to bite you. "And I have the marks to prove it," he laughs.

◆◆◆◆

IT WAS the morning of the Champion Hurdle and one that Mullins will never forget. Not just because of the arctic air that sat on the Cotswolds like clingfilm, but because of an incident after the Mullins battalion finished their morning stretch.

"David [Casey] and I were putting back the tack when we heard a roar," Carlisle says. "It was Willie coming from the Fly's box. He left a bucket of water in with him but he turned his back on

▶▶ (From left) Crossing the line in the Champion Hurdle, arriving in the winner's enclosure and with groom Gail Carlisle after winning at Punchestown

HISTORY BOYS

Willie Mullins equalled Tom Dreaper's record of Cheltenham Festival winners for an Irish trainer with Hurricane Fly's second Champion Hurdle success. By the end of the meeting he had the outright record on 29

Hurricane Fly became only the second horse to lose and regain the Champion Hurdle crown, winning in 2011 and 2013. He joined Comedy Of Errors, the winner in 1973 and 1975

Champion Hurdle victory took Hurricane Fly past Moscow Flyer as Ireland's highest-earning jumps horse. By the end of the season his total was €1,731,788 (£1,469,629)

With his Punchestown Champion Hurdle victory in April, Hurricane Fly joined Kauto Star on a record 16 Grade 1 wins over jumps

him for a second on the way out and that's when Hurricane Fly spotted his opportunity."

Mullins says: "He certainly showed his wellbeing all right and I still bear the scars. Thankfully everything went right on the day, even though it didn't . . ." He is almost anticipating the next question.

Mike Cattermole's commentary on the 2013 Champion Hurdle was peppered with concern for the way Hurricane Fly was travelling through the race and punters watching and listening from the grandstands followed with audible trepidation. Mullins, too, shifted from foot to foot, watching anxiously.

"There were stages during the race where I wondered to myself 'is he travelling at all, is he going to be okay?' A lot of viewers were definitely very worried at different stages and I was too. But maybe it is that his style of racing is changing. We'll see this season and if that is the case we'll adjust for that, but there was no doubting his class when he turned in. He is a remarkable horse and we're lucky to have him."

Before Grandouet fell four out, Hurricane Fly was a little detached from the leading group of four but rounding the turn at the top of the hill he closed up on Rock On Ruby, Zarkandar and Countrywide Flame. By the second-last he was pressing Rock On Ruby for the lead and he took over as they turned into the straight. From there, hard as the 2012 winner tried, Hurricane Fly was not going to be beaten.

For Carlisle it was the moment in her career that she thinks and hopes she will remember most. "There was a huge degree of satisfaction," she says, "and then he was even more like himself when he came back to Punchestown the following month. You'll put up with getting your toes stood upon for days like that."

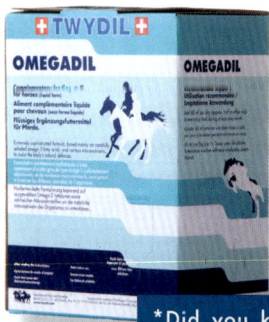

THE YOUNG ONES

Our Conor went from jumps debutant to Champion Hurdle joint-favourite with Hurricane Fly in the space of four months but he wasn't the only first-season hurdler to impress in a crop of enormous potential

By Nick Pulford

THE racing life of a thoroughbred is extremely short. A mere fraction of time is spent doing what they are trained for, much less than in other sports, and yet the preparation for those fleeting moments on the racecourse encompasses years of hard work, worry and hope. For the lucky few, the highest hopes will be fulfilled but there will always be worry.

Dessie Hughes understands that

▸▸ Continues page 62

better than most. The former top jump jockey is in his 35th year as a trainer and he knows what a good horse looks and feels like. He also knows how easily things can go wrong. That's why, in the long months and years before Our Conor made his debut over hurdles, Hughes suffered with ulcers. He may be a veteran of Champion Hurdle victories as a rider and trainer, but this was pressure of a different order. The pressure of knowing this young horse could be 'the one'.

From the first time Our Conor schooled as a two-year-old, Hughes was always looking deep into the future. "He was exciting all right, the most exciting horse I've had," he says. "He always schooled exceptionally well, he just really likes jumping. I couldn't wait to run him in his first three-year-old hurdle and, when I did, it was just a canter for him." From that moment, in November 2012, what Hughes had known for almost two years became apparent to everyone else: here was a hurdler with the talent to go right to the top.

In the space of four months Our Conor raced for only a little more than 16 and a half minutes, yet that was enough to stamp himself a hurdler of rare class. He won four out of four,

RARE TALENTS

How the top five novice hurdlers of 2012-13 compare

Champagne Fever
Best RPR 164 Grade 1 wins 2
Best performance Victory over My Tent Or Yours and Jezki in the Supreme at Cheltenham

Our Conor
Best RPR 164 Grade 1 wins 2
Best performance Runaway win in the Triumph at Cheltenham by 15 lengths

The New One
Best RPR 164 Grade 1 wins 1
Best performance Close second to Zarkandar in the Aintree Hurdle, having won the Neptune at Cheltenham

My Tent Or Yours
Best RPR 163 Grade 1 wins 0
Best performance Nothing to choose between Betfair Hurdle win and Supreme second

Jezki
Best RPR 162 Grade 1 wins 3
Best performance Champion Novice Hurdle win at Punchestown, with Champagne Fever third

'He was exciting all right, the most exciting horse I've had. I couldn't wait to run him in his first three-year-old hurdle and, when I did, it was a canter for him'

culminating in a 15-length victory in the Triumph Hurdle at Cheltenham, and ended the season disputing favouritism for the 2014 Champion Hurdle with Hurricane Fly.

The only surprise all season for Hughes was the manner of Our Conor's victory at Cheltenham. Standing in the hallowed winner's enclosure, he said: "I can't believe he won by 15 lengths. He was absolutely brilliant, he jumped marvellous and travelled, and the quicker they went the better he went."

Hughes's confidence in Our Conor was clear. "He's certainly a Champion Hurdle horse" was his bold statement and he should know, having trained Hardy Eustace to win two Champion Hurdles and ridden Monksfield to his second Champion victory in 1979. He does not shy away from measuring his rising star against Hardy Eustace and Our Conor does well from the comparison, matching him for jumping ability but with speed on top. "This lad has a lot of pace, loads of pace," Hughes says, with double emphasis.

Our Conor also has a high price tag, rumoured at €1 million, after leading Irish owner Barry Connell stepped in to buy him four days after Cheltenham. Achievement had brought more

THE YOUNG ONES

Our Conor went from jumps debutant to Champion Hurdle joint-favourite with Hurricane Fly in the space of four months but he wasn't the only first-season hurdler to impress in a crop of enormous potential

By Nick Pulford

THE racing life of a thoroughbred is extremely short. A mere fraction of time is spent doing what they are trained for, much less than in other sports, and yet the preparation for those fleeting moments on the racecourse encompasses years of hard work, worry and hope. For the lucky few, the highest hopes will be fulfilled but there will always be worry.

Dessie Hughes understands that

▸▸ Continues page 62

better than most. The former top jump jockey is in his 35th year as a trainer and he knows what a good horse looks and feels like. He also knows how easily things can go wrong. That's why, in the long months and years before Our Conor made his debut over hurdles, Hughes suffered with ulcers. He may be a veteran of Champion Hurdle victories as a rider and trainer, but this was pressure of a different order. The pressure of knowing this young horse could be 'the one'.

From the first time Our Conor schooled as a two-year-old, Hughes was always looking deep into the future. "He was exciting all right, the most exciting horse I've had," he says. "He always schooled exceptionally well, he just really likes jumping. I couldn't wait to run him in his first three-year-old hurdle and, when I did, it was just a canter for him." From that moment, in November 2012, what Hughes had known for almost two years became apparent to everyone else: here was a hurdler with the talent to go right to the top.

In the space of four months Our Conor raced for only a little more than 16 and a half minutes, yet that was enough to stamp himself a hurdler of rare class. He won four out of four,

RARE TALENTS

How the top five novice hurdlers of 2012-13 compare

Champagne Fever
Best RPR 164 Grade 1 wins 2
Best performance Victory over My Tent Or Yours and Jezki in the Supreme at Cheltenham

Our Conor
Best RPR 164 Grade 1 wins 2
Best performance Runaway win in the Triumph at Cheltenham by 15 lengths

The New One
Best RPR 164 Grade 1 wins 1
Best performance Close second to Zarkandar in the Aintree Hurdle, having won the Neptune at Cheltenham

My Tent Or Yours
Best RPR 163 Grade 1 wins 0
Best performance Nothing to choose between Betfair Hurdle win and Supreme second

Jezki
Best RPR 162 Grade 1 wins 3
Best performance Champion Novice Hurdle win at Punchestown, with Champagne Fever third

'He was exciting all right, the most exciting horse I've had. I couldn't wait to run him in his first three-year-old hurdle and, when I did, it was a canter for him'

culminating in a 15-length victory in the Triumph Hurdle at Cheltenham, and ended the season disputing favouritism for the 2014 Champion Hurdle with Hurricane Fly.

The only surprise all season for Hughes was the manner of Our Conor's victory at Cheltenham. Standing in the hallowed winner's enclosure, he said: "I can't believe he won by 15 lengths. He was absolutely brilliant, he jumped marvellous and travelled, and the quicker they went the better he went."

Hughes's confidence in Our Conor was clear. "He's certainly a Champion Hurdle horse" was his bold statement and he should know, having trained Hardy Eustace to win two Champion Hurdles and ridden Monksfield to his second Champion victory in 1979. He does not shy away from measuring his rising star against Hardy Eustace and Our Conor does well from the comparison, matching him for jumping ability but with speed on top. "This lad has a lot of pace, loads of pace," Hughes says, with double emphasis.

Our Conor also has a high price tag, rumoured at €1 million, after leading Irish owner Barry Connell stepped in to buy him four days after Cheltenham. Achievement had brought more

pressure but Hughes, ever patient, was still playing the long game. When the ground turned heavy at Punchestown, Our Conor was scratched from the Grade 1 Champion Four Year Old Hurdle. The season had been long enough, Hughes reasoned, and he was encouraged by the positive effect of the enforced break after a cough prevented Our Conor from running at the Leopardstown Christmas meeting.

In hindsight Hughes believes that was a blessing in disguise and, in the long run, missing Punchestown might help Our Conor. Simply put, "it was this season we had to concentrate on," he says.

◆◆◆◆

THE 2012-13 season would have been memorable for the emergence of Our Conor alone, but he was only one of an impressive group of first-season hurdlers.

While Our Conor laid waste to the four-year-old division, the all-age novice hurdles produced a series of outstanding performances, mixed with some disappointments. At the end of the season, the arguments were still raging over who was the best of them, but what was not in dispute was the rare talent of this crop of novice hurdlers.

As the season opened, Willie Mullins had the 2012 Champion Bumper winner Champagne Fever in his strong team and Nicky Henderson's budding stars included My Tent Or Yours, but the talent wasn't confined to the championship-winning stables.

Like Hughes with Our Conor, Nigel Twiston-Davies could not wait to see what The New One would do over hurdles. As soon as a saddle was put on him, Twiston-Davies says, "he was going up the gallops as fast as anything else". But even as The New One started to prove Twiston-Davies right in his belief that this was the best horse he had trained, the pressure only grew.

When the big moment came, in the Neptune Novices' Hurdle at the Cheltenham Festival, years of patience were boiled down to five and a quarter minutes of make or break. The New One handled the occasion with aplomb, but Twiston-Davies spent most of the race in the toilets with "terrible gutache", emerging only to see The New One jump the last and go clear for a four-length victory. It was hardly a case of basking in the glory, considering all the waiting that had gone before.

Within four months of first being tacked up, The New One was on a

▸▸ (From left) Cheltenham Festival scorers Champagne Fever, The New One and Our Conor, Betfair Hurdle winner My Tent Or Yours and Jezki after his Grade 1 success at Punchestown

racecourse, winning a bumper, and four months after that he was sixth in the Champion Bumper at the Cheltenham Festival. It would transpire that he was one of three future Grade 1-winning hurdlers in the field – along with Champagne Fever, the winner, and eighth-placed Jezki – and yet Twiston-Davies felt the race could have gone better for The New One. His conviction was proved right at Aintree, where The New One won the Grade 2 bumper from My Tent Or Yours, another who would prove a top-level novice hurdler.

While the other leading bumper horses stayed at two miles over hurdles in the 2012-13 season, Twiston-Davies framed The New One's novice campaign around the longer Neptune at Cheltenham. He didn't doubt The New One's speed but went down that route "because bumper horses normally seem to need two and a half miles".

By mid-January The New One had won his first three starts over hurdles, including a Grade 2 contest at Warwick, and was disputing favouritism for the Neptune with the Mullins-trained Pont Alexandre. Twiston-Davies felt he needed more experience and sent him to the Cheltenham trials meeting, but on
▸▸**Continues page 64**

heavy ground the experience wasn't what the trainer had hoped for. The New One quickened clear but then became bogged down and was overhauled by the strong stayer At Fishers Cross, who would go on to land a pair of Grade 1 wins.

Sam Twiston-Davies blamed himself for going too early but there was no disgrace in defeat in conditions that suited At Fishers Cross and his father remained as convinced as ever that The New One was the best he had trained. Reflecting in the summer on what the defeat had taught them, he said: "I don't think we learned anything, just that he's a very fast horse."

The New One proved that on his return to Cheltenham for the Neptune, when he quickened off a slow pace to score convincingly from Rule The World and 6-4 favourite Pont Alexandre. He was clearly established as the best novice at the intermediate distance of two and a half miles and Twiston-Davies felt there was nothing more to prove against his peers. Like Hughes, he was already looking towards the next season and decided to pitch him into senior company in the Aintree Hurdle, where a group of experienced rivals included Countrywide Flame and Zarkandar, fresh from finishing third and fourth in the Champion Hurdle.

"We thought he was ready for it and we could win the race," Twiston-Davies says. "That was his best run of the season, without a doubt." The New One lost out to Zarkandar in a titanic tussle but won the admiration of Ruby Walsh,

Zarkandar's jockey, who said he was "very impressed" with the runner-up.

Twiston-Davies's faith was only enhanced by The New One's novice campaign and he looks forward to the next chapter with relish. He is certainly unconcerned about dropping back to two miles in order to aim for the Champion Hurdle.

"We watched the replay of the Neptune with the owners one day and the way he quickened between the last two was absolutely phenomenal. An awful lot of Champion Hurdle winners have won that race. The Champion Hurdle is normally run at a hell of a pace and the winner has to be a good stayer to win it. He has proved he's got plenty of speed and I'm more than happy with two miles."

◆◆◆◆

THE NEW ONE and Our Conor may have emerged as clear winners of their divisions, but the two-mile novice division was less clear-cut. At the end of the season Champagne Fever, the Supreme Novices' Hurdle winner, was top-rated on an RPR of 164 – level with The New One and Our Conor – but close behind were My Tent Or Yours on 163 and Jezki on 162.

The Supreme was the crucial race in ratings terms and victory for Champagne Fever justified Mullins' decision to send him hurdling for a season rather than take him straight from bumpers to chases. There had

'The Champion Hurdle is normally run at a hell of a pace and the winner has to be a good stayer to win it. He has proved he's got plenty of speed and I'm more than happy with two miles'

been hiccups along the way – defeat by Jezki in the Grade 1 Royal Bond at Fairyhouse in December and a poor run the following month at Naas – but he bounced back to take the Grade 1 Deloitte at Leopardstown in February and improved again at Cheltenham.

"I thought the game was up at the second-last," Mullins admitted, and Champagne Fever's willingness to battle up the hill against speedy rivals marked him out as a first-rate chaser in the making. For the placed horses, My Tent Or Yours or Jezki, there were questions still to be resolved.

When My Tent Or Yours won a four-runner Grade 2 race at Aintree the following month, it didn't prove much apart from the looming decision facing his connections. "He's got to be in the 'contenders' bracket for next year's Champion Hurdle," Henderson said. "We'll see what everyone wants to do. He'll jump a fence if we want him to but I'd like to talk to AP [McCoy] and see what he thinks."

Jessica Harrington was more than disappointed by Jezki's third place in the Supreme. She was perplexed then and still is. She had nurtured Jezki for two years in preparation for a hurdling career and, once he had started with a debut win at Naas in October 2012, his progress had been swift. By Christmas he was a dual Grade 1 winner and Harrington was convinced Jezki was the best she had trained at this age.

Early in the new year JP McManus, having liked what he saw, bought him

GO racing in IRELAND

Whenever you are in Ireland, you're never far from a race meeting and if you want to understand one of our country's great passions and meet the Irish at play, choose from over 300 race meetings at any of the 26 racecourses around the country and have a day you'll always remember.

2014 RACING FESTIVALS

LEOPARDSTOWN
January Jumps
25th - 26th January

CORK
Easter Festival
19th - 21st April

FAIRYHOUSE
Easter Festival
20th - 21st April

PUNCHESTOWN
National Hunt
Festival
29th April - 3rd May

KILLARNEY
Spring Festival
11th - 13th May

CURRAGH
Guineas Festival
24th - 25th May

CURRAGH
Irish Derby
Festival
27th - 29th June

BELLEWSTOWN
July Festival
4th - 6th July

KILLARNEY
July Festival
14th - 17th July

CURRAGH
Irish Oaks Weekend
19th - 20th July

GALWAY
Summer Festival
28th July - 3rd August

TRAMORE
August Festival
14th - 17th August

KILLARNEY
August Festival
20th - 23rd August

**LEOPARDSTOWN
& CURRAGH**
Irish Champions
Weekend
13th - 14th September

LISTOWEL
Harvest Festival
14th - 20th September

DOWN ROYAL
Northern Ireland
Festival of Racing
31st October -
1st November

FAIRYHOUSE
Premier Jump
Weekend
29th - 30th November

LEOPARDSTOWN
Christmas Festival
26th - 29th December

LIMERICK
Christmas Festival
26th - 29th December

To plan your day at the races or for a FREE racing information pack, please call the **Marketing Team on + 353 45 455 455** or visit **www.goracing.ie**

facebook.com/goracing   twitter.com/@goracing

goracing.ie
The Horse Racing Ireland Website

HORSE RACING IRELAND

and Silviniaco Conti had tuned up with victory in the Denman Chase at Newbury. Yet the Hennessy form would prove remarkably robust, with subsequent Grade 1 winners Tidal Bay and First Lieutenant having filled the places, and so would Bobs Worth.

Geraghty had feared beforehand that the soft ground would be detrimental to his chance of victory, but as usual he had the most willing partner at Cheltenham. "Between five and six out I was in trouble and I knew jumping three out they had got six or seven lengths clear of me," the jockey recalls. "But they weren't getting any further ahead and I could feel my fellow filling up. So I just nursed and nursed him and didn't go for everything. I was driving in fourth gear and saving fifth gear until the second-last.

"What came into my head between the last two fences was that once this horse got his head in front he hadn't been headed. I was praying it wasn't going to happen for the first time that day." It wasn't. Bobs Worth was fit and ready for the battle, just as Henderson had promised after the Hennessy.

◆◆◆◆

MALCOLM KIMMINS, 76, lives near Lambourn and knows Henderson better than most. As one of five co-owners of Bobs Worth, known as the Not Afraid Partnership, Kimmins is well placed to appreciate Henderson's talent. "Nicky's attention to detail is faultless," he says. "He has the ability to mentally store every little bit of information about a horse filtering in from those involved every day. He's nothing short of a genius and his achievement with Bobs Worth is a fine example of that. Bob, rightly, has a reputation for being one of the toughest horses in training, and indeed he's as tough as old boots, but he can be fragile in that if there's the slightest little thing wrong with him it tends to be a major problem. That's why he'll have physio on his muscles from Philippa James most days."

Kimmins has owned jumpers for more than 40 years, initially with Fulke Walwyn in partnership with brother-in-law Christopher Pilkington, and at times cannot believe he has won a Gold Cup. Several rooms at his home, including the downstairs cloakroom, are adorned with pictures of Bobs Worth. "It's no exaggeration to say he has changed my life. We've had such fun. Please don't ask me how many times I've watched the replay of the Gold Cup because the answer is ridiculously embarrassing. On so many evenings I

tell Jane [his wife] that I'm off to watch the television news, but I press replay. She, of course, knows exactly what I'm up to and comes to watch it with me."

Never at ease watching a runner live, Kimmins was riddled with nerves at Cheltenham. "During the race I had Jane hold me up on one side, with Charlie [his son] on the other. At the top of the hill it wasn't looking at all good. I'd not been intelligent enough to notice that he hadn't been travelling well for most of the race. I did notice, however, that the leading group had quickened away from him after the fourth-last fence and I knew we were in trouble."

Coming round the home turn, Long Run led against the rail with Sir Des Champs challenging strongly on his outside. The Giant Bolster, runner-up the previous year, was plugging on in third and Bobs Worth appeared to be doing the same just behind him. In the straight it was a war of attrition and Geraghty's soldier was armed and ready. Long Run briefly appeared to have repelled Sir Des Champs, but all the time Bobs Worth was gaining ground.

"Although I doubt too many noticed it, he pinged the final two fences," Kimmins says. "I know people say he's all about stamina, but he has speed too. Barry told me that after he'd worked at Kempton before the Gold Cup. What happened after he hit the front became something of a blur. I felt as if I was in some kind of time warp. We celebrated at Nicky's and then, when I arrived home, I watched the race eight times, before going to bed at 3am."

In landing the Gold Cup, Bobs Worth became Henderson's 50th winner at the Cheltenham Festival. He was also the first since Flyingbolt almost 50 years earlier to win three different races at consecutive Cheltenham Festivals. Many greybeards insist Flyingbolt was the equal, or almost the equal, of his stable companion Arkle. Bobs Worth is not as close in ability to the best in his stable, the brilliant Sprinter Sacre, but he is a star in his own right and in Henderson he has a trainer who understands him and knows how to get the best out of him.

"In the string you'd never know he's there," the trainer says. "He's not one of those flashy types always wanting to get noticed. He's much the same in a race, buried in the mid-division just mooching along and then, all of a sudden two fences from home, up he pops. He's the most remarkable horse."

With a most remarkable dossier of achievement.

LONG HAUL

Barry Geraghty guided Bobs Worth from yearling to Gold Cup winner

"Barry has what I can only describe as a telepathy with the horse. He never bullies him, just lets him find his stride and strike into a rhythm." The words of Malcolm Kimmins could be applied to any number of the big-race winners partnered by Barry Geraghty, whose innate horsemanship has made him one of the foremost race-riders of his generation, but they have never been more apt than with Bobs Worth.

Geraghty bought his future Gold Cup winner as a yearling, raised him for two and a half years before selling him to Nicky Henderson, and now rides him for a syndicate headed by Kimmins.

But it was more an act of kindness than a specific desire to have Bobs Worth join his team that led to Henderson making the final bid at £20,000 for the then unraced four-year-old by Bob Back at Doncaster Sales in May 2009. Geraghty had bought him at Tattersalls Ireland in November 2006 for €16,500. In the summer of 2008 he was led out unsold at Goffs in Ireland at €24,000. Whichever way Geraghty was looking at this pinhooking exercise, he faced a deficit after all the costs of keeping the horse.

Henderson, always the busiest of trainers at the Doncaster May sale, where he sells and restocks with stores, takes up the story. "I was pottering about and bumped into Barry, who, knowing I like Bob Back's progeny, asked if I'd seen his horse. He got him out of the box and trotted him up and down. He was on the small side and I can't say I was thinking 'I must have this horse', but Minty [agent David Minton] and I both liked him.

"The horse was making no money and I suspect my final two bids were more to help out Barry than a desire to take the horse home. I had at the back of my mind, however, that at least he was a four-year-old and therefore a season closer to racing than most of the younger ones at that sale."

Then came the job of finding an owner. "He was by no means the first I sold that summer. The Not Afraid Partnership was a syndicate started by the late Nigel Clark, who was president at Kempton and did so much for racing and charitable causes. When, sadly, Nigel died in 2007, management of the syndicate was taken on by Malcolm Kimmins, who had been a great friend of Dad's."

The other members of the syndicate are Caro Wells, John Jarvis, Nick Deacon and David Nash, who together had owned the smart hurdler Afrad. The quintet arrived at Seven Barrows in hope of finding another horse as good as him and Henderson remembers the choice came down to two. "I can't recall the name of the other one, but it was Caro was selected Bobs Worth.

"We've had a wonderful summer celebrating the Gold Cup win. They are such an enthusiastic team. Malcolm has hosted lots of dinner parties to celebrate and at the end of the evening will always say 'let's watch the race just once more'."

Kimmins says "it was an extraordinary bit of luck" that Bobs Worth was the chosen one. But, from then on, luck has played no part. It has been down to the talent of Henderson and his team, Geraghty's understanding of his partner, and the horse himself.

privately from owner-breeder Gerard McGrath. McManus already had My Tent Or Yours, but the talent in this crop of novice hurdlers was so obvious that big-money interest was inevitable, as it would be with Our Conor later in the season.

While Tony McCoy chose My Tent Or Yours over Jezki in the Supreme, Harrington believed she had McManus's best chance. It is a measure of her confidence in Jezki, and particularly his killer turn of foot, that she expected victory in such a hot championship race. With a Grade 1 win over Champagne Fever before Cheltenham, and another afterwards at Punchestown, Jezki justified her faith everywhere except at Cheltenham.

"I'm still mystified about why he ran so badly at Cheltenham," Harrington says. "I thought after the last he'd scamper away from them. Okay, he made a bit of a mistake at the last but he was never going to scamper away from them like he did at Punchestown and at Leopardstown over Christmas. In all his other runs he just changed gear at the last and went away from them. Punchestown was great – that's what I was expecting him to do at Cheltenham."

Harrington is only ten miles down the road from Hughes's Curragh stable and she is looking forward to crossing swords with Our Conor and the other up-and-coming Champion Hurdle hopefuls, as well as title-holder Hurricane Fly. She remains confident

Jezki can more than hold his own.

"It's hard to know until they all meet," she says. "Our Conor's a year younger than him, Hurricane Fly's older than him, and until they all meet we won't know the pecking order. You would imagine he would step up again. He did very well over the summer and came back in great nick. He's got speed, he jumps well, he relaxes now in his races and he just seems to have a good attitude. He's a real smashing horse."

Jezki's ability to settle had been a question mark, as it was for My Tent Or Yours even after his impressive Betfair Hurdle win against seasoned handicappers in February. Faster-run races against better opposition seemed to bring improvement from the McManus pair and that is one factor that may help them to step up to a new level this season.

Ground conditions may also determine the pecking order. Most of the big races last winter were run on going that had 'soft' or even 'heavy' in the official description and several of the top hurdling prospects are unproven on good ground.

The rain that fell at Cheltenham before the Triumph was seen as a boon for Our Conor but Hughes believes faster going will not be a hindrance, even though good to soft at Cheltenham was officially the quickest he raced on in his first season. "It was quick enough at Leopardstown when he won, it was real good jumping ground," Hughes says. "He doesn't need soft or heavy ground."

THE RPR VIEW

As a group the novice hurdlers from last season were probably the strongest in the history of Racing Post Ratings, with no fewer than five horses breaking the 160 barrier.

The fences-bound Champagne Fever (164) took the notable scalps of Aintree/Punchestown winners My Tent Or Yours (163) and Jezki (162) in a vintage Supreme Novices' Hurdle, while Neptune winner The New One (164) went on to beat all bar Zarkandar in the Aintree Hurdle.

The New One, My Tent Or Yours and Jezki all have the potential to develop into the 170 performers needed to land an average Champion Hurdle.

However, it was the juvenile Our Conor (164) who made the biggest impression, his wide-margin win in the Triumph Hurdle ensuring he replaced the 1999 Supreme Novices' Hurdle winner Hors La Loi as the highest-rated four-year-old Cheltenham Festival winner.

Given normal weight-for-age improvement, Our Conor looks sure to develop into a 170+ hurdler this season and Hurricane Fly, who turns ten this season, may struggle to maintain his dominance.

▶▶ (From left) Jezki wins at Punchestown, Our Conor on the gallops, Tony McCoy drives out My Tent Or Yours in the Betfair Hurdle, The New One powers up the Cheltenham hill and Champagne Fever shows his wellbeing in morning exercise at Cheltenham before his Supreme Novices' win

Twiston-Davies is equally confident about The New One. "I'm sure he goes in any ground," he says. "He has proved he's very good, there's no doubt about it, and he's still very young." Worry has been submerged for now but soon it will bubble to the surface again as long-held hopes face the acid test.

For jump racing fans, there is only excitement at what lies ahead. The best crop of novice hurdlers for many years, possibly ever, is laden with possibilities. Where they go from here promises to be one of the most compelling narratives of the new season.

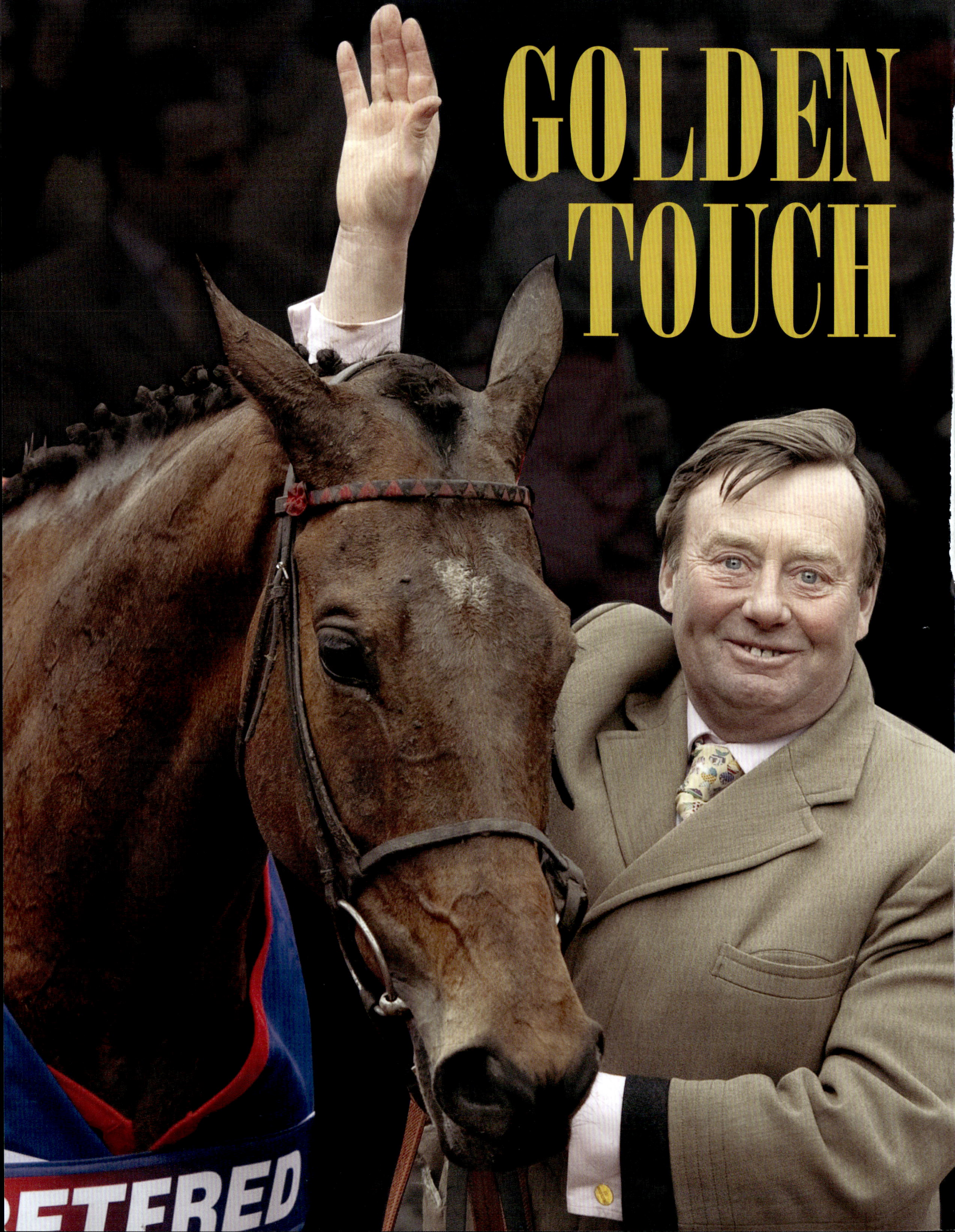

GOLDEN TOUCH

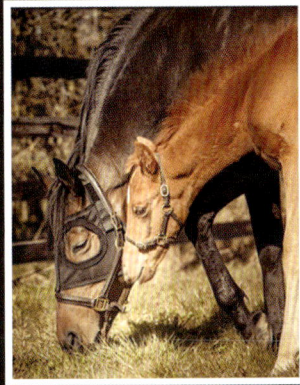

CHELTENHAM
in pictures

1 A bird's eye view of the National Hunt Chase from Cleeve Hill

2 Journalists scramble for Willie Mullins' reaction to Hurricane Fly's victory in the Champion Hurdle

3 Cue Card and Joe Tizzard win the Ryanair Chase

4 The Duke and Duchess of Cambridge watch the action on Gold Cup day

5 The 24 runners in the Pertemps Final set off on the three-mile trip. The 25-1 shot Holywell won the race for Jonjo O'Neill and Richie McLernon

6 Colman Sweeney hugs Salsify after winning the Foxhunter Chase for the second year in a row

7 Barry Geraghty (left) and Ruby Walsh line up for the RSA Chase. Irish champion Davy Russell won the race on the Jim Culloty-trained Lord Windermere

8 Bookmakers and punters in the betting ring on Gold Cup day

9 Davy Russell celebrates his RSA Chase win on Lord Windermere

10 A touch of glamour on ladies' day, the second day of the festival

11 Holywell powers up the hill in the Pertemps Final

12 The water jump in the Cross Country Chase won by Big Shu

13 The Venetia Williams-trained Carrickboy on his way to victory in the Byrne Group Plate. He was the first festival winner for jockey Liam Treadwell

14 Celebrations after Hurricane Fly's triumph in the Champion Hurdle

15 Taking a break

SCANDAL

After all the positive headlines generated by Frankel, racing was mired in negative publicity in 2013

By Mark Storey

IN 2013 a seven-letter word again dominated British racing. But this time it had nothing to do with Frankel. Scandal was not the name of the Arc winner or a thrilling two-year-old to hang your winter hopes on. No, scandal was a theme, polluting racing's waters.

In 2012 we were watching the horse of our dreams beat everything. But then bitterness and badness took over, humans playing dirty to get an edge, bending the rules, cheating.

The moment Frankel scooted past the winning post for the final time in the Champion Stakes and did a right turn out of Ascot for the Newmarket breeding sheds, we all began to wonder what would fill the void.

No horse could, so in stepped racing's dark attendant, creeping from the sidelines to centre stage. Jockeys throwing races, horses getting pumped with steroids, and everywhere, bans, bans,

bans. The year was pockmarked by BHA bulletins containing yet another development in a series of overlapping sagas. Compelling, but not in a good way.

◆◆◆◆

THE year started badly with Frankie Dettori already four weeks into a six-month ban after testing positive for cocaine at Longchamp, a major embarrassment to racing even if the drug was not performance-enhancing. But at least it could be regarded as one man stepping out of line and getting caught, an episode revealing human frailty rather than a faultline in racing. It did not speak of anything deeper than a personal journey for a jockey who by the summer of 2013 would be back riding some of the best horses in the world for owner Sheikh Joaan Al Thani.

But early in 2013 things took a more iniquitous twist. The year was just 25 days old when Andrew Heffernan *(above centre)* was banned

for 15 years in a case centred on nine races at Britain's four all-weather tracks in which the 24-year-old jockey's beaten mounts were laid to lose on betting exchanges. In serving bans totalling more than 70 years to nine people, the BHA claimed to have bust "an elaborate network of corruption", in a case that gained attention beyond the racing pages with footballer Michael Chopra, then with Championship side Ipswich Town, warned off for ten years for his part.

As the winner of 96 races in Britain, Heffernan was a moderately small fish landed by the BHA. As a former champion Irish apprentice and the rider of more than 1,000 winners in Britain, as well as a Classic winner in the 2011 Irish St Leger, Eddie Ahern *(above left)* was something bigger.

The 35-year-old jockey was handed a ten-year ban in May in a case centred on the laying of five horses. Again a footballer was involved, and again the headlines mushroomed as a result, with former

West Brom defender Neil Clement banned for 15 years.

As these cases concerned modest horses in poor races, those defending racing's corner could at least argue they were primarily a reflection of temptations that have always swirled about in the sport. The offences were serious but, in a wider sense, did they stop people going racing because its integrity had been compromised? Probably not. But the Mahmood Al Zarooni affair cut to racing's core. This was no case on the outer margins of the sport but went to the heart of one of the world's greatest racing establishments, involving top-class horses.

In little more than 48 hours in April the Godolphin trainer was charged and banned for eight years for doping 15 horses with steroids, including unbeaten 1,000 Guineas hope Certify. Al Zarooni *(above right)* admitted his guilt, pleading ignorance of the rules. A BHA investigation unearthed seven more positive tests, including on 2012 St Leger winner Encke. But it also

Ahern ban shame

Godolphin in crisis over drugs scandal

CHOPRA'S HIT BY LONG BAN

By DAVE MITCHELL

IPSWICH TOWN striker Michael Chopra (left) and jockey Andrew Heffernan were among nine people banned from racing for up to 15-years yesterday.

Chopra, who has publicly admitted to be battling gambling ... was found guilty of c... ...tish Horseracing

SHEIK'S MAN IS SHAMED

Eight-year ban for the ringleader of doping scandal

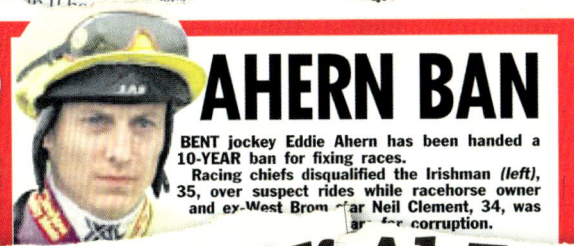

by MARCUS TOWNEND

AHERN BAN

BENT jockey Eddie Ahern has been handed a 10-YEAR ban for fixing races.

Racing chiefs disqualified the Irishman (left), 35, over suspect rides while racehorse owner and ex-West Brom star Neil Clement, 34, was ... for corruption.

from top left: Commander, ...eonniere, Sprinter ...ctuaire, Hurricane ...ular.

Heffernan banned for 15 years

By Graham Green

8yr ban for dope cheat

By CLAUDE DUVAL

DISGRACED trainer Mahmood Al Zarooni has been banned for EIGHT YEARS in horse racing's biggest doping scandal. Al Zarooni, employed by Turn to Page 58

GUNNERS

Ten-year ban for Ahern

Jockey's career in ruins after ... finds him guilty of stopping a ...

By Andrew Scutts

Al Zarooni hit with eight-year drug ban

Disgraced trainer feels full wrath of BHA 'on dark day for racing'

---

concluded the trainer had acted alone and without the knowledge of his employers.

The disease had been cut out, then. Godolphin was clean, said the BHA, even if the speed of their work in condemning Al Zarooni raised eyebrows.

The case also flushed out more trouble. In a wretched spring for the sport it emerged steroids were knocking about elsewhere in Newmarket, as news broke of the BHA's Sungate investigation into the use of a product containing the drug, designed to improve joints, being given to 43 horses. Nine trainers were found to have acted on the advice of vets and cleared, but more damage to the sport's image had been done.

◆◆◆◆

WITH so many negative stories surfacing, it looks like racing has issues. Or maybe the detectives have just got better. Adam Brickell, the BHA's director of integrity,

legal and risk, argues they have. He even believes the level of corrupt activity in the sport has declined, with potential wrongdoers deterred by both a greater chance of being caught and the tougher punishments being dished out.

Brickell points to the BHA's extensive intelligence network, close co-operation with betting operators and law enforcement agencies, and the routine review of every race for running and riding offences and suspicious betting. The rise of social media has also helped in the search for fingerprints.

In one sense the past 12 months have seen the ugly flowering of sins sown earlier in the decade, with both the Heffernan and Ahern cases, for instance, based on races straddling 2010 and 2011. But Brickell feels it would be naive to think the age-old issue of corruption has been cracked, a view given substance by the BHA's decision in the autumn to reverse spending cuts on their anti-doping work.

"There will always be people

prepared to take the risks of cheating," Brickell says. "But hopefully fewer will do so when they realise there is an increased chance of being caught and severely punished. Every prosecution either maintains or raises the deterrent effect. It is difficult to measure, and will take time, but we are confident that the message is very clear."

In order to prosper, racing relies on its relationships with all its stakeholders, from owners and sponsors to punters through the gates. That relationship is built on trust, which for now seems intact.

Despite a year that has been more challenging than the era marked by the marketing godsend called Frankel, Rod Street, chief executive of Great British Racing, believes that unwritten contract is not under threat. Yet.

"It is unrealistic to think that any sport will be without bad publicity from time to time," he says. "So how racing, via its governing body, acts when difficult circumstances arise defines it, and in the case of the Al

Zarooni and Sungate affairs it acted swiftly and decisively.

"The BHA's handing of a significant ban to Eddie Ahern also demonstrated a zero-tolerance approach to wrongdoers. Such actions provide customers with confidence that the sport is clean and well policed. In our opinion, these difficult moments did not damage racing's profile with the general public.

"Where there is risk, however, is at a corporate level, where brands may wish to avoid being associated with negativity. If racing is in the headlines too often for the wrong reasons it may deter investment from sponsors and that is something we need to take seriously. The current landscape, though, seems healthy, with racing attracting new brands and commercial partners."

A year of bad headlines can be tolerated. But somewhere comes the tipping point. If the corruption-laced tweets from the BHA keep coming, racing knows it has a problem.

SHOCK TO THE SYSTEM

Godolphin's reputation was rocked on April 22 when it emerged that 11 horses trained by Mahmood Al Zarooni had failed dope tests. The trainer was quickly banned but the damage to racing and Sheikh Mohammed's flagship operation could not be removed so easily

By Nicholas Godfrey

"GODOLPHIN truly represents Dubai," says the legend on the organisation's website, emphasising the massive role played by Sheikh Mohammed's personal racing team in advertising the tiny Gulf emirate of which he is ruler. The label is designed to make explicit the link between the mould-breaking outlook of the most international racing stable the world has ever seen and the remarkable transformation of its homeland from a relatively unknown dot on the map into a truly 21st century city.

Established in 1992, Godolphin was created to embody the positive aspects of Dubai as it emerged from its cocoon. Any mission statement from Godolphin's driving force would have stressed a determination to be the best, competing in the most prestigious races wherever they are. Despite the occasional wobble, any objective evaluation of the organisation's first 20 years could only judge the project a success according to many of its central tenets. Crucially, Godolphin has been responsible for a who's who of superlative racehorses, among

them Balanchine, Lammtarra, Daylami, Swain, Halling, Fantastic Light, Sakhee and the sheikh's personal favourite, the great Dubai Millennium.

"The Maktoum family's pioneering and respected horseracing stable has diffused the essence of Dubai around the globe," the Godolphin website says. "The city of Dubai has risen rapidly from the desert sands, emerging as a modern, thriving metropolis built upon a foundation of innovation and uninhibited achievement, upholding a vision that is truly international in scope. Godolphin, in encapsulating those same values, exemplifies Dubai and plays a meaningful role in representing the emirate to the world."

With that in mind, one can only wonder precisely what image of Dubai it was that Godolphin portrayed to the world in April when that same website broke the news that one of its employees, Mahmood Al Zarooni, one of the most high-profile trainers in European racing, had been systematically cheating by administering anabolic steroids to his horses. The news signalled the start of a doping scandal that attracted

attention beyond the confines of racing and brought the sort of notoriety more usually associated with the grievously tainted worlds of professional cycling and athletics.

It is no exaggeration to suggest that Sheikh Mohammed's involvement in British racing was called into question as shame and ignominy engulfed his private, hand-picked team and persistent innuendo surrounded other areas of his equine activity. In the eye of the storm, the British Horseracing Authority was criticised for its handling of a sensitive case and its entire anti-doping strategy came under scrutiny as the shockwaves radiated throughout the industry.

Against that background, anything that happened on the racecourse seemed almost incidental for Godolphin. If they were expecting a tumultuous year in the aftermath of their parting of the ways with Frankie Dettori after nearly two decades, it is fair to say they got one.

◆◆◆◆

GIVEN his determination to showcase Dubai to the world, Sheikh Mohammed has always been keen

▸▸ Continues page 78

to promote his countrymen within the Godolphin structure, most notably in the choice of long-serving trainer Saeed Bin Suroor, a former policeman. Former stable groom Mahmood Al Zarooni was a similarly unknown name in March 2010 when he was hired to run a sister stable to that of Bin Suroor in both Dubai and Newmarket. Bin Suroor continued to train at Godolphin Stables (Stanley House) in Newmarket, with Al Zarooni taking charge of a high-powered team at nearby Moulton Paddocks; while Bin Suroor handled his horses at Godolphin's famous Al Quoz Stables, close to the city of Dubai, Al Zarooni's Marmoom base was located in the desert.

Al Zarooni had previously assisted trainer Mubarak Bin Shafya, who took the Dubai Racing Carnival by storm in 2009, when he saddled Gladiatorus and Eastern Anthem to win valuable Group 1 races on World Cup night. Bin Shafya's name was blackened in 2011 when he was banned from the discrete sport of endurance racing over the use of stanozolol, one of the steroids that Al Zarooni later admitted using. There is no suggestion Bin Shafya ever used such substances on thoroughbreds and, in any event, he never trained for Godolphin.

Al Zarooni moved from Bin Shafya to join Bin Suroor as an assistant before Sheikh Mohammed appointed him in 2010 to take over about half the string racing under his Godolphin banner. He hit the ground running when he saddled Calming Influence to win the Godolphin Mile on Dubai World Cup night and Group 1 events in Germany and Italy later that year, after which his ascent was little short of meteoric.

He took his first British Classic in May 2011 with 1,000 Guineas winner Blue Bunting, who went on to claim the Irish Oaks. Rewilding beat So You Think at Royal Ascot, while back on home ground Al Zarooni saddled Monterosso to win the world's richest race, the Dubai World Cup, in March 2012. Six months later, he enjoyed his highest-profile triumph when 25-1 shot Encke won the St Leger to deny Camelot the Triple Crown.

If the sheikh's intention was to promote the idea of competition within his own ranks, then it worked to the extent that Al Zarooni rather than Bin Suroor was receiving the pick of the Godolphin string. The trainer's habitual use of the new golden boy Mickael Barzalona was later cited by Dettori as a primary factor in the long-time stable

jockey's abrupt departure at the end of 2012.

Dettori, who said Al Zarooni had "ruined" his career, had enough problems of his own, but he could perhaps have been forgiven for thinking he was better off divorced from his former employers when a statement on April 22 on godolphin. com dropped the bombshell that 11 horses trained by Al Zarooni had failed dope tests. The gravity of the charges could be transmitted in just two short clauses: the horses at the centre of the controversy included leading 1,000 Guineas hope Certify and Gold Cup runner-up Opinion Poll; the substances involved were the anabolic steroids ethylestranol (used on fillies) and stanozolol. Therefore we were talking about the biggest horses at the most high-profile stable in the world and we were talking about the most notorious of performance-enhancing substances.

Although the rules differed in places like Australia, the USA and significantly Dubai, where steroids were allowed for out-of-competition horses, under British racing rules anabolic steroids are outlawed at any time, whether in racing or just in training. Legitimate veterinary use is rare indeed: anabolic steroids help develop muscle mass, they can aid recovery from injury, they enable a horse to be trained harder. Even if the obvious effects wear off (and are untraceable) after a few months, their effect on a horse's frame could theoretically be fine-tuned long afterwards by any trainer

▶ Mahmood Al Zarooni celebrates victory with Monterosso in the 2012 Dubai World Cup

'Because the horses involved were not racing at the time, I did not realise that what I was doing was in breach of the rules of racing'

minded to flout the rules.

A dark shadow was thus cast over Al Zarooni's Classic-winning achievements: sages of the 'told-you-so' philosophy readily pointed to horses who left their form in Dubai, with some, like World Cup hero Monterosso and runner-up Capponi, having demonstrated marked improvement there. There was no evidence of wrongdoing with either horse but Al Zarooni had forfeited the right to object to those questions being posed.

The BHA revealed that it had taken samples from 45 horses trained by 37-year-old Al Zarooni at Moulton Paddocks on April 9; subsequent analysis by the Horseracing Forensic Laboratory confirmed the initial findings. Al Zarooni held his hands up, immediately admitting culpability to what he described as "a catastrophic error". Although he expressed "deep regret", he also claimed, laughably, that "because the horses involved were not racing at the time, I did not realise that what I was doing was in breach of the rules of racing".

At best, then, Al Zarooni stood accused of rank stupidity, although that was probably the least of his employers' worries on what racing manager Simon Crisford described as a "dark day" for the Dubai team. Sheikh Mohammed was in an invidious position, having been vocal in his opposition to a permissive drugs regime in the United States, where Darley representative Ollie

▶ Continues page 80

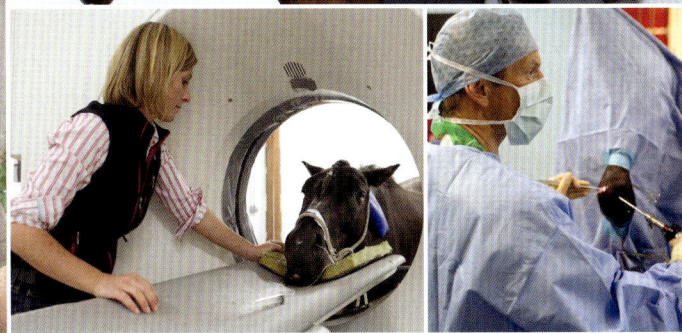

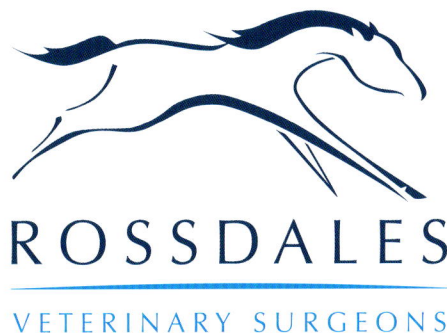

Tait had only a month before resigned from the Breeders' Cup board over the decision not to enforce a Lasix ban. That anti-bleeding medication, it could almost go without saying, is rather more benign than steroids.

What is more, while the sheikh may hold an advantage when it comes to resources, he has always taken immense pride in his reputation as a sportsman. How had that sense of fair play been dented now? As damage-limitation exercises go, Godolphin faced a testing assignment. "We are all shocked by what has happened," said Crisford, charged with undertaking an urgent review of Godolphin's controls and procedures. "His highness Sheikh Mohammed was absolutely appalled when he was told and this is completely unacceptable to him. We will await the outcome of the BHA inquiry before taking any further internal action."

◆◆◆◆

WE DID not have to wait long for the outcome of the inquiry as less than a week after the initial news had broken, the BHA banned Al Zarooni for eight years. His rap sheet had been extended to 15 horses after he admitted administering steroids to four more unraced horses that had not been tested by the BHA; all 15 were banned from racing for six months. Sheikh Mohammed put Moulton Paddocks into lockdown and issued an impassioned statement in which he continued to emphasise the link between Godolphin and Dubai.

"I was appalled and angered to learn that one of our stables in Newmarket violated Godolphin's ethical standards and the rules of British racing," he said. "I have been involved in British horseracing for 30 years and have deep respect for its traditions and rules. There can be no excuse for any deliberate violation. I built my country based on the same solid principles.

"I can assure the racing public that no horse will run from that yard this season until I have been absolutely assured by my team that the entire yard is completely clean. I have worked hard to ensure that Godolphin deserves its reputation for integrity and sportsmanship, and I have reiterated to all Godolphin employees that I will not tolerate this type of behaviour."

To some observers, the speed with which the Al Zarooni inquiry had been concluded smacked of undue haste, although it was a totally uncontested verdict as the disgraced trainer described how he brought the drugs into Britain

from Dubai in his luggage and passed syringes through his car window to a junior member of staff to inject five horses. The BHA defended itself against the criticism by claiming Al Zarooni was such a risk that he had to be removed from his stables as soon as possible.

With Al Zarooni cast as a dangerous rogue element within Godolphin, Crisford said he felt "betrayed" by a trainer he had personally recommended to his boss. The racing manager also stressed this was an "isolated case", adding: "He has tarnished the Godolphin brand so badly that it's going to take a long time to recover. I think we'll get there because Sheikh Mohammed is passionate and loves horses and horseracing. He's going to make sure everything is done to ensure the stable is absolutely 100 per cent clean before any horses get transferred to any other trainers. We're working with the BHA to make damned sure there aren't any more. I have no evidence to suggest there are. Mahmood has told us there aren't, but we have to check."

In a tricky situation given British racing's dependence on the Maktoum family, BHA chief executive Paul Bittar was at pains to stress the level of Godolphin's co-operation in the investigation. He added his hope that the bans would "serve to reassure the public, and the sport's participants, that use of performance-enhancing substances . . . will not be tolerated".

But if the combination of swift justice, uncharacteristically emotive language from the sheikh and pledges from racing's rulers were intended to put

▶ Sheikh Mohammed shelters from the rain before the 2,000 Guineas at Newmarket on May 4. Dawn Approach won the Classic for Godolphin but that success provided only brief respite from the scandal swirling around the organisation

to bed a sordid affair, then a few people were going to be severely disappointed. In the wake of Dawn Approach's victory in the 2,000 Guineas at Newmarket, nine days after the Al Zarooni judgement was handed down, Clare Balding asked Sheikh Mohammed some reasonable, if uncomfortable, questions. Here was an opportunity for him to speak his mind about a controversial subject and reassure the public, but instead he cut short the interview.

Hopes that Al Zarooni would go gently into the good night seemingly evaporated as the whole affair came close to farce when he suggested he would be appealing against the severity of the ban amid support on his Facebook page. Support from whom, precisely? Malaysian-based trainer Malcolm Thwaites, evidently. Be that as it may, Al Zarooni did indeed lodge an appeal, which was withdrawn almost as soon as it appeared. He was not heard from again, which was significant in light of revelations that emerged in the middle of May, when the true scale of the steroids scandal came to light.

◆◆◆◆

BHA tests taken from 391 Newmarket-based Godolphin horses between April 29 and May 2 gave the all-clear to the entire Bin Suroor string – indeed, one thing the Al Zarooni scandal did was to enhance his former colleague's unsullied reputation. On the other hand, seven more horses at Moulton Paddocks tested positive for anabolic steroids, including none other than the St Leger winner

▶▶ Continues page 82

EL FAMILY
A *VISUAL* CLIMAX

Your eyes, which are well-trained in spotting rare bird species, have already enabled you to enjoy many wonderful sights. But if you increase your visual acuity using SWAROVISION technology, you'll get the most out of every birding experience. The EL family takes long-range optics to a new level. The field flattener lenses in every pair of these binoculars ensure perfect edge-to-edge sharpness, and the HD optics impress with brilliant, lifelike colours. And thanks to their unique wrap-around grip, the EL binoculars fit perfectly in your hands – no matter what size binoculars you choose. Enjoy moments even more – with SWAROVSKI OPTIK.

SEE THE UNSEEN
WWW.SWAROVSKIOPTIK.COM

SWAROVSKI
OPTIK

Encke. Royal Ascot winner Energizer and Derby hope Steeler were others, and so was Improvisation, which cast a harsh light on the weaknesses of the BHA testing programme as he had won a maiden as recently as the Craven meeting, where it emerged he had not been post-race tested. Now in full-on firefighting mode, the BHA soon insisted Encke had been clean when he beat Camelot at Doncaster, having twice been tested after racing in 2012 with negative results.

"Clearly what has happened involves one trainer, and it is not endemic throughout Godolphin," said Crisford. "This revolves around one stable, and one stable alone, and the other stables haven't been affected in any format whatsoever."

Sheikh Mohammed pledged to help restore Godolphin's battered reputation by drawing up legislation to make the use of anabolic steroids a criminal offence in equine sport in the United Arab Emirates, although it did not proceed as quickly as was originally suggested. Whereas decrees issued by the sheikh are usually implemented rapidly, his declaration on anabolic steroids required a change of UAE law and, months later, the matter was still being studied by lawyers and the country's cabinet.

One of the more welcome consequences of the steroids scandal was a toughening of the rules elsewhere in the racing world as places like Australia, South Africa and New Zealand fell into line with the European zero-tolerance stance, but in North and South America there was resistance to a ban on steroids being used away from the racetrack.

The BHA proposed a minimum three-month stand-down period in all jurisdictions for horses found to have been given anabolic steroids, although Bittar admitted: "We're never going to get complete harmonisation of the rules on steroids, but we can establish a set of minimum standards."

Britain's position was soon to be muddied by a second steroid-related investigation involving the veterinary product Sungate. A total of 43 horses from nine different yards were found to have been administered Sungate – which contains stanozolol – since early 2010. The use of Sungate was first uncovered by the BHA on February 20, after nine horses trained by Gerard Butler tested positive for stanozolol. Butler was the only trainer to face charges. Since there were no positive samples, and the treatments were all advised by and

▸▸ Continues page 84

BRIGHT SPARKS

Amid all the damage to Godolphin's reputation, the performances of new trainer Charlie Appleby and star horses Dawn Approach (above left) and Farhh provided some cheer

DAWN APPROACH Godolphin's flagbearer for most of the year was not in the care of either of their regular trainers. Rather, it was the sole horse in Jim Bolger's stable to carry the famous blue silks who offered the Dubai team a glimpse of light amid the darkness.

Within days of the Mahmood Al Zarooni steroids scandal breaking, Dawn Approach slammed his rivals in the 2,000 Guineas on his seasonal debut and, after a disastrous Derby run in which he pulled like a freight train, he scored another Group 1 mile victory in a St James's Palace Stakes thriller against Toronado.

But his season tailed off after that ferocious battle. He was beaten fair and square by Toronado in the Sussex Stakes before a lacklustre display in the Jacques le Marois, where he again refused to settle. For good measure, he reportedly returned with mucus in his lungs. On his final run before retirement he was 2-1 favourite for the Queen Elizabeth II Stakes but finished fourth to Olympic Glory.

Godolphin racing manager Simon Crisford said: "He has won four of the top races in the calendar and has done all we have asked of him. He has been a great horse for Godolphin."

FARHH The admirable Farhh may have been restricted to two outings in 2013 but he certainly made the most of them. His pair of Group 1 wins, in the Lockinge and the Champion Stakes, were notable high points for his beleaguered team.

While Classic winner Dawn Approach was acquired as a 'made' horse and continued to ply his trade from Jim Bolger's yard, Farhh was Godolphin through and through. The Darley homebred came up through the ranks with Saeed Bin Suroor, whose abilities must have been sorely tested by the fragility that restricted Farhh to just ten races over four seasons.

By necessity, Farhh has always gone well fresh and so it proved again in an epic running of the Champion Stakes, where the five-year-old held on gamely from Cirrus Des Aigles and Ruler Of The World. That victory ensured Godolphin were able to claim the owners' title, which must have been a blessed relief in an ill-starred season.

"He is all heart and wants to fight and wants to race," said Simon Crisford. "It makes Godolphin champion owner for the ninth time in 17 years, so this victory is very sweet."

CHARLIE APPLEBY Clean-cut with a clean reputation, Southampton-born Appleby was promoted after 15 years at Godolphin to take over from the disgraced Mahmood Al Zarooni. The decision proved one of the more successful decisions of a troubled 2013 for his employers: Appleby, 38, was a safe pair of hands.

After the BHA confirmed it was happy Appleby had no knowledge of Al Zarooni's wrongdoings, the former assistant trainer was officially installed at Moulton Paddocks on July 25, having already set about implementing some procedural changes alongside fellow Godolphin trainer Saeed Bin Suroor.

Appleby's debut runner finished last of eight at York on July 27, but he did not have to wait long to hit the mark as Expressly took a maiden at Ascot the following afternoon. Four days later at Glorious Goodwood he recorded his first Pattern winner when Cap O'Rushes squeezed home in the Gordon Stakes.

As his string approached the 50-winner mark, Appleby – who previously worked for Susan Piggott before joining the David Loder branch of Godolphin – was able to reflect on a satisfactory transition. "All Sheikh Mohammed said to me when he asked me to take over here was 'do your best and go forward', and so far I feel I'm achieving that," he said.

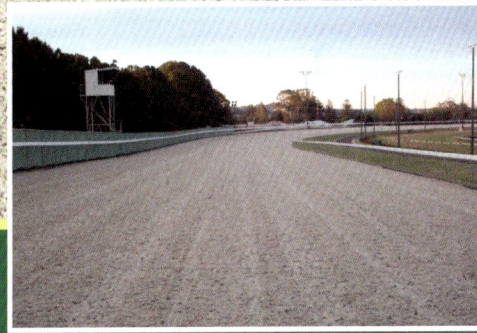

administered by veterinary surgeons and were recorded in medication records, the investigation concluded there were no grounds for charges to be brought against the other trainers, who were never officially named.

Back at Godolphin, Bin Suroor's string swelled to about 400 as he took over training the former Al Zarooni horses that hadn't been banned. Al Zarooni's assistant Charlie Appleby, his personal record totally unblemished, took over at Moulton Paddocks later in the summer, making his presence felt almost immediately with the Gordon Stakes victory of Cap O'Rushes at Glorious Goodwood at the end of July.

That move came a week after the long-awaited completion of the BHA's inquiry into the Godolphin affair, where it was announced the Dubai team would face no further charges. Although it was shared with Godolphin, the full report was not made public; a press release was deemed information enough.

What was clear, though, was that the Dubai team's reputation was about to receive another savage blow: while the investigation's findings reinforced the image of Al Zarooni as solely responsible, it also identified key failings in a damning assessment of chaotic management structure and procedures at Moulton Paddocks.

The BHA said there was no evidence of any other parties beyond those pinpointed at the original April inquiry being involved in the distribution of anabolic steroids, but it strongly criticised the structures that enabled Al Zarooni to carry out the offences without being detected. It was said Al Zarooni had been able to marginalise senior staff and "excluded many loyal employees from his inner circle". He "was doing whatever he wanted, with no accountability to anyone" and the "lack of individual accountability and transparency" created an environment in which, with the help of two foremen and a vet's assistant, he masterminded the steroids regime.

"The investigation process has been a complex and challenging one," Bittar said. "However, I am satisfied that the conclusions reached are an accurate reflection of events. Fortunately cases such as this – both in terms of scale and profile – are incredibly rare. However, there are areas where we can learn from the issues raised."

Critics weren't slow to hit out at the BHA's alleged failings. Why hadn't they interviewed Al Zarooni since April, especially after the emergence in May of the seven new cases including

Encke? According to Bittar, attempts to make contact had been "unsuccessful" and "it was not considered best use of funds and resources" to ensure he was interviewed again.

"Surely it would not have been that hard to track down the disgraced former trainer?" asked Graham Cunningham in his Racing Post column. "The issue for Bittar is simple. Cycling and athletics have paid a heavy price for failing to police their doping problems with maximum vigilance and racing simply cannot afford to do likewise."

With the Sungate controversy also rumbling on, Bittar soon announced that planned budgetary cuts in the drugs-testing programme would be reversed. They weren't about to be beefed up, however, and few believed the procedures as they stood were rigorous enough. Steroids may be illegal within racing, but the law is virtually unenforceable, because all any trainer minded to flout the law need do is to remove a horse from their yard and take it to a non-licensed establishment, where the testers have no jurisdiction.

Critics continued to question the 'lone assassin' theory in the Godolphin case, as well as the BHA's ability to investigate serious corruption, especially when one of the sport's key figures was involved. Some believed the issue would not fade away

▶ Simon Crisford at the press briefing after Mahmood Al Zarooni's hearing at the BHA offices in High Holborn, London, and (below) Al Zarooni leaves the hearing

as quickly or completely as the BHA appeared to hope.

The BHA was by no means alone in hoping to move on from the steroids issue. Crisford, a popular figure within the sport, spoke on behalf of Godolphin after the BHA inquiry's findings were announced. He stressed they had already set about cleaning up their act; their critics, and they've seldom been short of them, might have suggested Hercules faced a more straightforward job at the Augean stables.

"We read the BHA report in detail and have had extensive discussions with BHA officials over the past few months," Crisford said. "We had already identified and addressed shortcomings in our internal processes and procedures, and accept the observations and criticisms of the BHA made in that regard. Today's report again confirms that Mahmood Al Zarooni was acting alone. The time has now come to draw a line under this episode. It's finished, it's gone, it's happened."

Crisford should be so lucky. Given the unfortunate innuendo that continued to surround Sheikh Mohammed's equine interests, with particular reference to the endurance-racing world, the steroids scandal still had a distance to run.

The season ended on an upbeat note as Godolphin claimed the owners' title in Britain for the ninth time in 17 years, thanks mainly to Farhh and Dawn Approach, but it remains to be seen how long it will take to repair the damage done to the reputation of Sheikh Mohammed's flagship operation. It is likely to be more than a few short months.

"Novellist in dazzling show of German horsepower"

Racing Post, 28.07.2013

NOVELLIST
a BBAG Yearling
Sale graduate

King George VI and Queen Elizabeth Stakes, Gr.1
Grand Prix de Saint-Cloud, Gr. 1
Grosser Preis von Baden, Gr. 1

Sales Dates 2014

Spring Breeze Up Sale: 30th May 2014
Yearling Sales: 5th September 2014
Sales & Racing Festival: 17th to 18th October 2014

www.bbag-sales.de BBAG

THE
BIGGER
PICTURE

A work rider gives his mount a hug on
the snow-covered exercise grounds at the
Curragh in early February
**PATRICK McCANN
(RACINGPOST.COM/PHOTOS)**

By Nick Pulford

CLASSIC hopes always fill the spring air at Ballydoyle and this year was no different. The names that had most excited everyone going into the winter – Kingsbarns, Mars, Cristoforo Colombo, Battle Of Marengo – were the ones that punters were waiting to hear news of, waiting to see. In the background, however, was an unraced colt who would upstage all of them by giving Aidan O'Brien his fourth Derby triumph.

His name was Ruler Of The World and even among the Ballydoyle set he wasn't the focus of attention. "Earlier this year he wasn't on my radar," admitted co-owner Michael

Tabor after the Derby. "The only thing I would say is that Aidan told me 'we have four or five very nice horses that haven't appeared yet'. I always know Aidan has some good ones in the locker and it just depends on when he wants to bring them out. This one was a late developer."

Whenever they are ready to start, however, O'Brien's top colts are invariably pointed towards the Derby. John Magnier, head of the Coolmore organisation, still operates by the old maxim of the importance of 'one piece of wood – the winning post of the Epsom Derby' and that explains why Ruler Of The World was at Epsom, along with four other Ballydoyle colts, on June 1, less than two months after his racecourse debut.

"This is what it's all about," Magnier said after Ruler Of The World had given Coolmore a third successive Derby, following the victories of Pour Moi and Camelot. "An interesting thing about the Derby is you never know how good horses are at this time of year. If you try to find out who's best at home you're not going to win the Derby. We bring horses here if they look as though they are good enough to be here."

On the day Ruler Of The World was not just good enough to be there, he was good enough to win too, although it was an unsatisfactory race at the time and even more so in hindsight. For a start the best horse finished last, for the simple reason that he pulled hard

and didn't last home in a slowly run race. When Dawn Approach trailed in 33 lengths behind Ruler Of The World, the strength of the race was immediately open to question.

The analysts in the Racing Post described it as "messy" and "muddling". With the first seven covered by less than four lengths and Ballydoyle having provided five of the 12 runners, it didn't look the most convincing form. Jamie Spencer, who rode seventh-placed Chopin, gave probably the most damning verdict: "You can't have an opinion on such a stupid race."

◆◆◆◆

RULER OF THE WORLD did not appear on a racecourse until April 7, when he won a mile-and-a-

RULER FOR A DAY

In the space of two months Ruler Of The World went from unraced to Derby winner but he failed to win again despite a gallant effort in the Champion Stakes at Ascot

quarter maiden at the Curragh, but his late introduction to racing was not deliberate, far from it. He had a middle-distance pedigree – a half-brother to five-time Group 1 winner Duke Of Marmalade by Galileo, O'Brien's first Derby winner in 2001 – but he was precocious enough to be considered for Royal Ascot as a two-year-old. He would have gone too, but was ruled out at the last minute by a cough that turned into a persistent problem for the rest of the year.

That put him behind the other Derby hopefuls who filled the barns at Ballydoyle and to catch up he would have to learn quickly. He was "babyish" at the Curragh, O'Brien felt, and the best place to continue his fast-track education was Chester,

with its tight turns, downhill run into the straight and big crowd. "Lazy" and "sleepy" were two more words O'Brien was using to describe Ruler Of The World and that led him to put on cheekpieces for the Chester Vase. A six-length win showed Ruler Of The World was moving in the right direction.

Tom Segal, in his Pricewise column in the Racing Post two days before the Chester Vase, had advised Ruler Of The World at 33-1

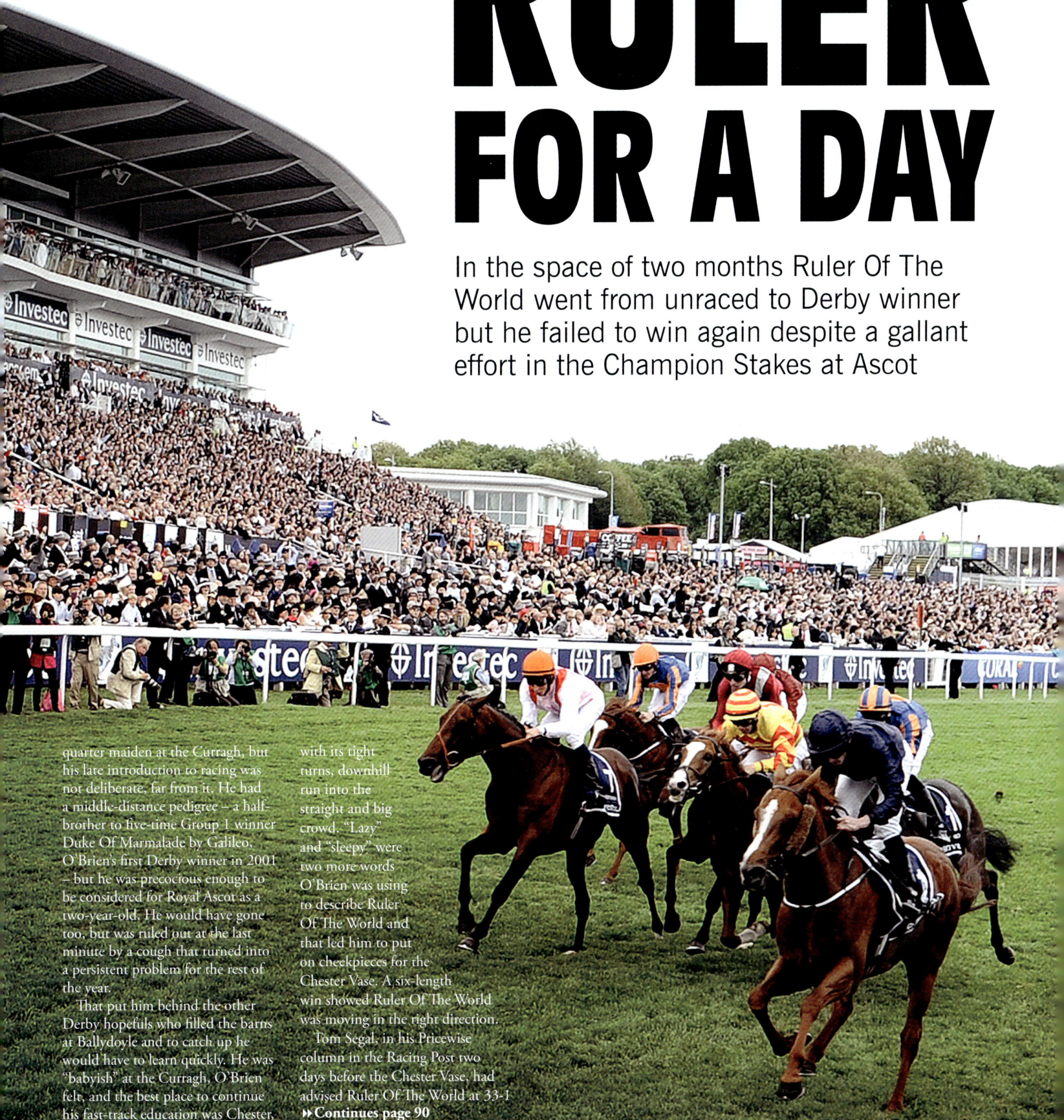

▶ **Continues page 90**

ante-post for the Derby and now the twice-raced colt was down to a best-priced 10-1 fourth favourite.

By the day that had contracted further to 7-1, but Joseph O'Brien opted for the better-fancied Battle Of Marengo from the Ballydoyle five. Ryan Moore, having won the Chester Vase on Ruler Of The World, was on the 'second string', who wore cheekpieces again. The question was how to beat Dawn Approach and the answer, as strange as it appeared, was not to make the race a test of stamina, but instead to make it a test of tractability.

Battle Of Marengo dawdled along in front and Dawn Approach, used to the strong pace of mile races, could not settle under Kevin Manning. "He was more or less out of control," said Jim Bolger, the favourite's trainer.

Lack of pace in the race would have been seen as a handicap beforehand for Ruler Of The World – a certain stayer after his Chester Vase victory – but he quickened up well from the rear to collar Battle Of Marengo a furlong and a half from home. He never looked likely to be caught, even if he didn't stretch away in the manner of a top-class Derby winner.

"He quickened well off a slow pace and was in front from a long way out – he had to tough it out in front of a big crowd and he's still learning," Moore said. "Time will tell how good he is."

For a long time, what we learned about Ruler Of The World and the Derby form was not very positive.

◆◆◆◆

RULER OF THE WORLD'S victory raised the usual hopes that the race had anointed a new middle-distance king but it wasn't to be. Quite the opposite, in fact. Through the long hot summer, as a succession of older horses ripened in time for the big prizes, the Derby form wilted. By late autumn it was almost the forgotten race; a near irrelevance compared with the feats of Treve and Novellist. Apart from Dawn Approach, back at his proper distance of a mile, none of the Derby horses had imposed themselves at Group 1 level.

In one sense, that was not so surprising. Racing Post Ratings put Ruler Of The World on 121 for his Epsom performance, at the bottom end of Derby winners this

millennium. Yet even below-average Derbys can produce high-class performers and, in Ruler Of The World, there was hope of better to come. He was the first Derby winner since Commander In Chief 20 years earlier to have been unraced at two and his Epsom victory made it three out of three in a career that had spanned little more than eight weeks.

O'Brien certainly hoped for improvement when Ruler Of The World lined up as 4-5 favourite in the Irish Derby. "We have been very happy with him," he said. "He impressed us at Epsom and we think the Curragh will suit him even better."

Ballydoyle had won the last seven Irish Derbys and every one of O'Brien's three previous Epsom heroes – Galileo, High Chaparral and Camelot – had come home to win the Irish Derby, but this time he was left bitterly disappointed. Ruler Of The World, who got warm before the race, was off the bridle before the straight and was beaten ten lengths into fifth place by Trading Leather, Dawn Approach's stablemate.

"There's a big chance the gallop caught him out [at the Curragh]," O'Brien said. "At Epsom they went slow and he kicked and won, but he wasn't going away at the finish. He could be more of a mile-and-a-quarter horse at the top level."

In the autumn, after a two-and-a-half-month break, Ruler Of The World was kept at a mile and a half and aimed at the Prix de l'Arc de Triomphe. He ran a good trial in the Prix Niel, finishing a short-head second to Japanese Derby winner

Kizuna, but in the Arc itself he was a well-beaten seventh. Both runs were given a mark of 115 on Racing Post Ratings, 6lb below his Derby figure, and it seemed clear Ruler Of The World was a long way behind Treve, the year's dominant middle-distance Classic winner.

◆◆◆◆

WHAT O'Brien hadn't tried was the mile-and-a-quarter trip he had been thinking about after the Irish Derby. When he did, in the Champion Stakes at Ascot, Ruler Of The World gave his best performance yet.

In finishing a close third behind older rivals Farhh and Cirrus Des Aigles, having been trapped out wide for a long way, Ruler Of The World ran to an RPR of 126, 5lb better than his Derby mark and the best by a three-year-old colt in the European middle-distance division.

It had taken more than four months, but at last the Derby winner had stood up and counted for something. O'Brien said it was "some run for a three-year-old" and now there was fresh hope that the Derby might just have been the start for Ruler Of The World as a force in big races. "Hopefully he is a horse we can look forward to next year," the trainer said.

Looking back, Ruler Of The World had a long debut season with seven races in six months and at the end showed the potential to be better as a four-year-old. But, whatever happens next, he was still king for a day at Epsom and that means everything to Ballydoyle and Coolmore.

HARD ACTS TO FOLLOW

Ruler Of The World (left) was the tenth Derby winner trained at Ballydoyle (four by Aidan O'Brien and six by Vincent O'Brien) and only the third who did not land further big-race success as a three-year-old

1962 Larkspur No win in three starts

1968 Sir Ivor Won Champion Stakes and Washington DC International

1970 Nijinsky Won Irish Derby, King George and St Leger (completing Triple Crown)

1972 Roberto Won Benson & Hedges Gold Cup

1977 The Minstrel Won Irish Derby and King George

1982 Golden Fleece Did not race again

2001 Galileo Won Irish Derby and King George

2002 High Chaparral Won Irish Derby and Breeders' Cup Turf

2012 Camelot Won Irish Derby

2013 Ruler Of The World No win in four starts

NAME GAME

Ruler Of The World, like the other horses who go to Ballydoyle, was named by John Magnier's wife Sue early in his juvenile year and his promise was evident even then, more than 12 months before he appeared on a racecourse.

"Even before he came to Ballydoyle he must have been highly rated to be given such a name and he's always been a stunner with an unbelievable pedigree," Aidan O'Brien said after the Derby. "With a name like that I must have been scared to run him as a two-year-old."

John Magnier said: "The horses are rated on pedigree and as individuals, and Sue names them in February or March. Then we monitor them and this horse obviously made his way to the top – sometimes we get it right and sometimes we don't. We've had a lot of bad American presidents."

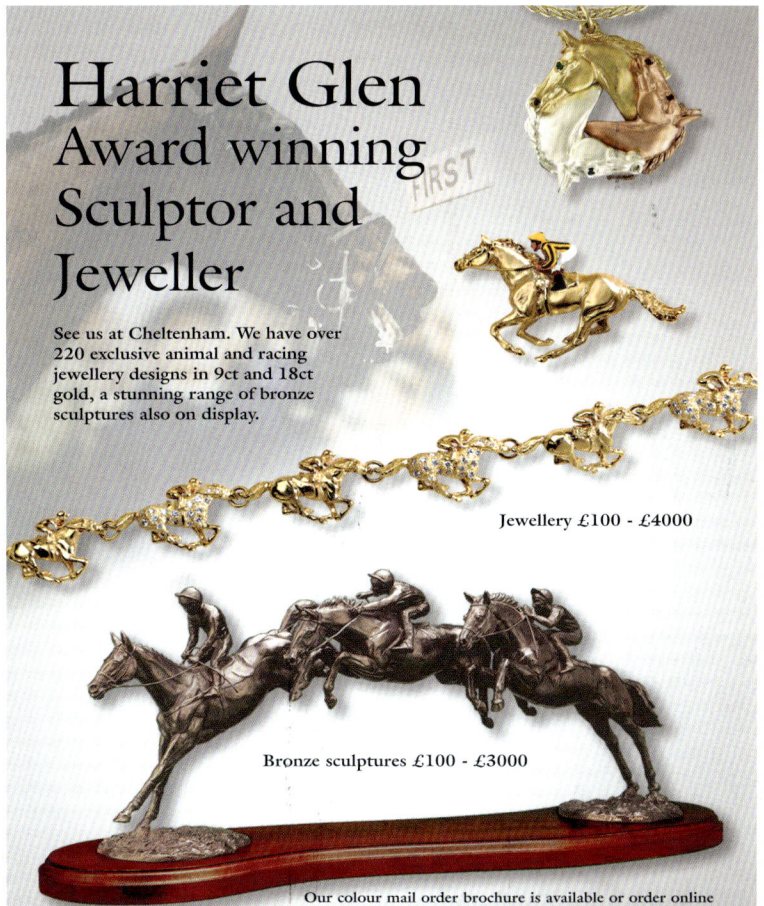

THE
BIGGER
PICTURE

Runners in the Grand Handicap de Chantilly race around the bend against the timeless backdrop of Les Grandes Ecuries. The race, part of the French Derby card on June 2, was won by the Elie Lellouche-trained Pinturicchio
EDWARD WHITAKER
(RACINGPOST.COM/PHOTOS)

PRIMARY COLOUR

By Peter Scargill

Greys enjoyed a spectacular year with big-race victories from the Classics to major handicaps and Cheltenham to Royal Ascot

IT'S OFFICIAL, grey is the new black – not to mention bay, brown and chestnut. The big, wide world has Fifty Shades Of Grey and the silver fox Jose Mourinho, while racing has been on trend with its very own grey revolution. Everywhere you looked in 2013, from Cheltenham to Royal Ascot, there were grey winners and they weren't just making up the numbers. Champions and Classic winners were among them too.

Right from day one the greys made sure 2013 would be theirs with Tarquinius and Eight Chimes scoring at Fairyhouse on January 1. From then on the silver soldiers won battles all over the place, led by Simonsig (Arkle Chase), Champagne Fever (Supreme Novices' Hurdle), Sky Lantern (1,000 Guineas, Coronation and Sun Chariot), Style Vendome (Poule d'Essai des Poulains) and Lethal Force (Diamond Jubilee and July Cup).

So are we living in the age of steel?

According to Peter Wright, horse registry analyst and international co-ordinator at Weatherbys, greys are not so much winning more races as winning better races.

"The percentage of grey winners from British and Irish foal crops has remained at around 5.5 per cent for the last five years but there seems to be an increase in the number of class one and class two wins," he says. "Greys are winning more than their percentage share of better-quality races than they used to. Whether that's an indication of more high-quality greys, I couldn't be sure, but there definitely has been an increase in what they have won quality-wise."

Grey winners stand out and even more so when they are flamboyant pacesetters, as Desert Orchid was over jumps and the Clive Cox-trained Lethal Force was this year in the major Flat sprints. Robin Craddock, who had the pleasure of owning Lethal Force with his father Alan, agrees that racegoers and owners alike are attracted by greys.

"I have always liked grey horses and I think most people do," he says.

"A lot of people, particularly girls, like the colour on horses. Lethal was our first grey horse and he was very lucky for us. When Clive rang up from the sales to say he had just bought a little fella for €8,500 who was grey and would we like him, I instantly said yes. I would have said yes anyway but as soon as he said he was a grey I wanted him.

"I think people like Lethal because he is a dashing grey in the same way that Desert Orchid and One Man were. People like to see them go from the front like that. He has the same 'come and get me if you think you're hard enough' attitude."

Unlike other coloured racehorses, Lethal Force and his fellow greys truly are family. All grey thoroughbreds trace their ancestry back to the Alcock Arabian, who was born in 1700 and had a mere five recorded foals before dying. Fortunately for him – and us – one of those foals was Crab. He became a prominent sire in the 18th century and many of his daughters were kept for breeding, helping the grey gene to spread.

Foals receive two genes for colour – one from each parent – and grey is a dominant gene. That means if a horse carries a grey gene for colour they will be a grey even if they are born a darker colour. The genes passed on by Crab's daughters to their sons and daughters meant the colour clung on in there against the odds.

Even so, the grey was hardly flourishing when cattle tycoon Edward Kennedy imported a run-of-the-mill stallion named Roi Herod from France to stand in Ireland in 1910 and bred him to a mare named Vahren. The result, however, was The Tetrarch, a fabulously fast racehorse and a true saviour of the greys as he went on to produce a number of high-class offspring.

Today the grey gene is carried on by leading sires Dom Alco, Dark Angel, Clodovil, Mastercraftsman, Verglas and Linamix. The latter two are both pure-breeding greys, which means they can only pass on grey genes to their offspring. That boosts the pool of grey horses to go out into the racing and breeding world but emphasises the cyclical nature of success for the grey population.

For now, the trend is upwards and, while Lethal Force has been retired to stud, grey fans can look forward to years of prominence over jumps for Simonsig, Champagne Fever and the other young stars. They are racing's very own nifty shades of grey.

GREY WONDERS

Grey winners of major Group/Graded races and big handicaps in 2013

Champagne Fever Supreme Novices' Hurdle (G1), Deloitte Novices' Hurdle (G1)

Danchai John Smith's Cup

Diakali Champion Four Year Old Hurdle (G1), Prix Alain du Breil (G1)

Dynaste Mildmay Novices' Chase (G2)

Galician International Handicap

Gregorian Hungerford Stakes (G2)

Lethal Force Diamond Jubilee (G1), July Cup (G1)

Lightning Cloud Buckingham Palace Stakes

Masamah Betfred Mobile Sports Handicap

Outstrip Champagne Stakes (G2)

Prince Of Johanne Coral Challenge Handicap

Quentin Collonges Bet365 Gold Cup (G3)

Simonsig Racing Post Arkle (G1)

Sky Lantern 1,000 Guineas (G1), Coronation Stakes (G1), Sun Chariot Stakes (G1)

Style Vendome Poule d'Essai des Poulains (G1)

Tominator Northumberland Plate

▸▸Simonsig wins the Arkle Chase at the Cheltenham Festival and (clockwise from top left) Tarquinius wins at Fairyhouse on January 1; dual Grade 1 scorer Diakali; Outstrip takes the Group 2 Champagne Stakes at Doncaster; Lightning Cloud wins the Buckingham Palace Stakes at Royal Ascot; handicap star Galician; Dynaste at home; Tominator wins his second Northumberland Plate; Quentin Collonges gets a kiss from Andrew Tinkler after the bet365 Gold Cup

LETHAL WEAPON

The European sprint scene was set alight by Lethal Force, whose exhilarating Group 1 wins gave trainer Clive Cox a dream season

CLIVE COX already believed. Spring had barely taken the baton from winter but Cox knows his horses like a father knows his son and he was sure something special was on the horizon for one member of his equine clan.

Those residents with top-level aspirations tend to stay at Cox's Beechdown Farm, perched high above the Lambourn Valley, through the winter months, and Lethal Force had been among them. Solid, rather than spectacular, had been the verdict on his three-year-old campaign in 2012 but Cox hoped there was more to come. As the winter wore on, hope turned to belief.

"Physically it was clear that he'd strengthened considerably through the winter," recalls Cox, who even at this early stage was mapping out a route that would take in all the top six-furlong races, even though Lethal Force's last five starts as a three-year-old, including a Group 2 win in the Hungerford Stakes, had all been over a furlong further. The Hungerford had been regarded as a fluke win in many quarters, and the blinkers Lethal Force wore had been taken as a sign that he was ungenuine, but Cox knew different. Above all, he was confident Lethal Force would leave his three-year-old form behind.

So, too, was work rider Kevin Harris, who during his days with Godolphin had partnered Lammtarra, unbeaten hero of the Derby, King George and Arc. "The work he was doing in the spring, we knew there was a big race in him," Harris said. Adam Kirby, who had won the Hungerford on Lethal Force, was impressed too. "He'd gone from a frame to a big bull of a horse over the winter," says Kirby, casting his mind back to those pre-season work mornings when 'power' was the word that most often came into his head.

Yet Lethal Force started the season behind the other top sprint prospects, even in his own yard. Reckless Abandon, after two Group 1 wins as a juvenile, was rated 6lb higher than his year-older stablemate and in the early betting on the top Royal Ascot sprints he was regarded as the best of the British contenders, while Lethal Force did not make the top 25 in the Diamond Jubilee lists. While they could be kept apart, with Reckless Abandon running over five furlongs and Lethal Force over six, the bigger hopes appeared to lie with Cox's younger sprinter. When the Racing Post's 'Stable Tour' stopped off at Beechdown Farm in early April, however, Lethal Force was listed as the 'trainer's choice' and Cox's

words would prove prophetic. "He was underestimated before and after his Hungerford win but he won't be for much longer."

◆◆◆◆

THE FIRST proving ground for the sprinters is Royal Ascot and there is no denying it is a difficult place for the three-year-olds. So it proved for Reckless Abandon, who started 4-1 second favourite for the Group 1 King's Stand Stakes over five furlongs on the opening day but could finish only fifth. He was the best of his generation in the race and the first two – Sole Power and Shea Shea – were six-year-olds already proven as Group 1 winners in all-age sprints, but defeat still left Cox's team deflated.

Lethal Force wasn't exactly plan B in the Diamond Jubilee four days later, when he was only sixth in the betting at 11-1 and it looked difficult for him

▶ Celebratory scenes at Royal Ascot after Lethal Force blitzes the field in the Diamond Jubilee Stakes (above) and (left) Clive Cox's grey notches another Group 1 triumph with a course-record time in the July Cup

to reverse the form of his first-time-out head second at York to Society Rock, the 4-1 favourite, who was 5lb better off this time. There was, however, an element of plan B in the way Kirby had to ride the race. Taking the race by the scruff of the neck wasn't the intention, but in doing so Lethal Force was a revelation.

"The race was completely back to front," Kirby says, recalling the opening exchanges of Ascot's final-day feature. "I wanted to hold him up but he hit the gate and got into his stride." The stride was every bit as powerful as the spring workouts at Beechdown had suggested and, as Kirby pressed on the gas, the challengers faded away. Society Rock made a late run to move within two lengths of the charging grey but could get no nearer. In truth it was a case of Lethal Force first, the rest nowhere. "It was all very easy for him," Kirby says.

▶ **Continues page 98**

"He was wandering around and getting a bit lonely but if something had come to him, which they were never going to with the form he was in, he'd have gone again. I said it then and I'll say it again, he had an easy race at Ascot."

It was a first Group 1 win for Kirby and the fourth for Cox, to go with Gilt Edge Girl's 2010 Abbaye and Reckless Abandon's juvenile double, and already it was clear they might have a European champion sprinter on their hands. "It wasn't the plan to be in front like that and I was a bit worried," Cox said in the winner's enclosure. "But when Adam sent him to the front he was explosive. It was a very authoritative victory."

◆◆◆◆

"YOU can go racing on your own, but if you win, who do you slap on the back or have a drink with?" asks Robin Craddock, who owns Lethal Force with his father Alan. With that in mind, and aided by the prize-money Lethal Force had scooped for his close second at York, Craddock decided to take a box for 18 people at Royal Ascot. Optimism was high but nothing could prepare him for meeting the Queen after watching his father's pink and burgundy silks carried to victory in one of the most prestigious sprints of the season. To this day he still can't remember what he said to her.

Craddock has a long association with racing and was once stable lad to former trainer and best mate Norman Babbage, but it is down to the success of the family business, Lakes Bathrooms, founded by his father in 1986, that they were able to join the ownership ranks.

With Babbage, Craddock first became accustomed to riding horses of a decidedly moderate persuasion before owning many of the same ilk. When Babbage was seriously injured by falling hay bales in 2007, the father and son were forced to search for a new trainer. With a string of glowing references to his name, Cox was chosen and was sent the Craddocks' pride and joy of that year, a filly called Covert Decree. "She never made it to the track at two," Craddock says, "and when Clive said he was going to the sales in September I asked him to find us one for about ten grand to have a bit of fun with. That was Lethal. It's unbelievable."

The Craddocks were hurt by suggestions after the Diamond Jubilee that Lethal Force had not won fair and square. The place to prove the doubters wrong was obvious – Newmarket and the July Cup – and Lethal Force would do it in a style that brooked no argument. Making the running had

not been the plan at Royal Ascot but on July 13, the hottest day of the year so far, Kirby's sole intention was to burn off his rivals.

As it turned out, the biggest threat to Lethal Force was himself. In the pre-parade he was so wound up that he bounced from hoof to hoof, foam forming at the mouth, and the first test for Kirby was getting him to the start. The second came on the way back, when Lethal Force jinked about a furlong and a half from home. "He was half looking around," Kirby says, "so I gave him a flick and he half jinked and half lost his action. I thought, 'If he's ever going to get beat, this will be it'. But even after that he found another gear and went again. That's why he's special; he's got a very high cruising speed but he doesn't just pick up once, he picks up twice."

This time Lethal Force finished a length and a half clear of Society Rock and his winning time of 1min 9.11sec was four-tenths of a second faster than any other horse in history had scorched the July Cup's six-furlong course, breaking the record set by Stravinsky in the July Cup 14 years earlier. His Racing Post Rating of 124 at Newmarket, 1lb better than at Royal Ascot, was proof of his status as the best in Europe, even if he was still behind Black Caviar, with 128.

"I felt quite hurt after Royal Ascot when all the pundits, if I can call them that, inferred Adam stole the race and that the other riders were not awake," Alan Craddock said afterwards. "He proved conclusively today he didn't steal the race."

▸▸ Gordon Lord Byron (right) storms home in the Haydock Sprint Cup. Lethal Force, unsuited by the good to soft ground, is left well behind in ninth place

'He found another gear and went again. That's why he's special; he doesn't just pick up once, he picks up twice'

The only 'steal', it might be said, was the price tag of €8,500 on Lethal Force, whose earnings for the Craddocks went on to top £750,000 before his retirement to stand at Cheveley Park Stud in 2014.

◆◆◆◆

ALL the later Group 1 sprints took place on good to soft or soft ground, which was not in Lethal Force's favour. He was beaten by Moonlight Cloud over six and a half furlongs at Deauville and again when he dropped back to six furlongs in the Haydock Sprint Cup. The latter race was a washout for Lethal Force, who trailed home ninth of 13 behind Gordon Lord Byron, and Cox blamed himself. "It was one of those situations where the track walked a lot better than it rode and it was plain to see he didn't handle it," he said a few days after the race. "I feel responsible and should have taken him out, but I thought we'd get away with the ground."

In almost every respect, however, Cox's handling of Lethal Force was exemplary. His eye for a horse and training skill have been obvious for years, and the Group 1 winners have come with a rise in the quality of his string, but this was proof positive of his ability to mould a divisional champion. In that sense, Lethal Force was a breakthrough horse for the 49-year-old trainer. Looking back at his dream season, Cox says: "It means everything. To be in those races with a chance and to be associated with a horse like this

▸▸Continues page 100

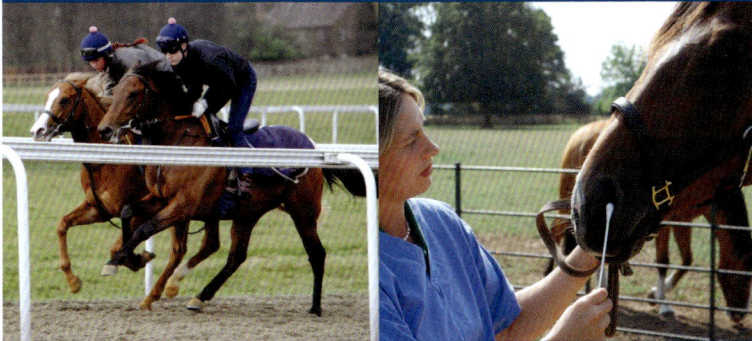

is what I dreamed about achieving in my training career. The whole journey, with great owners who are genuinely grateful to have a horse like this, has been amazing."

Cox had suffered another blow before the Sprint Cup when Reckless Abandon, who had been absent since Royal Ascot, was ruled out with a pulled hamstring. An injured Society Rock also missed the race and it was left to another old favourite to pick up the pieces, although the manner of Gordon Lord Byron's success suggested the result would have been the same no matter who was in opposition.

Runner-up the previous year and fourth in the Diamond Jubilee, Tom Hogan's consistent five-year-old ran as straight as a gun barrel down the far rail, finishing unchallenged under Johnny Murtagh with a yawning three-length gap back to another emerging force in the sprinting ranks, Slade Power, who bettered his third-place finish at Newmarket.

After fracturing his pelvis on his debut in 2010, Gordon Lord Byron has fought back from the brink under the patient guidance of Hogan, who admitted he was surprised by how effortless the win was for his stable star. "Lethal Force is a serious horse and I thought if ever we were going to beat him that would be the day, but I didn't think it would be that easy," he said.

◆◆◆◆

ANOTHER comeback from a nasty injury was achieved in rather quicker time by Jwala, who caused the upset of the sprint season with her 40-1 victory in the Nunthorpe Stakes at York.

The four-year-old filly, trained in Newmarket by Robert Cowell, appeared on the up when she won over York's five

MAAREK THE MARVEL

Ireland enjoyed a fantastic year in the Group I sprints and the most remarkable backstory came with Maarek, whose Prix de l'Abbaye victory added to the earlier wins of Sole Power and Gordon Lord Byron.

Maarek delivered an extraordinary victory for trainer Barry Lalor, who during a career restricted by two spells of leukaemia had not enjoyed success in his home country for almost 20 years.

Lalor, 52, from Fethard, County Tipperary, had taken over the training of Maarek from David Nagle only in August and the transfer came with a ready-made assistant, Evanna McCutcheon. As her father Peter runs the syndicate that owns the six-year-old, she knew Lalor's new stable star inside out.

Success came quickly when Maarek landed a Group 3 at Newbury – Lalor's first victory in Britain – and then it was on to Paris. Maarek, as usual, tested the nerves of his connections with a late challenge in the Abbaye but got home by a short neck from Catcall. Further back were two of the year's Group I winners: Jwala in fourth and Sole Power in sixth.

"A day like today makes it all worthwhile," Lalor said. "I had the offer to take Maarek into our yard, plus a number of other horses. Evanna became my assistant because she has a wonderful knowledge of Maarek. It's because of her hard work that we're here today."

▶▶ Jwala (centre, white face) lands a 40-1 surprise in the Nunthorpe at York and (below) Maarek wins the Prix de l'Abbaye

furlongs in July but then she finished last on her next run in the Group 2 King George Stakes at Goodwood. The bare facts told nothing of the story, however, as Cowell explained after the Nunthorpe.

"At Goodwood she went down in the gate, lifted her head up and fractured an eye-socket and just ran punch-drunk," Cowell said. "It has been a big effort after what happened last time. This wasn't really a surprise. She is uncomplicated, has a huge turn of foot and a high cruising speed. Those are the ingredients you need for a real good sprinter."

In holding on bravely by half a length, Jwala inflicted a third defeat of the summer on Shea Shea, who started favourite for the King's Stand, July Cup and Nunthorpe but had to settle for a minor placing each time. The South African star, winner of the Al Quoz Sprint in March, had been expected to dominate in Europe but this was the year the British and Irish sprinters held back the tide.

Admittedly the overseas raiding party was thinner than usual, but none of the Group 1 sprint prizes departed Europe – something of a rarity in recent years.

There was rarity value, too, in Europe's divisional leader. Lethal Force was only the fourth sprinter in the past two decades to complete a Royal Ascot-July Cup double in the same season and the manner of his victories will live long in the memory. Exactly where he fits among the best sprinters of recent times is open to debate, but few have been more exhilarating in full flight. As Kirby says, "He gave you some buzz".

THE DARLING OF DEAUVILLE

Moonlight Cloud had a brilliant season for trainer Freddy Head and jockey Thierry Jarnet, capped by a remarkable Group 1 double at France's seaside track

FRANCE'S celebrated Head family had quite a year with fillies. While Criquette Head-Maarek took Treve to top billing in front of an international audience at Longchamp in the autumn, her brother Freddy had the star of the summer in Moonlight Cloud. On consecutive Sundays in early August she was the darling of Deauville, the summer playground of the Paris elite, as she achieved an unprecedented Group 1 double in the Prix Maurice de Gheest and Prix Jacques le Marois.

For good measure, Moonlight Cloud blasted to another Group 1 victory in the Prix de la Foret. But on Arc day, as good as she was, she could be only a bit-part player in the Treve show; at Deauville, she made the stage her own and the Marois was her crowning moment. In producing the best run of her life on Racing Post Ratings, she won one of the races of the season.

In 2012 the double had eluded her. After almost causing the upset of the season against a dramatically slowing Black Caviar at Royal Ascot, she had won the Maurice de Gheest but come up short in the Marois behind Excelebration. Perhaps her Diamond Jubilee effort had left a mark when she finished fast for fourth in the Marois, and later when failing to give her running in the Breeders' Cup Mile, and this year Freddy Head was determined that another crack at the Deauville double would not be compromised by a return to Ascot.

A deliberately low-key warm-up at Longchamp led connections to declare her faster and stronger than ever. She proved it with a clear-cut victory over Lethal Force and Gordon Lord Byron in the Maurice de Gheest, her third straight victory in the six-and-a-half-furlong contest, but she would have to be better in the Marois. Could the mare that Head described as "running like a little rabbit" really see off all-comers over a trip plenty still felt exceeded what she was really designed to do?

Looking around the Deauville parade ring before the Marois, it was easy to have doubts. The 2,000 Guineas and St James's Palace Stakes winner Dawn Approach was there, along with fellow Royal Ascot hero Declaration Of War. Across the tightly packed oval from them was Intello, who was attempting to add a top-flight win over the commercially crucial distance of a mile to his Prix du Jockey Club triumph. A few steps further back came Elusive Kate and Olympic Glory. Group 1 winners all.

Amid the throng, Head and veteran jockey Thierry Jarnet, his long-time ally, gave the impression of being somehow more relaxed than their opponents, while the object of their unhurried preparation, Moonlight Cloud, seemed almost asleep. Head had warned that her Maurice de Gheest exertions in track-record time might have left their mark – "you don't run 1min 14sec just like that, she's had a hard race and she gives all she has" – but on reflection Jarnet is of the opinion that the key to her Marois triumph was the ease with which she had won the first leg.

"She has so much class and in the end she never had to go to the limit," he says. "She broke the record but she didn't exhaust herself at all. It was like a piece of morning work. But there was pressure before the Marois. It was such a great challenge to try to win back-to-back like that. You have to manage that pressure because it's important to concentrate and put the mare in the right place to do what she is capable of."

The 'right place' was, in most observers' imagining of the race, for Jarnet to be sitting and waiting to play his hand as late as he dare. But by not much past halfway it became clear a different plan was needed.

Elusive Kate, four times a winner at Deauville, had grabbed her favourite rail position under William Buick but there were already distress signals. Even more surprisingly, Dawn Approach was also being chided by Kevin Manning, soon to back out of the argument tamely.

Intello was travelling powerfully on the rail, while to the outside, almost unthinkably early, Jarnet was about to thread Moonlight Cloud through a fractional gap and then set her free. "They went quite quick and she had lots of gas and felt full of running," Jarnet says. "When she came through she was going so easily – almost too easily."

To roars of encouragement from the crowd, Moonlight Cloud bounded past the wilting Dawn Approach, who shifted left for a couple of strides – just long enough to briefly halt the freewheeling Olympic Glory and Frankie Dettori.

Jarnet is insistent that his partner hadn't begun to run out of steam during that final furlong. "When she went to the front she thought her work was done. She showed brutal acceleration and then she slightly pulled herself up."

A week earlier Head had pointed out that it was the mare who chose her own velocity, regardless of her rider's urgings. "She's the kind of filly that, even if you push her more or whip her, she won't do better," he had said.

Jarnet is one of the least stick-happy jockeys in the weighing room and his rhythmic reminders weren't much more than flicks as Dettori and Olympic Glory bore down. It was, of course, the reverse of the previous season's Ascot drama, with Moonlight Cloud now promoted from understudy to the principal role previously played by Black Caviar.

Jarnet picks up the story at its almost unbearable climax. "She wasn't at the end of her rope, she just relaxed," he says. "She went past them and then for her it was finished." Moonlight Cloud had held on by a little more than the minimum distance.

"I wasn't sure we'd won and when the result was announced it was a huge relief," Jarnet confesses. "The emotion was intense. And it was a really joyful moment because I knew I was sitting on a champion. You have to savour every moment because you don't ride horses like her every day. Each time I ride her it's magical."

On Arc day, through a stroke of good luck for him and ill fortune for Dettori, Jarnet got to ride two magical fillies. An hour and a half after his Arc win on Treve, he scored again on Moonlight Cloud with a three-length victory over old rival Gordon Lord Byron in the Prix de la Foret.

On Racing Post Ratings she was behind Treve and also behind Black Caviar, even on 2013 form, but Jarnet would have loved a rematch with the great Australian mare. "I think we would have beaten her this year. Last year with a better trip Moonlight Cloud might have beaten her in England and this year she was on another level again," he says.

"She's among the best horses I've ridden during my career. It's extraordinary because she's only small but she has an amazing engine. Very few horses can accelerate like she can."

Throughout the season, and especially on that historic day in the Marois, France's grande dame proved she was something special.

AUGUST ACHIEVER

Moonlight Cloud's Deauville double took her record at the seaside track to five wins from six starts, stretching back to her debut success in a maiden as a two-year-old

Prix de la Motte Sassy
Aug 15, 2010 1st

Prix Maurice de Gheest (G1)
Aug 7, 2011 1st

Prix Maurice de Gheest (G1)
Aug 5, 2012 1st

Prix Jacques le Marois (G1)
Aug 12, 2012 4th

Prix Maurice de Gheest (G1)
Aug 4, 2013 1st

Prix Jacques le Marois (G1)
Aug 11, 2013 1st

THE
BIGGER
PICTURE

Salisbury specialist Sunny Future races in last place as the field head out into the country in the mile-and-a-half handicap on June 11. The Malcolm Saunders-trained seven-year-old went on to score by three-quarters of a length, the first of three wins at the track in a seven-week purple patch

**EDWARD WHITAKER
(RACINGPOST.COM/PHOTOS)**

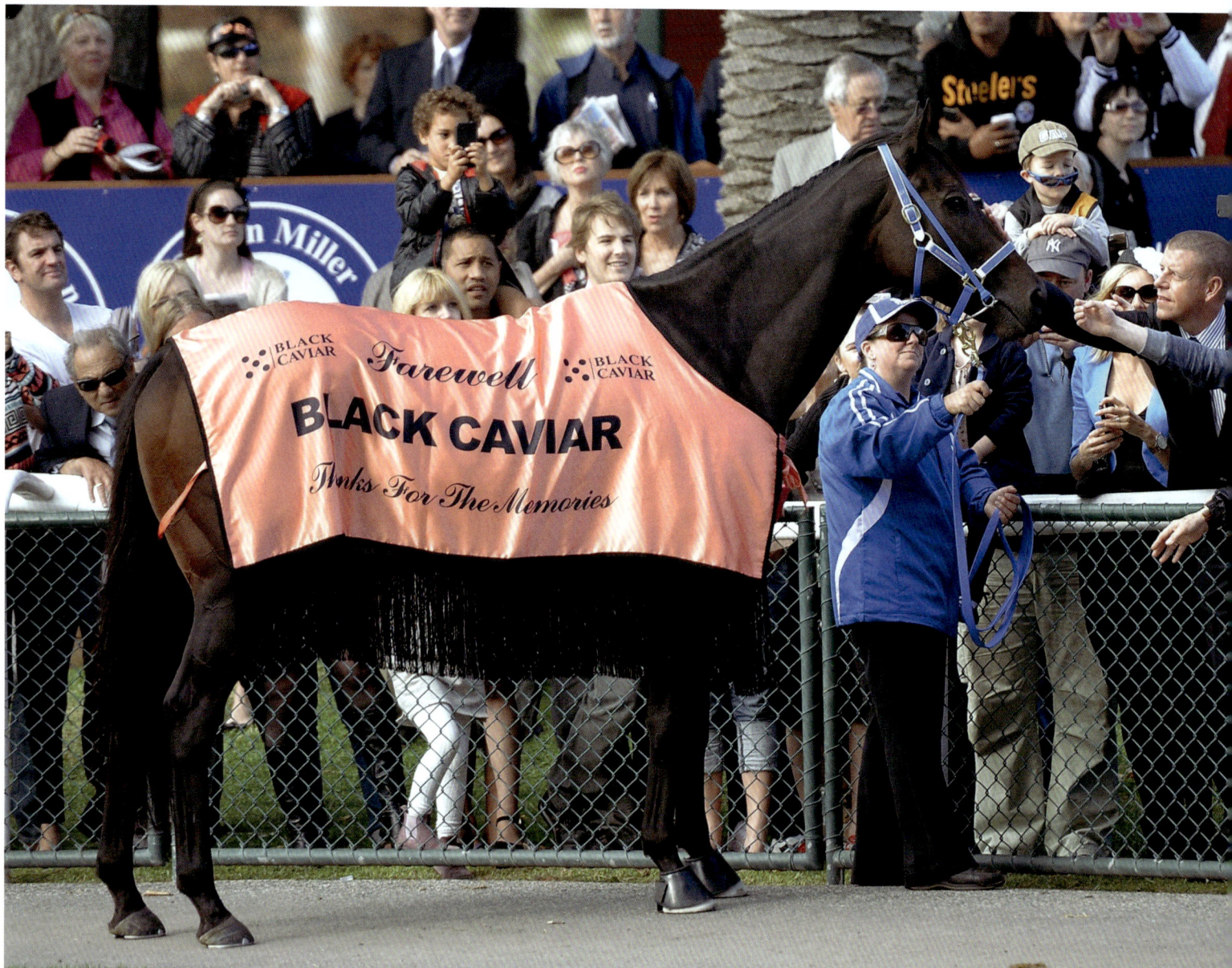

BLACK MAGIC

Black Caviar took a long time to recover from her Royal Ascot exertions but was as dominant as ever on her return. And then she was gone

By Nicholas Godfrey

THE visual impression was confirmed by the race commentary. "Black Caviar is completely in control. It's the Black Caviar of old all right," came the reassuring words as Australia's wonder mare entered the final 300 metres of the Group 1 Lightning Stakes, the country's most prestigious sprint. For almost eight months her adoring public had wondered if she would race again and, if she did, whether she would be as good as before. By the end of the race there was no doubt.

In a breathtaking display befitting a 1-10 favourite, she broke the track record with a time of 55.42sec for 1,000 metres (just short of five furlongs), bettering a mark that had stood for 25 years. By any standard, this was a superlative comeback, better than anybody dared imagine, and only 5lb off

her career-best according to Racing Post Ratings.

"I am proud to have her back," said Peter Moody, her trainer. "It was the first time I have been nervous for a long time and I am just so proud of her and my team. I am getting a little bit emotional for the first time. Geez, it's good to have her back."

The sense of relief was palpable at the end of a long road back from Royal Ascot the previous summer. The 'Wonder from Down Under' may have extended her unbeaten sequence to 22 in the Diamond Jubilee Stakes but she was battered and bruised, muscles torn apart by the twin exertions of an arduous transglobal trip and the hardest race of her life.

Moody feared Black Caviar's career was over. "I thought she was stuffed after Royal Ascot," he said, days before her return to the fray in February. "I told the owners it had come to an end

25
Unbeaten starts

15
Group 1 wins

£4.8m
Total prize-money won

133
Highest Racing Post Rating

79.7
Aggregate winning margin in lengths

24
Number of times she started odds-on

1455
Days between her first and last wins

28min 1.96sec
Total time spent racing

but she travelled back from England really well, lost just seven kilos, really appreciated her time off and then had some time in the water-walker. She's a totally different horse – she's enjoying herself and that's what I wanted to see."

What the world wanted to see was the old Black Caviar, and they did. Soon it would be revealed that the international handicappers had given her a mark of 130 for the Lightning, putting her on course for a fourth world champion sprinter title.

Five weeks later she was back at another familiar stamping ground running around the tight turns of Moonee Valley, where she cruised home under the floodlights with a four-length victory in the William Reid Stakes over a substandard field.

Next came Sydney, where the opposition was much stronger in the TJ Smith Stakes and the weather offered an additional hurdle with rain-softened ground. But it mattered little: come rain or shine, fast or soft, Melbourne or Sydney or anywhere else, nothing had ever managed to beat Black Caviar, and so it was for the 25th time as she scored by three lengths over a pair of Group 1 winners, Epaulette and Bel Sprinter. Among the also-rans were multiple top-level scorers Sea Siren and Hay List, plus Sydney soft-ground specialist Rain Affair. Put simply, Australia has the best sprinters in the world, and for years Black Caviar annihilated all of them.

Luke Nolen, such a shellshocked figure after the Diamond Jubilee, was now in jubilant mood. "They were going to make her earn it today but she still kicked their arse," he said. "If there are any knockers today they can come and see me and I will sort them out."

By now Royal Ascot was being discussed again as a target and talks on the subject were scheduled for the following week. They duly took place,

▶▶ Clockwise from main picture: Parading at Caulfield in April after her retirement; fans at Flemington; in the parade ring at Randwick in April before her final race; Luke Nolen in the winner's enclosure at Randwick; the enormous crowd at Moonee Valley in March to see Black Caviar win her 24th straight race; storming home in the Lightning Stakes

with an unexpected outcome: to the surprise of virtually everybody outside her immediate circle, Black Caviar was immediately retired to the paddocks. "The connections of the horse and I decided 25 was a great number," said Moody. "We thought long and hard about racing on and we talked about Ascot but we believe she has done everything we asked of her. She's in great shape and that's the way we wanted her to bow out."

Moody, for all his wariness over a second visit to Ascot, admitted it hadn't been easy to call time. "It was a hard decision but we just thought the time was right," he said. "We've done our job, she's more than done hers, she's been a great advocate for the sport. She brought interest to our sport that hasn't been there for decades. Black Caviars don't come along every day."

You can say that again. We won't see her like again in a hurry, that's for sure.

POWER POINT

Johnny Murtagh's impeccably timed win on Sole Power at Royal Ascot proved he could handle the twin pressures of being a jockey and trainer, and it was just the start of a glorious summer

By Jonathan Mullin

THE pancake-flat 5,000 acres that make up the Curragh, Ireland's most famous plain and the home of the horse, provide the country's most strapping horizon. The sky feels further away here and, as Johnny Murtagh and his team rattle through evening stables, night-time keeps a respectful distance. With three days to British Champions Day at Ascot, Murtagh is as busy as ever – this man doesn't do still life.

"Nearly every horse in the yard is in action over the next few days," he says, chasing around box to box. "The horses heading to Ascot are getting electrolytes to help them handle the trip; that will get hydration into them before they lose it. They leave on the early ferry tomorrow morning. And the rest of the team are entered at Cork or at Naas. It has been a great season and I want it to finish strongly."

It's evening time, too, on a season that saw Murtagh craft the most unusual season a rookie trainer has ever experienced.

In 2012 he orchestrated an Irish St Leger win from his yard with legendary jump jockey Tommy Carmody, his assistant, holding the name on the licence. Now the one-time champion jockey has his own name over the door – if you want your horse ridden, he's your man; if you want it trained, he is also your man. Johnny Murtagh: General Merchant.

"At the start of the year so many people were telling me I couldn't do both, that I couldn't be a trainer and be a jockey, that it wasn't possible. I was thinking 'I wonder, can I?' It was only when I started riding the winners and then the training was going so well with Group winners in Ireland, that I knew it could be done. Those people who were saying it, maybe they couldn't do it – but I can."

Murtagh rattles off like an Uzi, but if one of those bullets could be opened up and emptied, dust thrown out on the table to decipher just what his targets were for 2013, they probably would be this: one, make a right go of his new career as a trainer; two, as a jockey, stay relevant. Starting at Royal Ascot, Johnny wasn't just relevant, he was much more than that.

◆◆◆◆

DAY ONE of Royal Ascot and it's like old times. The same faces, the same sounds and smells. Murtagh is not the dewy-eyed type, but his back catalogue at Ascot leaves a feelgood residue. The big day has always suited him.

Murtagh has never been the quietest, but the 43-year-old hasn't been around the weighing room as much recently. The big rides haven't been coming his way for the big races and maybe he finds himself a little quieter than usual.

As he departed from Dublin airport that morning he did so knowing he was certain to ride only four horses over the five days. Bookmakers made him a 33-1 shot to finish the meeting as leading jockey and no layer was bundled off his butter box by punters looking to get on. Four rides: Sole Power in the

▶▶Continues page 110

King's Stand, Simenon in the Gold Cup, and two more.

In the weighing-room canteen at Ascot he runs into Matt The Tea Man, who asks about his best chance of a winner. "Sole Power, that's the one," Johnny says, "but I tell ya, it's going to be hero or zero today. Eddie Lynam is either going to sack me this afternoon or I'm going to be the king – I'm coming late on this fella." He wouldn't lie to Matt.

"I was after riding Sole Power a good few times," Murtagh explains, "and he's got a real good burst, but just one burst. I felt a few times that I got there a bit soon. He won the Palace House Stakes at Newmarket in May getting there too soon but he was just better than them.

"I said to Eddie: 'I'm really confident today Eddie, really confident.' He knows me now and he just leaves it to me. He takes that gamble.

"Sometimes a trainer gets a bit itchy on the day, saying 'you won't be able to pick up five lengths on these good horses, so be a bit closer'. I know from being a trainer that it's so hard to get horses there that if you miss, if you get beat, you'll be thinking to yourself: 'Jaysus, why didn't you sit a bit closer?'

"But this horse, I knew him so well and I knew what I had to do. I knew I had to hold him up for one late burst. The likes of Eddie trust you in the big races.

"It all happens so quick but I distinctly remember never having a worry at any stage. Jamie Spencer was travelling really well in front of me on Pearl Secret and, rather than go with him, I sat and let him go. And when he faded I just moved across to his left.

"I always feel that the stands side at Ascot is a huge advantage. I don't know what it is; I just love the stands side. When a big field comes out and I'm drawn stands side I love it. Maybe it's just me, and I think you need the speed to be on that side. I had the speed to switch left and I knew my fella would run straight and true.

"But it was like a slingshot," Murtagh says, his arms held together now as if he is riding the race all over again. "I was just holding him up and holding him up, but when I let him go the run was going to get him there and get him to win. And it did."

On one side was Shea Shea, the South African sprinter, and Sole Power was on the other. The distance between them was almost the width of the track. "You always know when you're up, the same when you know you are beat. And I knew I was up."

▶ (Clockwise from top left) Murtagh's fab four at Royal Ascot: Sole Power, Extortionist, Forgotten Voice and Thomas Chippendale

SIX OF THE BEST
Flat rides

Johnny Murtagh Sole Power, King's Stand Stakes Inch-perfect late thrust executed at high speed

Richard Hughes Sky Lantern, Coronation Stakes Defied wide draw to come from last to first

James Doyle Al Kazeem, Prince of Wales's Stakes Won a magnificent duel with Paul Hanagan and Mukhadram

Richard Hughes Toronado, Sussex Stakes The master of Goodwood at his brilliant best

Ryan Moore Almost Gemini, Kempton June 5 Moore looked the most unlikely winner of four but would not be denied

Silvestre de Sousa Farhh, Champion Stakes Simply refused to yield to Cirrus Des Aigles and Ruler Of The World

And there it was, like old times, Murtagh's winning smile melting into the cheering grandstands, the two arms aloft after his 40th win at the most prestigious fixture in the calendar. "It was Royal Ascot, it was Sole Power, it was super, and Eddie Lynam was the only Irish trainer that really stood by me when I went training myself.

"That's more the reality of competition, I suppose. And maybe other trainers were a bit worried that you were trying to take their owners. I don't know. That's a natural way to think.

"But Eddie doesn't seem to mind, he seems to know that he's getting Johnny Murtagh the jockey when he books me. That's good enough for me and that made it all very sweet."

Murtagh could scarcely wait to get back into the weighing room for the banter. "I let them know. I told them: 'This riding is easy lads, wait until you start training.' I get on well with a lot of them, so a lot of them were genuinely happy for me.

"I'll walk around as if I own the place, and especially now that I'm back riding the Group 1 winners again. Not in an arrogant way – in a way more to push them a bit. 'I keep hearing how good you are, let's start seeing it.' There are loads of good riders but they need to push themselves a bit more too. I'm only doing it for their benefit – 'let's see what you've got because whatever you have I'm ready for you.'"

◆◆◆◆

SOLE POWER was just the start, not only at Royal Ascot but for the rest of the summer as Murtagh enjoyed a glorious season. "From just four rides we managed to pick up a few more rides for the week and from Sole Power on, that's when everything seemed to happen. I suppose you can only ride one horse in every race and I picked up a few good spares during the year."

Murtagh was top jockey at Royal Ascot after adding to Sole Power's victory on Extortionist (Windsor Castle Stakes), Forgotten Voice (Wolferton Handicap) and Thomas Chippendale (Hardwicke Stakes). The King George on Novellist, the Haydock Sprint Cup on Gordon Lord Byron, the Cambridgeshire on Educate: Murtagh's Saturday spares quickly translated into newspaper headlines on summer Sundays.

"You just need to be getting on the good horses. I suppose after Ascot it confirmed to me that 'all you need is the horses Johnny, if you get on them you can do the business'. A lot of people probably thought I was part-time, that I didn't care anymore. After Ascot everything turned around.

"I've never been more relaxed going into big races or as prepared. I'm trying to give everyone the best chance, whether it be in a Group 1 or a maiden at the Curragh, because I realise now how hard it is to get them there, how much the owners are putting into it and how much they are depending on you.

"I don't mean that in a bad way but when you're a jockey and you're chasing around from ride to ride, you often don't think of that. It couldn't be more on my mind now."

◆◆◆◆

THREE days later and the rain that defines the fault line between autumn and winter batters the windscreen of the three-stall horse lorry as Orla Murtagh makes her way to Cork racecourse in Mallow.

Mrs Murtagh is an integral part of the training operation and as such she doesn't mind the whirr of the wipers as she meanders down the M8 motorway. Their runner in Cork's feature race, a Listed race, is Rich Coast, and every drop that falls between now and post time serves only to fill her with confidence.

On Friday evening she was at Dundalk and today she is down south despite the fact that the yard's flagbearers are in the salubrious surrounds of Ascot. The boss is away with the yard's progressive filly Belle De Crecy and the game Royal Diamond, but with so many runners this weekend the Murtaghs are split. With Orla holding the licence to drive the lorry – and, let's face it, Johnny riding the horses in Ascot – she is left behind.

Not that she minds, and once between the Cork villages of Kildorrery and Doneraile, her mobile phone emits a beep. Then another, and then another. In the back of the lorry, daughter Caroline roars: "Royal Diamond has won mammy!" It might look like another day on the road to another race meeting, but Orla Murtagh knows this day could be special.

The security guards at the gate of Cork's stable yard welcome her with congratulations for what has happened at Ascot and soon those greetings are redoubled after Rich Coast foils the

odds-on favourite in the big race. A smile hasn't left her face for hours and she gets home around 8pm, feeds the horses and by 9pm her smiling husband is back from Ascot too.

No champagne, no nightclubs – this is an evening to be enjoyed as a family, much like the mucking out the following morning is. They gather around the television to watch the recorded re-run of a day they will never forget.

And they start with Royal Diamond. After all this was the horse that defined the early months of a new career. An Irish St Leger in 2012, a Group 3 in 2013 and now this – a victory on British Champions Day at Ascot in the Long Distance Cup with Johnny as both rider and trainer. What are those who said he couldn't do two jobs thinking now?

The family watch the post-race television interview where the carefree Murtagh is no longer, replaced by a reflective one. The words, clotted by emotion, don't come so easy.

"This is probably the best day of my life," he says. "I'm lucky in that I'm doing something I love with wonderful staff, a great wife and lovely kids."

In the background the big screen shows a re-run of the finish again and there is Murtagh, lying across the back of his horse during that last critical stride, exhausted and deathly still in a moment of blurred commotion. A perfect, peaceful end to a season without compare.

'I'm lucky in that I'm doing something I love with wonderful staff, a great wife and lovely kids'

▸▸ Murtagh celebrates after Royal Diamond's Group 3 win on Champions Day at Ascot in his dual role as trainer and jockey

MURTAGH'S YEAR

MARCH 24 Wins the Irish Lincolnshire on the opening day of the Irish turf Flat season on Sweet Lightning, trained at Murtagh's yard by Tommy Carmody

MAY 25 First runners as a trainer, Fort Knox and Ask Dad, finish ninth and tenth in the Irish 2,000 Guineas

JUNE 1 Has his first winner as a trainer when Benbecula scores at Tramore

JUNE 18 Wins the Group I King's Stand on Sole Power and completes a Royal Ascot opening-day double on Windsor Castle scorer Extortionist

JUNE 22 Ends Royal Ascot as top jockey with four winners, the others being Forgotten Voice (Wolferton) and Thomas Chippendale (Hardwicke)

JUNE 30 Another Group I victory on the Roger Varian-trained Ambivalent in the Pretty Polly at the Curragh

JULY 20 Wins his sixth Irish Oaks, and 15th Irish Classic in all, on Chicquita for Alain de Royer-Dupre

JULY 27 Lands his fourth King George with a five-length victory on Novellist, having been third choice for the ride

AUGUST 24 First Group winner as a trainer when Royal Diamond takes the Group 3 Irish St Leger Trial at the Curragh, with Murtagh in the saddle

SEPTEMBER 7 Rides his fifth Group I winner of 2013 as Gordon Lord Byron lands the Haydock Sprint Cup

SEPTEMBER 14 Trains and rides Belle De Crecy to win the Group 2 Blandford Stakes at the Curragh

SEPTEMBER 28 Wins the Cambridgeshire at Newmarket by a short head on the Ismail Mohammed-trained Educate

OCTOBER 19 Trains and rides Royal Diamond to win the Group 3 Long Distance Cup at Ascot on British Champions Day and in the same dual role finishes second on Belle De Crecy in the Group I British Champions Fillies & Mares. Later in the afternoon the Murtagh-trained Rich Coast wins a Listed race at Cork

THE
BIGGER
PICTURE

Snow Fairy takes a swim in June in preparation
for a comeback, but the following month she
was retired after a tendon injury flared up
again. The Ed Dunlop-trained mare won six
Group 1 races and £3.9m in prize-money
EDWARD WHITAKER
(RACINGPOST.COM/PHOTOS)

▶▶Auroras Encore and Ryan Mania (left) at the last with Oscar Time (centre) and Teaforthree

FAME AND FORTUNE

Auroras Encore was 66-1 for the Grand National but hard work and several twists of fate combined to produce a thoroughly deserved victory

By Nick Pulford

RYAN MANIA had a decision to make. It wasn't the hardest he had faced in his career, but it would be life-changing, even though he didn't know it at the time. As he looked towards the two Aintree-style fences specially built in Malton to school Grand National aspirants, Mania felt a buzz that usually comes only at the start of a race. Underneath him, Auroras Encore felt it too.

Over the next half an hour, in the early-morning chill of the last Friday in March, Mania took Auroras Encore over the pair of fences five times. He did the same with Mr Moonshine, the other National contender from Sue Smith's yard, and by the end of the exercise he had his answer: Auroras Encore would be

his first ride in the Grand National eight days later.

"The schooling at Malton was extremely important," Mania recalls. "When I got there I was surprised. They weren't small schooling fences, they rode like the normal National fences, they'd built them up properly. I was very impressed. I was still in two minds what I was going to ride at Aintree but riding Auroras that day – schooling him over the fences and seeing how well he was – made my decision. It was a no-brainer really. He lit up when he was jumping them, he really enjoyed it, and it gave me a lot of confidence for Aintree."

The session was important for Smith too. The bleak midwinter had been difficult for all trainers but conditions had been particularly tough at Craiglands Farm on Bingley Moor, West Yorkshire, which stands exposed to the elements at 275m above sea level. Her husband Harvey, the other half of a redoubtable training team, worked hard to keep the gallops clear but for long periods it was a losing battle.

Waiting for the weather to relent did not fit with the Smiths' training philosophy. "We struggled to find races but you can't just have one run and go to the Grand National because, like any athlete, a racehorse has to be match-fit to go to the races," Sue says. "We knew Auroras Encore was a spring horse but you can't just run when the ground's good in October and then not run him any more until the spring. We don't work like that; we feel horses have to go to the races because it keeps their mind sharp, it keeps them jumping fit, it keeps them in good order. When you're going for those long-distance races, they have to be very fit."

The difficult winter helps explain why Auroras Encore, who had been touched off in heartbreaking fashion under Mania in the Scottish Grand National 12 months earlier, would be dismissed as an outsider at Aintree. He had five races in his National build-up but, with conditions against him, he seemed out of form. "Difficult to enthuse about," said one national newspaper guide to the big race on the day. Another gave him a one-star rating, which was helpfully translated as "don't waste your money".

Auroras Encore and Mr Moonshine may have been 66-1 shots, but the Smiths left no stone unturned in their determination to send them to Aintree as well prepared as any of their better-fancied rivals. By late March the training partners were looking for every opportunity to tune up their National contenders. Two days before the schooling session at Malton, they went to Wetherby for a post-racing gallop.

"It was a struggle because we had severe frosts and snowdrifts over certain parts of the gallops, up to 4ft high," Sue recalls. "We have a big indoor school and Harvey kept us going on one part of the gallop, but we needed to do a full-up piece of work and Wetherby were very kind in allowing us to do that after racing. We still needed to get another good bit of work into them, but at the very last the weather relented a little bit and we were able to do that at home on the Tuesday before the National. It all worked out very well in the end. We couldn't have had them any fitter.

"Going to Malton was a definite bonus too, because with the frost we weren't able to use our own fences. Auroras has always been a good jumper, over fences and hurdles,

▸▸ **Continues page 116**

but once I'd seen him jump those schooling fences I had no concerns at all about Aintree."

◆◆◆◆

GRAND NATIONAL day dawned cold but bright and Mania walked the course – as he had on the previous two days of the meeting – in a positive frame of mind. The 23-year-old Scot had another crucial decision to make: how to tackle his first National ride. Later he would tell Sue Smith he had a plan, although she never asked what it was. She was happy to leave it to him.

The mutual trust between the Smiths and Mania was a cornerstone of what they would achieve that day. Eighteen months earlier, having taken the gut-wrenching decision to leave the sport through lack of opportunity, Mania had been acting as whipper-in for the Fife Hunt but the thrill of racing lured him back. Even then, making his way was hard without the comfort of regular rides from previous supporters Peter Monteith, who had died, and the warned-off Howard Johnson.

Harvey Smith, among many other things, is a talent-spotter of riders as well as horses and he liked what he saw in Mania. "I've seen a good lad riding," he told his wife. Within a fortnight of the young jockey's return to the weighing room, he was riding out for the Smiths. The relationship blossomed and now he

goes to the yard three or four times a week through the winter, travelling down from his home in the Scottish Borders or often staying overnight. Last season the Smiths provided half of his rides and almost two-thirds of his winners, including the most important of his life.

"You need a good yard behind you," Mania says, "and I can't even imagine where I'd be if Harvey hadn't asked me to ride for them. It was a life-changing moment. There's every chance I'd be finished again if that hadn't happened. Harvey's help and advice has been paramount. If I wasn't riding for Sue and Harvey, I don't know who I'd be riding for because there just aren't the opportunities in the north that there used to be. I couldn't have done it without them."

Mania's plan for the National was simple, as the best plans often are. "I just wanted to lie up as handy as I could, follow someone who'd been there and done it before, go down the middle and not worry about riding a race until I got to Becher's second time. I only decided at the start who I was going to follow. I lined up behind Ruby Walsh and I thought I couldn't be in a bad place if I went where he was."

As it turned out, Mania was soon riding his own race, with Walsh just behind him on the fancied On His Own. It was an early sign of how well Auroras Encore was going.

▶Continues page 118

SAFETY FIRST

The Grand National was on trial and the verdict was positive, as the latest course modifications earned widespread approval

Fate has not always been as kind to Sue and Harvey Smith at Aintree as it was in the 2013 Grand National. The Last Fling and Goguenard, two of their early runners in the race, lost their lives in successive Nationals in 2002 and 2003 – a double blow that Sue Smith admitted was distressing but did not dim her enthusiasm for the race.

Patient to wait for the right horse, she was back at the National in 2013 for the first time in seven years but it was a different kind of National. After four fatalities in the previous two years and a raft of course modifications, the race was under scrutiny like never before. Thankfully, it passed the test.

Only two horses were classed as fallers (Tatenen at the 12th and On His Own at the 25th) and 17 of the 40 starters completed the course. The major talking point was the small number of casualties on the first circuit – every horse made it to the Canal Turn first time and 33 were still in the race at the end of the first circuit.

The most notable change in 2013 was a reduction in the race distance to four miles, three and a half furlongs, which was caused by moving the start forward by 90 yards, away from the crowds and grandstands. The move was regarded as a principal reason behind the safer race.

"The jockeys were brilliant," said John Baker, the Jockey Club's regional director for Aintree and the north-west. "The start set the tone, they were sensible, and they pulled up when they should have done."

RSPCA equine consultant David Muir agreed. "The jockeys played their part," he said. "They didn't go loopy at the beginning, jumped the horses round and pulled up when they were no longer in contention. These are all elements which make the race safer."

Other changes included the levelling out of some landing areas, notably at the first fence and Becher's Brook, and 'softer' fence designs using plastic birch instead of wooden stakes, although fence heights were unchanged.

Harvey Smith, usually a thorn in the side of the authorities, praised the changes. "Full marks to the Aintree set-up," he said. "They've all worked hard, they've got the track safe. Onwards and upwards now for the Grand National. The public love this race. This race will go on forever."

An Interest for Life

If you are looking for a new rewarding life interest that can take you all over the world and mix with the elite – come and join horse racing, The Sport of Kings

Peak Racehorses offers a private and confidential service from Start to Finish, for you to become a racehorse owner. We outline the possibilities in this exciting sport, you decide what suits you. We'll present possible horses that will fit your expectations, you choose the horse you want, it's name and location. We will also help you find the right training establishment. In other words – we advise, you decide.

Where would you like your horse to race? From Ascot to Melbourne, Paris to New York and anywhere in between – you and your race horse lead the way.

The young rider and the old horse were always in the front rank as, remarkably, 33 of the 40 starters made it round the first circuit. When Auroras Encore sailed over second Becher's in fourth place, Mania switched to race mode as he had planned. With only eight fences left to jump, he had a real chance.

"I thought, 'Bloody hell, I'm at Becher's second time and I'm still travelling. Oh God, I never really planned for this.'" Months after the event, there is still boyish incredulity and excitement in his voice. "I couldn't believe my luck. My next target was to get to the Melling Road. He winged the fence before the Melling Road and I knew I had loads left. I knew he'd gallop home from there."

The race was boiling down to the National specialists and Auroras Encore was in the thick of it. Welsh National runner-up Teaforthree and Oscar Time, second in the National in 2011, were just in front, while the group behind included Cappa Bleu, twice placed in Nationals, and former Irish National fourth Rare Bob. Stamina would decide the National and Auroras Encore had it in spades.

"The two lads kicked on in front and I was happy to take a lead from them," Mania says. "Coming to the second-last I was delighted because I thought I was going to get placed. Then going to the last the front two just stopped in front of me and I couldn't believe what was happening."

Many dreams have been shattered on the long run-in past the Elbow and Mania couldn't help thinking back to his heartbreaking defeat in the Scottish National, when Merigo snatched victory on the line. "Halfway up the run-in I still thought I was going to get chinned on the line. I was too scared to look behind me," he says. But his lead was growing to nine lengths over the staying-on Cappa Bleu and, with the 17 finishers including three of the leading fancies, there was no fluke about the result.

"It was one of the fairest Nationals there's been for a while," Mania says. "People can say what they like about the course being easier, but it still takes a lot of getting round. The best horse won on the day. There's no way to describe what it feels like to win. I was just in shock. You try to savour it, but it was like an out-of-

NATIONAL MILESTONES

Perhaps it is a sign of the times, but Sue Smith's gender did not figure prominently in reports of her Grand National triumph. For the record, she was only the third woman to train a Grand National winner after Jenny Pitman (Corbiere 1983, Royal Athlete 1995) and Venetia Williams (Mon Mome, 2009)

Smith was the first trainer based in Yorkshire to win the National since Neville Crump of Middleham with Merryman in 1960

Auroras Encore is one of four 66-1 winners of the National, bettered only by five 100-1 shots – Tipperary Tim (1928), Gregalach (1929), Caughoo (1947), Foinavon (1967) and Mon Mome (2009)

body experience. I didn't believe it was actually happening to me. It was pretty awesome. No matter what happens with the rest of my career, I've won the Grand National. It's something I can boast about for the rest of my life."

◆◆◆◆

UP in the stands, Jim Beaumont couldn't believe his luck either. He had been the owner of Auroras Encore – along with Douglas Pryde and David Van der Hoeven – for little more than three months, having bought him in a private deal when the previous owners, Warren and Alicia Skene, decided to sell owing to health issues.

Beaumont watched the race with his daughter Nicki, who had flown in from her home in Majorca, in the old stand reserved for owners with runners in the National, and their excitement left no doubt who they were. "Do you know, as the horse passed the post I turned to go up the steps and the whole crowd parted to let me through," Beaumont recalls. "I ran to where the horses were circling on the course. I couldn't wait to see Ryan. I led the horse back in. It was absolutely bloody marvellous."

Having had one previous runner in the National, Beaumont and Pryde had set out to buy another horse for the race. They did not know the Smiths, but they were aware of their skill with staying chasers and their first choice was Mr Moonshine.

When the price was too high, they were offered Auroras Encore and brought in Van der Hoeven, a business acquaintance of Pryde, as a third partner. Beaumont and Pryde eventually went back to buy Mr Moonshine as well but in this story of so many twists of fate Auroras Encore would turn out to be the one. Perhaps the luckiest of the three partners was Van der Hoeven, for whom the National was his first win as an owner.

As Beaumont says: "It was all good fortune."

◆◆◆◆

AS much as it was a hometown triumph of sorts, this was a victory made in Yorkshire. Auroras Encore was the first National winner trained in the county since Merryman in 1960. Shortly before the race there was another auspicious moment when Gerry Scott, Merryman's rider, bumped into Sue Smith and wished her luck. But, as much as good fortune is needed in the National, the journey there was all about old-fashioned values of horse sense and hard work.

While the owners and Mania jumped on board later, Auroras Encore and the Smiths were together from the very beginning. The little Flat-bred son of Second Empire did not seem typical of the stayers the Smiths are renowned for, but as an unraced three-year-old he had something that caught Harvey's eye and at 9,500gns he would prove

to be a bargain. Even before the mammoth payday at Aintree, his willing attitude had brought earnings of £177,291 in 43 starts.

"We broke him and he's been a special horse for us," Sue Smith says. "He's only 16 hands, but he's a little tank and it was obvious from his early days he was going to get a trip. As we stepped him up he always found it easy." He had speed as well, enough to win a Listed handicap hurdle over two and a half miles at Aintree's big meeting as a six-year-old, which remained his most valuable success until the National.

Two days after that hurdles win he turned out again at Aintree and finished fifth, an early sign of the toughness that is perhaps his defining characteristic. "He doesn't give up, he's not frightened of doing anything," the trainer says. "He's not a soft horse. If the weather's bad he comes out with a smile on his face and if it's sunny he's just the same. He'll fight to win; he likes to be a racehorse."

Harvey Smith's Yorkshire grit has been passed down to the little horse he brought back from the sales eight years ago and, all being well, Auroras Encore will be back to defend the National title as a 12-year-old in 2014. It will be a tough test after the 11lb rise that so irked Harvey and which he could not handle in the Scottish Grand National, where he was pulled up by Mania.

The fates may not smile as kindly again on Auroras Encore but on that April day it was far more than luck that was the defining factor. In Mania and the Smiths, he was in the perfect hands when opportunity knocked.

'No matter what happens with the rest of my career, I've won the Grand National. I can boast about that for the rest of my life'

GRAND DESIGNS

Aintree could be on the agenda in 2014 for the Welsh, Scottish and Irish National winners

IMPULSE BUY
Monbeg Dude, Welsh National
By Nick Pulford

HE was the horse they didn't mean to buy but Monbeg Dude did his rugby-playing owners and trainer Michael Scudamore proud by winning the Welsh National. And they liked the feeling so much they are aiming for a repeat bid in the new season, followed by a possible crack at Aintree.

Given one of the rides of the season by Paul Carberry, Monbeg Dude was brought with an exquisitely timed challenge in the Chepstow marathon to overhaul 11-4 favourite Teaforthree and go on to a half-length victory. It was a scrum in the winner's enclosure afterwards as the celebrations started for three of Monbeg Dude's four co-owners – Scudamore, Gloucester centre James Simpson-Daniel and Nicky Robinson, a fly-half then with Wasps before moving to Bristol.

Scudamore, who has a rugby pedigree himself having played for Wales under 19s, was the third generation of his family to win Wales's biggest race. His grandfather, also Michael, won on Creelo II in 1957, while his father, Peter, won the race four times as a jockey. "What's

the plan?" the trainer said afterwards. "To get to the pub as soon as possible."

The fourth co-owner, Mike Tindall, Zara Phillips' husband, was unable to be at Chepstow as he was playing for Gloucester that day. He finished on the losing side but when one of the team's substitutes said to him, "Winner, winner, chicken dinner", he knew Monbeg Dude must have done well, although he was cautious enough to assume it meant a place, not victory.

Simpson-Daniel, ruled out of the match by injury, was given permission to go to Chepstow by Gloucester rugby director Nigel Davies as long as he kept a low profile. "And then he goes and wins," said Simpson-Daniel.

Both victor and vanquished agreed the winning ride was something special. Monbeg Dude made mistake after mistake and lagged behind for much of the race, but Carberry never gave up.

"It would have to be among my best rides," Carberry said. "When you ride them like that, if the horse is good enough the tactics come off. If the horse isn't, they don't." More ruefully, Coral director John O'Reilly, one of Teaforthree's owners, said simply: "Carberry, what a ride."

The story behind Monbeg Dude's purchase is unusual, to say the least.

SIX OF THE BEST
Jumps rides

Paul Carberry *Monbeg Dude, Welsh National* The head waiter at his best as he timed his challenge to perfection

Ryan Mania *Auroras Encore, Grand National* Well planned and well executed by National debutant

Ruby Walsh *Champagne Fever, Supreme Novices' Hurdle* Tactically astute front-running ride in top-class race

Tony McCoy *Wayward Glance, Worcester, August 28* Had to work for the whole two-and-a-half-mile trip to win claiming hurdle

Ruby Walsh *Quevega, Mares' Hurdle* Picked up the great mare off the floor to ride her into history

Barry Geraghty *Bobs Worth, Gold Cup* Nursed his mount before making a relentless run from the turn

At a post-racing Cheltenham auction in January 2010, Tindall put in a bid just for the hell of it. Moments later the horse was his, which was not how he had planned it at all.

"I had no intention of buying him," he recalled. "We just thought it would be fun to say we had at least put in a bid for one horse. I put my hand up at £12,000, which I don't think any horse had been sold for that day, but this one did and we ended up with him. Even the auctioneer knew I wasn't keen because he announced that they didn't have a particularly enthusiastic buyer. Fortunately it has worked out well and the horse has been a good boy for us."

Tindall was more decisive when it came to sticking with the Welsh National as Monbeg Dude's target after the race was abandoned at Christmas and moved to January 5. "I wanted to go to Cheltenham on New Year's Day," Scudamore said after the race, "but Mr Tindall, who is bigger and stronger than me, wanted to come here."

The plan now is a return to Chepstow in December. "The Welsh National was only his sixth race over fences and I'd hope there is still improvement in him," Scudamore says. "His jumping wasn't great at Chepstow but he did better later in the season and over the summer he went to Zara Phillips to do some more schooling. If everything goes well he'll get an entry at Aintree. It's certainly in our minds."

So far every decision, intended or not, could not have worked out better.

▶▶ Paul Carberry and Monbeg Dude (left) get the better of Teaforthree

HOMECOMING KING
Godsmejudge, Scottish National
By Lee Mottershead

WHEN it was suggested to Alan King on the first Saturday of March that it was not long until the start of the Cheltenham Festival his reaction was that it was also not long until the end of the season. At that point he could not wait for the campaign to close, but after what happened over the coming weeks, most notably on home soil at Ayr, King viewed the season just gone rather differently.

For much of the autumn, winter and spring there was little for King to smile about. Some good horses got injured, other good horses found sodden ground conditions against them and the good horses that were left were simply not good enough. Then, however, came Cheltenham and Aintree, both of which brought reasons to cheer, as most definitely did Ayr's showpiece jumps fixture, at which a proud Scotsman, relocated to English soil, celebrated one of the most magical moments of his career.

You could tell from King's face, let alone King's words, what the victory of Godsmejudge in the Scottish Grand National meant to him. The master of Barbury Castle Stables was born in Lanark and brought up near Hamilton, just an hour from Ayr racecourse. As an 18-year-old he went to work for John Wilson, whose Cree Lodge Stables were a short hop across the road from the track. He still regards going back to Scotland as going home.

"This means a huge amount," said King, who is not averse to the

RACING POST ANNUAL 2014 **121**

▶ Liberty Counsel (blue, main picture) scores in Ireland and (above) Scottish winner Godsmejudge

odd display of emotion and was once again incapable of hiding the pleasure victory had given him. Given much of what had gone before, nobody could blame him.

Even before the core part of the jumps season began, David Nicholson's long-time protege was forced to wrap up in cotton wool leading prospects Invictus and Batonnier. Other smart performers either failed to appear or disappointed when they did, but a glass half-empty became a glass half-full when Medinas led home Meister Eckhart for a stable one-two in Cheltenham's Coral Cup, L'Unique took the Grade 1 Anniversary Hurdle at Aintree and then Godsmejudge struck at Ayr for a yard in rampant late-season form.

"It's awfully special," said King, whose number-two rider Wayne Hutchinson once again proved an impressive substitute for the sidelined Robert Thornton. "Every winner at Ayr gives me a tremendous kick, but this one is extra special and right up there with my Champion Hurdle and Champion Chase victories at the Cheltenham Festival."

He meant it as well. The win ensured that the trainer moved from seventh to fourth in the championship table and took his season's earnings past £1 million. In the land of his birth King had reasserted himself and also laid down solid foundations for an assault on a Grand National that, although not staged in Scotland, is even more important than Ayr's – even to a Scotsman.

"I'd like to think in a year's time he might be a proper Grand National horse," said King, whose view was backed up by Hutchinson's

assessment of Godsmejudge. "He is relentless in his galloping, his jumping is very slick and he just doesn't break stride," the jockey said.

Such qualities are valuable in a Grand National challenger and King's record at Aintree – eight of his 23 Grade 1 winners have been at the National meeting – is impressive. The Grand National itself might be a Grade 3 but it is still well worth winning. In Godsmejudge, King might well have a horse who can win it.

UNLIKELY HEROINE
Liberty Counsel, Irish National
By Jessica Lamb

LIBERTY COUNSEL always had a big Fairyhouse win in her but the question from the off was whether it would be on the chase track at Easter or the cross-country course in May.

When the ten-year-old landed this year's Irish Grand National her odds of 50-1 made her the longest-priced winner in the 143-year history of the handicap chase and the victory was the biggest of Danish trainer Dot Love's career as well as a defining moment for Wexford conditional Ben Dalton.

Love comes from the eventing arena and her right-hand man is Ciaran Murphy, twin brother of Olympic eventer Joseph Murphy, while Dalton started out in show jumping. For a team brimful of equestrian knowledge and horsemanship, it is apt that the mare who has done so much for them is not a pure thoroughbred and was

considered an eventer as much as she was a racehorse.

Breeder Robert Honner explains: "Her dam, My Free Mantel, came to Clongiffen Stud to look after a thoroughbred foal who had lost its dam, but my dad Winston liked her so much he let her be covered by our stallion, Leading Counsel. Her owner decided he didn't want her anymore when she was in foal and we got her registered as a non-thoroughbred so that we could then register her progeny as thoroughbreds and use them to race.

"We were thinking they'd end up being nice horses for a bit of fun point-to-pointing or at the very least make good eventers. How wrong were we?"

Local man Bernard Murtagh bought a share in Liberty Counsel when she came of age and put her in training with the Honners for a point-to-point campaign – on one condition. "We weren't to tell his wife Helen," Robert says.

"Liberty Counsel would have been third to Seabass on her first run but for a tired fall at the last and we were gearing up then for a run at Loughrea, in Galway, when Bernard died suddenly from a heart attack."

Helen found out, but instead of discarding the secret racehorse she and her sister Irene Neale bought out the Honners to own her completely. They transferred her to Love's Westmeath base, local to them, and 16 months later, on her fourth outing, she landed the first of her six wins.

It was the fifth success, a handicap chase at Kilbeggan, that sparked the Irish National dream. "I kept telling her owners it was the race for her," Murphy says. "Staying trip, good

ground, light weight. It was perfect. They looked at me like I was mad but went along with it anyway and thank God for that.

"We fancied her in the Kim Muir at Cheltenham a fortnight before the Irish National, but the ground went and she was nursed around with Fairyhouse in mind. We had her as fit as we could get her and told Ben to keep the pedal down the whole way and burn the others out. He gave her a cracking ride. It was an unbelievable day."

Not only did Liberty Counsel's pedigree scream eventer, so too did her legs. The Irish National was only her 21st run, owing to three separate tendon injuries that Love and Murphy now have under control.

"We have to train her with long-term targets like Cheltenham and Fairyhouse in mind and keep her off the track," Love says. "Thankfully we have excellent facilities here and can have a horse race-fit without racing. She spends a lot of time out in the paddock with her darling friend Shadow Eile. She is something else and is such a good jumper that, personally, I would consider having a go at Aintree. Good ground is what makes all the difference to her. She really needs that wherever she goes."

Murphy adds: "She would get the trip at Aintree and she keeps getting better now that we're able to train her properly. It's in our minds all the time."

New season, new dream, for the unlikely heroine.

By Jonathan Mullin

COMING OF AGE

Bryan Cooper continued his rapid rise to the top with a string of big-race successes in the 2012-13 season, capped by Our Conor's romp to victory in the Triumph Hurdle

WHEN you are five-nil up, playing the football of your life, the last thing you want to hear is the half-time whistle. But come that whistle did for Bryan Cooper in May, loud and shrill. Three Cheltenham Festival winners and two Aintree successes had vaulted the 21-year-old from his relatively unknown status in Britain into the consciousness of the racing public, but then came the downside that is a fact of life in the jumps game.

Jockeys don't tend to like too much detail about their falls, understandably so. They will divide them into two categories – a simple fall or a heavy fall – and get on with it. While Cooper's fall from Tepalo, in a beginners' chase at Down Royal in May, might have been simple in its execution, the consequences were serious.

"It wasn't a bad fall, just a simple one. The ground was quite quick but I've had much worse falls and come out without a scratch," Cooper says. "I knew straight away my leg was broken, you could see it was gone. The first thing I thought was, 'How am I going to spend the next three and a half months?' While it was hard at the time, in one sense it could have been a worse fall and it could have happened at a worse time too – in September or October. I had all summer to get over it."

His broken left femur brought an abrupt halt to the whirlwind progress that had taken him to Cheltenham, Aintree and back home to Punchestown, where he was among the winners again. At the close of the season, he was fifth in the Irish jump jockeys' table with 61 winners. Not bad for a fast-maturing young man in only his second season without a claim.

"The injury gave me a chance to sit back and watch the races again and realise what I had achieved – having those winners at Cheltenham, Aintree and Punchestown. Just my overall number of winners alone – setting out at the start of the season I never thought that was going to happen."

The modest phrase "those winners at Cheltenham" does little to sum up Cooper's firecracker impact on the big spring festivals. The son of trainer Tom Cooper had been a star in waiting in Ireland ever since he shook off his claim like you wave away a housefly, winning the conditionals' title in 2011-12 just 18 months after riding his first winner, but his Cheltenham haul of three winners turned BJ Cooper into jump racing's hottest young prospect.

"I suppose in Britain they are so used to seeing the likes of Ruby and Barry in

all the big races," he says. "For me, being only 20 years old, and winning those big races, it was a bit of a shock to them." He had never ridden a Cheltenham Festival winner before, but the full range of his talent was evident in his never-say-die effort on Benefficient in the Jewson Novices' Chase, his confident display on Triumph Hurdle winner Our Conor and his well-judged hold-up ride on Ted Veale in the County Handicap Hurdle. Three different rides, all with the same result.

"I've watched back the Cheltenham races quite a bit, especially during the time when I was injured. I'd flick on one of those big races from the spring and that would pick me up again. It's great to have them there because if I never again ride a winner at Cheltenham, I can always say I rode three in one year."

Cooper broke his Cheltenham duck on Benefficient, already one of the most important horses in his young career after being his first Grade 1 winner as a novice hurdler in February 2012. "He put me on the map as far as riding in those big races was concerned," the jockey says. "He went to Cheltenham

'I suppose in Britain they are so used to seeing the likes of Ruby and Barry in all the big races. For me, being only 20 years old, and winning those big races, it was a bit of a shock to them'

and proved he was tough and gutsy, proved he was a good horse.

"I was lucky enough that the lads left me alone in front and let me have my own way and he settled well in front. When Dynaste and Captain Conan came around me turning in, I said to myself, 'I'll probably have to settle for a place here.' I just gave him a chance to get home and when I did he picked up a lot better than I thought he would.

"I suppose the jump at the last sealed it. I was a bit long at it but thank God he came up for me. When I got the gap up the inner on the run-in, I thought, 'It's do or die now'. To be fair to him he stuck his head out as well."

Even on a 20-1 shot who had just denied hot favourite Dynaste, Cooper received a hero's welcome. "That journey back up the walkway gives you shivers up your spine, particularly on an Irish horse when there are so many Irish there cheering for you. They're throwing out the Irish flag for you and no matter what winner it is, whether he is favourite or 50-1, they always get a great cheer coming in."

The next day took him to a different

level on Our Conor, who raised the roof with his effortless cruise to victory in the Triumph. "With Our Conor, it stands out vividly. He was one of the Irish bankers and so many people were there to see him. There were faces I knew and two or three people threw out a flag to me. I'll never forget that walk back."

What made it all the more special was the sudden release of pressure after all the expectation that had built up in Dessie Hughes's yard over the winter. "I was determined I was going to enjoy it, I wanted this one to soak in," says Cooper, who has been guided by Hughes for most of his career over jumps. "As I headed back in I was determined to remember as much as I could. There was a lad out of the yard, Johnny King, who had said from day one he wouldn't be beat in the Triumph, and I had kind of half said, 'Ah, he won't win, I don't think he'll win.' And then there was Johnny down at the bottom of the chute and he was roaring, 'I told ya so! I told ya so!'"

Before the walk came the victorious punch of the Cotswolds air, a show of emotion from Cooper at odds with his cool ride. "I suppose there was so much relief," he says by way of explanation. "We had such high expectations, yet people were questioning his ability and questioning just how strong the Irish juvenile form was. Personally, the pressure got a lot worse after Benefficient because after I won the Jewson I thought, 'Well, that's it, that's my winner got.' In my own head I was battling that when I came to ride Our Conor.

"I was very confident he had a lot of class and would take some beating, but I never dreamed he would win the way he did. He showed himself to be something else. The boss told me to jump him off handy and get him a position, but I didn't mean to be that handy at all. He was a little bit off the bridle earlier on in the season, but he came alive with me at Cheltenham and was a little keen over the first two hurdles."

Our Conor had won the major Irish trial, the Spring Juvenile Hurdle, by five lengths from Diakali but home punters put their trust in British form. Nicky Henderson's Rolling Star was 5-2 favourite and Our Conor, backed by

▶▶ The power of five (clockwise from above left): Our Conor, Benefficient (right), Ted Veale (left), Special Tiara and First Lieutenant – Cooper's quintet of winners at the Cheltenham and Aintree festivals

Irish money, was joint-second favourite at 4-1 with the Paul Nicholls-trained Far West. The market may have been competitive but the race wasn't as Our Conor came home by 15 lengths from Far West.

"It was only a piece of work to him," Cooper says. "I was getting a lead off Diakali and I jumped and jumped, and took a lead as long as I could. But suddenly there was nothing to take me any further. I was just hoping going down to the last that he wasn't going to empty, but he never did. When I turned in I knew nothing could beat me unless something came from the clouds.

"I have never experienced anything like it and I hope I will feel it again some time, but I doubt it. He has so much class and so many gears, and the way he jumps you can ride him with so much confidence. I didn't have to touch him. I just gave him a squeeze before the last and he took off again. He's very special."

Just over half an hour later came a victory almost as fluid on Ted Veale in the County Hurdle – another one for Benefficient's trainer Tony Martin – and at Aintree there were Grade 1 victories on Special Tiara for Henry de Bromhead and on the Mouse Morris-trained First Lieutenant in the Betfred Bowl. The spread of trainers trusting Cooper with their biggest chances is one of the clearest signs of the standing he has achieved in Ireland in a short time.

If there were low points in a year where Cooper grabbed the box seat and became box office, it would be that fall at Down Royal and the news of Our Conor's sale to owner Barry Connell. With Connell employing a retained jockey in Danny Mullins, the partnership that looked at Cheltenham's hill and laughed at its gradient would be no more.

"When I first heard, it hit me hard, I was devastated," Cooper admits. "He was something you would look forward to every single morning, riding him out every day. Look, that's racing. There will always be personal highs and lows. At least he's staying in the yard with Dessie.

"It's a long road between here and Cheltenham and it's a great buy for Barry Connell. It shows the amount of money he's putting into Irish racing. Our Conor probably will have to improve 10lb or a stone to beat Hurricane Fly on ratings, but he's only four and he's lightly raced, and I'm sure there's plenty of improvement to come from him."

Cooper is only just getting started too. Even without Our Conor, he is playing in the big league now and he looks a natural. His rise has been quick, but he's here to stay.

PRIZEFIGHTER

Even with Ruby Walsh back in Ireland full time, Davy Russell won't give up his title easily

By David Jennings

NOT even a punctured lung could stop Davy Russell clinching a second successive jump jockeys' title in Ireland, but in his bid for a hat-trick this season the reigning champion faces a much more serious obstacle: Ruby Walsh.

When you glance back at the business end of a race, the all-time leading rider at the Cheltenham Festival is the one man you don't want to see on your tail but it's a sight Russell had better get used to. Walsh parted company with Paul Nicholls in the summer in order to concentrate his efforts on home soil and it sets up a potential ding-dong duel with Russell in the months ahead.

"It's going to be very difficult as Ruby is going to be riding here a lot more frequently than in recent seasons," Russell admitted in October. "But we have a good spread of exciting horses in different yards and there is plenty to look forward to. We'll see how things go and, hopefully, he won't be too far ahead of me come the spring.

Russell won't give up his title easily, that's for sure. Not after all the pain he went through last season.

◆◆◆◆

IT still hurts. The punctured lung has long healed but it left behind a trail of destruction to Russell's big-race ambitions. When Un Beau Matin took a tired fall at the last in the Coral Cup on the second day of the Cheltenham Festival, little did Gigginstown House Stud's retained rider know the damage it would do to his season.

Russell didn't flinch at first. He felt fit enough to take his first two rides on day three but that was to be his last festival action. He had to forfeit the Gold Cup ride on Sir Des Champs, as well as Ryanair favourite First Lieutenant.

Success on the latter in the Betfred Bowl at Aintree was the only possible cure. "That was First Lieutenant's Gold Cup," Russell says. "All year it looked to be the one race that was tailor-made for him. Aintree was his track and three miles was his trip."

Russell was spot on. First Lieutenant, so often the bridesmaid in winter, got to throw the bouquet at Aintree. But it was Bryan Cooper and not Russell who shared the moment. The British Horseracing Authority denied Russell the right to ride at Aintree, a decision that came as a shock to the system.

"I thought I was heading over to London for a run-of-the-mill check-up. Show my face, say hello and that would be that. But I sensed straight away that the doctor wasn't happy and it wasn't going to be as straightforward as I thought. He reckoned the percentage chance of recurrence was too high and that was that. It was a shock, believe me."

The shock was understandable, given that Russell had already returned to race-riding in Ireland, but he had no option other than to stay at home while the big prizes at Aintree were being decided. When he should have been getting ready to ride Solwhit for Charles Byrnes in the Liverpool Hurdle on Grand National day, instead he was guiding Kates Benefit to victory in a mares' maiden hurdle at Navan.

The difference? Sixty grand or thereabouts, but it wasn't just about the money. After the heartache of his early exit from Cheltenham and missing out on First Lieutenant on day one of Aintree, here was a lost opportunity for a Grade 1 winner on the biggest day in the jump racing calendar.

"It was hard to take and even harder to watch," he admits. "It's all about Grade 1s at the end of the day. They're the big ones, the ones you want to be riding in. I've always loved Solwhit and I knew he had a massive chance of following up his win in the World Hurdle."

Solwhit stormed to victory, filling the hole left by the injured Big Buck's in the staying hurdle division. Paul Carberry filled in brilliantly for Russell too, just as Cooper had been doing on all the horses in Gigginstown's maroon and white.

Finally, at Punchestown, Russell got to play with his favourite Gigginstown gifts. If the punctured lung was affecting his strength in the saddle, it would have been pretty obvious in the Punchestown Gold Cup on Sir Des Champs, the 2-1 favourite who needed every last ounce of Russell's resolve to fend off Long Run. It was vindication.

Three days later, when the champagne was uncorked in the parade ring at the season finale, Russell was once again soaked. He had successfully defended his jockeys' title with 103 winners, two more than Walsh.

"It was every bit as sweet as the previous year," Russell says. "When you win it once people will say there was an element of fortune about it. That it was just a fluke. But when you win it twice in a row, the doubters dwindle."

The doubt over a potential recurrence of his lung problem was removed by an operation in the summer and Russell is looking forward to a big season in Ireland and Britain.

"I'm lucky to have a great team behind me. There are a lot of good young horses coming through, so the future looks bright."

But, more than ever, Russell knows he had better watch out for Walsh.

GOING THE EXTRA MILE

Solwhit stepped into the hole left by Big Buck's to take the major staying prizes of 2013

By David Jennings

THE best bit of rebranding since a Marathon became a Snickers. All anyone wanted on the two-mile hurdle shelf was Hurricane Fly, so Charles Byrnes decided to take Solwhit down, dust him off and bring him back in a different wrapper – this time as a stayer.

The timing, as it happened, was perfect because there was a gap in the market after injury put champion stayer Big Buck's out of the big events of 2013. Something new and different was needed, and Solwhit fitted the bill. The two big springtime staying hurdles at Cheltenham and Aintree, which have been reserved for Big Buck's in recent seasons, this time went to the reinvented Solwhit.

Byrnes felt there was no option but to move Solwhit up to three miles. "It was either stay at two miles and get our backside kicked by Hurricane Fly every time we ran or step up in trip," he says. "It was something we had been talking about for a long time. Davy [Russell] mentioned it a long time ago as he always felt that the further he went, the better he would be. I always thought he would stay too."

Not only did Solwhit stay, he devoured the extra mile. After the best part of two years off with a tendon injury, he returned on the final day of 2012 at Punchestown. Solwhit couldn't reel in the mud-loving Bog Warrior in the conditions hurdle over two and a half miles, but

there was sufficient promise in defeat to suggest he could be a force again.

Just shy of three weeks later, Solwhit showed up for the Grade 3 Limestone Lad Hurdle at Naas. A furlong less, a solid field of six and heavy ground. He ranged up alongside So Young at the last before sauntering four lengths clear. It could have been eight.

"We have no real plans as such," said a smiling Byrnes afterwards. Never play poker next to the softly spoken Ballingarry boy. Two months on and Solwhit, with Paul Carberry in the saddle, rocked up in the World Hurdle at Cheltenham.

Tom Segal knew. His popular Pricewise column had flagged up Solwhit weeks before at 16-1. That had whittled down to 17-2 by the off. There was no Big Buck's and no genuine Grade 1 performer among the dozen opponents, according to Byrnes.

"They were Grade 2 horses and we knew we had a Grade 1 horse. That's the way we were looking at it," he says. "Cheltenham is different to everywhere else. It's the be-all and end-all. We knew he was back to himself and we all knew what a good horse he is. Paul gave him a great ride and he won well in the end. It was fantastic. He is a genuine Grade 1 horse who rarely lets you down."

Not everybody was convinced by Solwhit. Some said he would be found out at Aintree in the Liverpool Hurdle, arguably a stronger race than the World Hurdle had been. He was favourite but 9-4 didn't scream superstar.

Carberry had the kid gloves

on again as he crept his way into contention and Solwhit didn't even know he had left his stable until the home turn. By that stage, half the field were cooked and it was Pertemps Final winner Holywell who put up the biggest fight. But Solwhit was the class act and he was three lengths clear at the line.

A bloody nose deprived us of an epic duel with Quevega at Punchestown. As the crowd held their breath in anticipation of a classic, Russell spotted some blood sneaking out of Solwhit's nostril down at the start. On further investigation it was just a scratch but caution prevailed.

Success in the Grande Course de Haies d'Auteuil, the French Champion Hurdle, in June would have been the perfect send-off to a sensational season but Solwhit's stamina ran out in the closing stages of that marathon on very soft ground and he was unable to get to Gemix. He still led the strong away challenge, with nine lengths back to Zaidpour in third.

"I couldn't have asked for more from him," Byrnes says. "It was a truly magnificent year and I just hope he can do something similar this season. Obviously we'd hope to be back in the World Hurdle but the three-mile hurdle at Leopardstown over Christmas has been upgraded to Grade 1 status and we'll go there, all being well."

Big Buck's is likely to be waiting at Cheltenham but Solwhit, rebranded and rejuvenated, won't be pushed aside without a fight.

PUNCHESTOWN
in pictures

1 An exuberant racegoer stands out from the crowd

2 The Noel Meade-trained Il Fenomeno and Paul Carberry win the bragbet.com Handicap Hurdle

3 Barry Geraghty signs racegoer Katie Cody's Sprinter Sacre replica silks

4 Lord Hawkfield is followed by a loose horse on his way to second place behind Zest For Life in the Sean Breen Memorial Chase

5 Moyle Park has a refreshing drink of water after winning the Goffs Land Rover Bumper for Willie Mullins

6 Runners tackle Joe's water splash during the Irish Field Chase. The cross-country race was won by Sizing Australia, who denied Zest For Life a festival double

7 David Pipe greets Jane Mangan after her victory on The Liquidator in the Betdaq The People's Exchange Champion Bumper

8 Willie Mullins and Ruby Walsh in the winner's enclosure after Quevega's fourth consecutive victory in the Ladbrokes World Series Hurdle

9 Barry Cash hugs Big Shu as they are led into the winner's enclosure after landing the La Touche Cup

10 Patrick Mullins holds his trophy after winning the Kildare Post Bumper on Turnandgo

11 All eyes on the action in the packed stands

12 Studying the form in the betting ring

13 The field passes the stands in the Louis Fitzgerald Hotel Hurdle with the winner, the grey Dalasiri (orange silks), in mid-division

14 Hurricane Fly fans after his victory in the Rabobank Champion Hurdle, the final chapter in a glorious unbeaten season

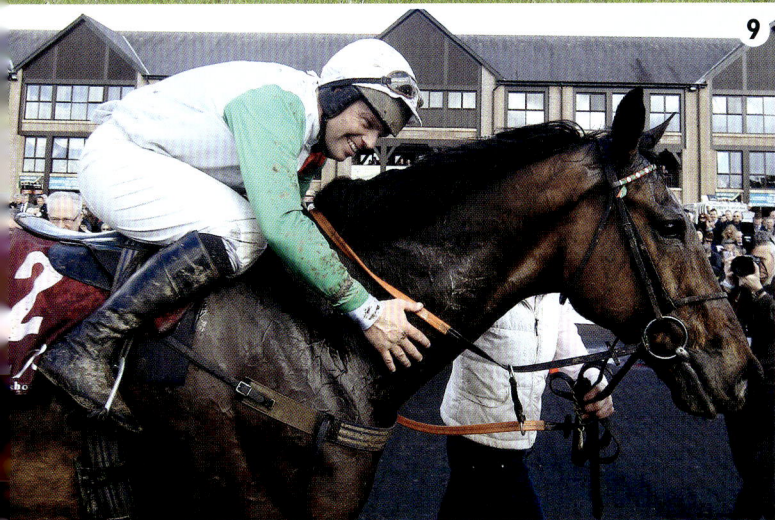

'Racing's pain at JT's plight is just as sharp now as it was when we first learned the terrible scale of his injuries'

John Thomas McNamara's catastrophic fall cast a shadow not only over the Cheltenham Festival but over the entire year

By Alastair Down

IN THE months following a bereavement, those who remain behind take a small degree of solace from the old adage "it doesn't get any better, but you get better at it". The theory being that, while time never truly cures the pain, the passing of weeks, months and years somehow eases the intensity of the ache and dissipates the shock.

But with John Thomas McNamara's paralysis since his fall at Cheltenham in March, time has brought no form of consolation. Racing's pain at JT's plight is just as sharp now as it was when we first learned the terrible scale of his injuries.

It was quite soon after his fall late in the afternoon on the third day of the festival, Thursday March 14, that you began to be gnawed by a feeling that something hideous was in the air. The routine bypassing of a fence is usually nothing to chill the soul, but as time went by and the focus of medical attention grew ever more intense you sensed a palpable and mounting seriousness that you could not quite quantify and feared all the more for that fact.

Then came the arrival of the air ambulance – often a saviour and to which one of my daughters owes her life, yet whose appearance is to be both welcomed and dreaded at the same time. Help is indeed at hand but the need and urgency has to be dire for the helicopter to take flight. The peril is immediate.

The last race was delayed by half an hour and run in a gathering gloom that never lifted from the rest of the meeting or, for some, ever since. As the evening wore on you heard from people who knew how desperate JT's situation was and it was clear that if he survived the immediate threats to his life he almost certainly faced a future of unimaginable restriction. This at the age of 37 and with a wife and three young children.

I never believed anything could ever take the joy out of Gold Cup day, but I learned differently in the most bitter way on that grey Friday that ended the meeting. Yes, the roars still went up, the bars were bursting, bonhomie and conviviality could still be found in corners of the course and the heroes of the hour were given the welcomes and accorded the admiration they deserved.

But for many the soul of the occasion had been sucked out.

Those with even the slightest clue of the battle being fought 30 miles away at Frenchay Hospital, near Bristol, had their minds elsewhere. The weighing room was in utter shock, you could see it in their faces, hear it in their words and feel it through their tears. In many respects the weighing room remains in shock still.

From the first hours of JT's ordeal, racing swung behind him. At seven the next morning Injured Jockeys Fund almoner Julia Mangan met Caroline McNamara, JT's wife, off her flight into Bristol and took her to Frenchay. Caroline never left JT's side until he returned to Dublin months later and Julia in her turn was always there for her in the darkest of hours.

Julia herself is no stranger to grief, having lost her jockey husband Roy in freakish circumstances 19 years ago, and she has been one of the heroines of this tale. JT's great friend and ally, Enda Bolger, paid tribute to her remarkable efforts. "Julia Mangan has been incredible and we don't have anyone in Ireland like her," he said.

While at Frenchay, JT was at first reluctant to let his children, Dylan, Harry and Olivia, see him reduced to a state of virtual immobility. You and I would wonder how an active sportsman begins to come to terms with such a predicament but just ponder for a second how you convey the new reality to three young kids who have spent their lives being picked up happily by Dad.

Yet even such extremes were not without a defiant vestige of a lighter side. Four-year-old Harry wanted to know what all the tubes attached to JT were for and whether it would be all right if he pulled them out.

And since the day after the accident Caroline McNamara has stood at the heart of this storm that has overtaken her family. Julia Mangan says: "Caroline has been just extraordinary – so strong, sensible and practical. Nothing seems to faze her and, while she has had to be tough, it has never for a moment masked how charming and lovely she is.

"I said to JT once: 'I'm sure you don't see yourself as being fortunate, but you are in having Caroline.' He smiled and said: 'Yes, I know.'"

The extent to which family, friends and the racing world at large have rallied round John Thomas quickly became the stuff of legend and at one time if you needed to find one of jumping's principal players the best way to do it was to stake out Frenchay, where Caroline kept a diary of every visitor.

But on his return to Ireland, despite the devoted medical care and the inspirational input of Dr Adrian McGoldrick, the Turf Club's

▶▶**Continues page 134**

senior medical officer, somehow the momentum of maintaining hope that there would be some form of limited recovery began to stagnate. It was nobody's fault but somehow the idea of going forward had become becalmed.

When people feel powerless they inevitably begin to feel angry and the frustration of some of JT's close friends in the weighing room became palpable. Something was needed to reinvigorate the process and in early October he was transferred back to Britain to continue his treatment at the North West Regional Spinal Injuries Centre at Southport on the Lancashire coast.

But at no stage has any momentum been lost on the fundraising front. A large number of events have been held on both sides of the water in aid of JT, whose care will cost all but limitless amounts in the years to come. And at Limerick on October 14 seemingly the whole of Irish racing united as one to raise money for JT and another badly stricken amateur, Jonjo Bright, who at the age of 18 was left in a wheelchair after a point-to-point fall in the same month as JT's accident.

The day generated in excess of €550,000 (£465,000), with the prospect of much more to come, and Julia Mangan says: "It was the most fabulous occasion with an extraordinary sense of coming together in a cause in which we all believe so passionately. It was one of the most uplifting occasions you could imagine."

Writing about JT and the challenges ahead is complex because even the most benign and sympathetic observer cannot escape the nagging feeling that one is intruding into private grief. Nor do I wish to inject even a scintilla of false hope into peoples' thinking about what lies ahead for a man whose world fell in on him just months ahead of a planned retirement from race riding.

But while the discreet bulletins from his friends had an air of gloom about them over the summer, there were suggestions of tiny steps forward after JT moved to Southport.

One of the central issues since the accident has been the fact that JT cannot breathe unaided and requires a respirator. But shortly after moving to Southport he managed to breathe for periods of 12 and 14 minutes unaided and this represents a faint glimmer of light. No more than a glimmer but hugely better than nothing.

If there is a target – and it is a bold call which nobody dares pretend will be easy and may, indeed, not prove possible – it is eventually to allow JT to breathe

▶▶ Limerick's charity raceday in October raised in excess of €550,000 (£465,000) in aid of the Jockeys Emergency Fund and its care for JT McNamara and Jonjo Bright. Andrew McNamara and Tom O'Brien get soaked during the tug of war and Nick Nugent conducts an auction that raised more than €250,000

without help for large parts of the day and go back on the respirator at night.

Some doctors believe the diaphragm has up to a year during which it is perhaps feasible to undergo some process of recovery; others are not so sure. All these judgements are knife-edge and we are operating at the outer limits of both hope and knowledge.

If there is to be one long-lasting and indisputably good thing to come out of the bleakness of recent months it must surely be the establishment and funding of an Injured Jockeys Fund for Ireland.

'There was an extraordinary coming together in a cause we all believe in so passionately'

In October, British racing celebrated the 50th anniversary of the Injured Jockeys Fund and celebrate it we should as it is our sport's brightest shining light. The reasons why Ireland has never established a direct equivalent to the IJF need not bother us. We cannot change the past but we can build the future.

Moves are already afoot and the wheels of decision making are slowly moving into forward gear. It will come into being one day and out of the darkness it will bring a torch of hope to light the way ahead.

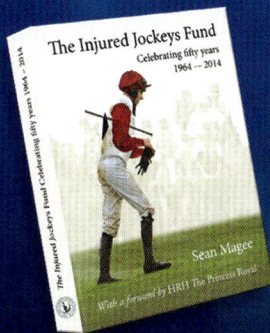

WAIT OFF HIS BACK

Richard Hughes finally won his first British Classic . . . and then his second

By Lee Mottershead

SOME of sport's highest achievers have been forced to accept they were destined to miss out on the biggest prizes. Colin Montgomerie never won a golf major, an Olympic gold medal eluded Colin Jackson and the one thing missing from John Francome's collection was the Grand National.

For years Richard Hughes seemed set to suffer the same fate. On January 11, 2013, he reached his 40th birthday – a watershed moment for many at the top level of sport – without a British Classic to his name. Two months before, he had been crowned British champion Flat jockey at long last but still the calendar turned for Hughes with the unwelcome tag of 'best current jockey never to have won a British Classic'. He had landed Classics in Ireland and France, but on his adopted home soil he was still waiting.

In total, 47 Classic races had passed him by. The record showed 15 defeats in the 2,000 Guineas, 11 in the 1,000 Guineas, eight in the Oaks, six in the Derby and seven in the St Leger. Nor had Hughes ever really troubled the judge, for although he had twice finished second in the 2,000 Guineas and once in the Oaks, none of those runner-ups came that close to glory.

The 2013 Classics campaign started in depressingly familiar fashion. Hughes went into the 2,000 Guineas as utterly certain as a jockey can be that Toronado

was going to win. He was wrong. Toronado and Dawn Approach, the favourite, eyeballed each other on the descent to the Dip, but climbing up the hill the Godolphin hope powered clear as Toronado's legs buckled. Fourth, a hugely deflating fourth, was the best he could manage.

Yet in racing there is always a tomorrow and on this tomorrow there was Sky Lantern, a Moyglare Stud Stakes winner at two, in the 1,000 Guineas. Hughes had endured a frustrating passage on her at the Breeders' Cup and there was another defeat on her reappearance when she failed to get past Hot Snap in the Nell Gwyn Stakes. No matter. Victory in the Nell Gwyn would have been only minor compensation. A Classic triumph in the 1,000 Guineas more than made up for American losses.

It was a typical Hughes ride, a veritable Hughesie special. The filly's trainer Richard Hannon once said of his son-in-law: "There's nothing you can do about his style. You just say 'Jesus' and hope everything goes right." Aboard Sky Lantern it did, but only just. At the foot of the Newmarket hill the willing grey still had three lengths to find on Just The Judge but with irresistible momentum she got her head in front where it needed to be. Cue a very emotional jockey.

"It's about time," said Sky Lantern's delighted partner, who had been sure the weekend would yield his first British Classic, and it did, but not quite in the expected manner. "This is a monkey off my back, especially after what happened with Toronado. But I've won some 50 Classics elsewhere and I knew I would do it one day. It's very special and I'm delighted my mum and dad were here to see it."

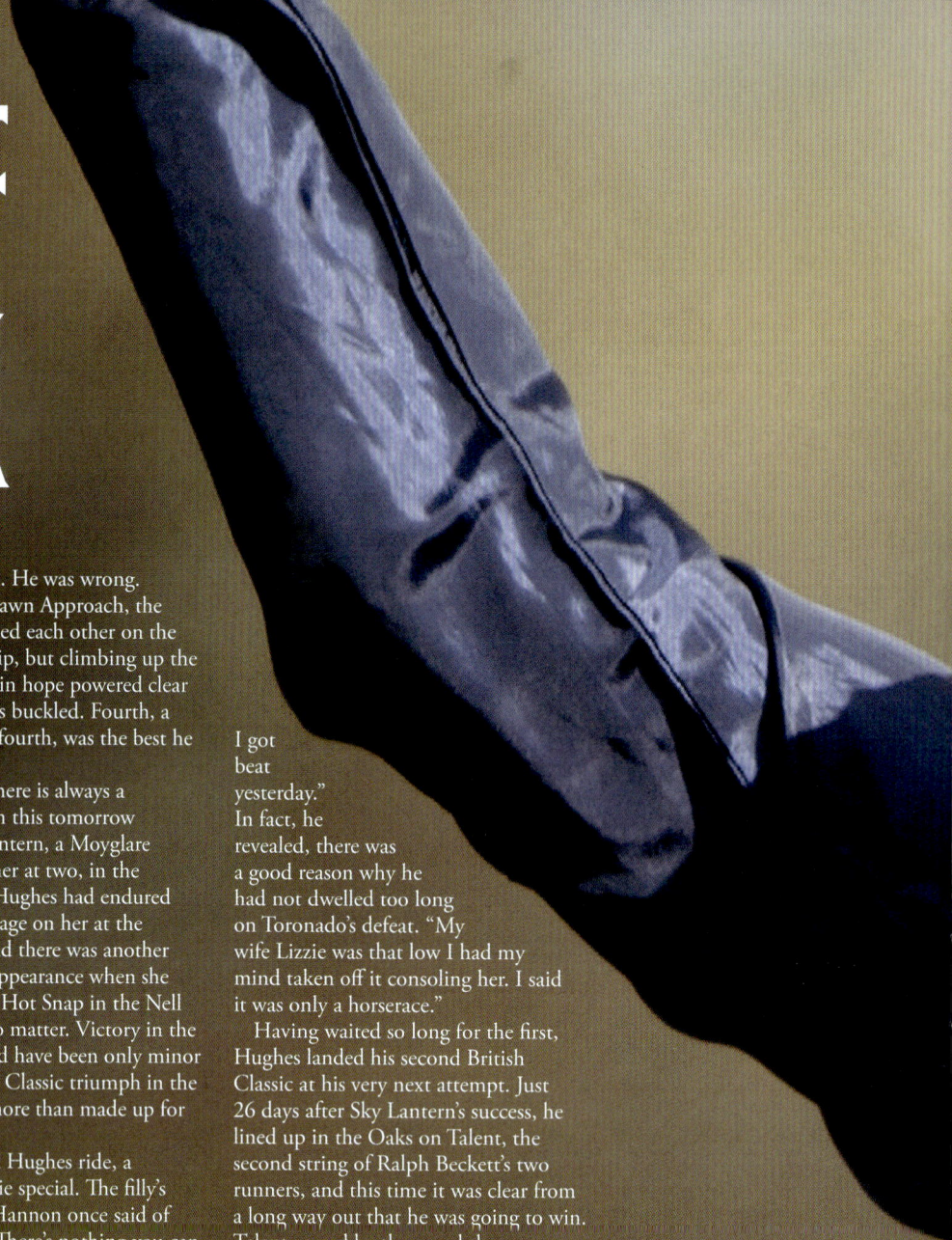

Hughes had the maturity to put the disappointment of Toronado out of his mind and do the job he was born to do. "I rode her the way I wanted to," he said. "I had to ride her with balls and drop her in, and ride her the right way. I didn't want to go panicking just because

I got beat yesterday." In fact, he revealed, there was a good reason why he had not dwelled too long on Toronado's defeat. "My wife Lizzie was that low I had my mind taken off it consoling her. I said it was only a horserace."

Having waited so long for the first, Hughes landed his second British Classic at his very next attempt. Just 26 days after Sky Lantern's success, he lined up in the Oaks on Talent, the second string of Ralph Beckett's two runners, and this time it was clear from a long way out that he was going to win. Talent scored by three and three-quarter lengths from stablemate Secret Gesture to give her trainer a memorable one-two and her rider back-to-back Classic wins. Once again, Hughes was at his most exquisite, biding his time and letting his mount nap at the back of the field as the leaders set punishing fractions. When those leaders had nothing left to give, Talent still had plenty and sailed past for an authoritative success. Suddenly for Hughes, winning Classics was like shelling peas.

But the hat-trick was not to be. Since Hughes first sat on a racehorse the biggest ambition has been to add his name to the Derby's roll of honour and a promising call-up for the Aidan O'Brien-trained Mars gave him hope. Sixth place, however, was one disappointment in another glorious season for Flat racing's most prolific rider.

The Derby might not elude him forever. After an astonishing couple of seasons that have seen his wish list whittled down considerably, Hughes knows that patience is a virtue.

'This is a monkey off my back but I knew I would do it one day. It's very special and I'm delighted my mum and dad were here to see it'

▸▸ Richard Hughes celebrates on Sky Lantern (main and top) and wins on Talent (bottom)

EASY RIDER

First ride for Dermot Weld, first Classic success for Chris Hayes. Surely it couldn't be this easy, but it was

"When I heard the commentator say I was six lengths clear, I knew I couldn't lose it," Hayes said after cruising to victory in the Irish St Leger on Voleuse De Coeurs.

Hayes has long had the trust of Lady O'Reilly, the owner of Voleuse De Coeurs, but came in for the Classic ride only after Weld's stable jockey Pat Smullen chose to partner Pale Mimosa. Riding for Weld for the first time cranked up the pressure, but Hayes was confident enough to tear up the trainer's plan and ride his own race.

"Mr Weld was very bullish," Hayes said. "He told me to be handy and try to arrive with my challenge about a furlong out, but things didn't work out as planned. They were stopping in front of me and I decided to take the bull by the horns. She was awesome and put the race to bed turning for home. When she hit the easier surface she sprinted away."

Hayes was especially pleased to win for Lady O'Reilly, who hired him as retained rider in 2007 after he had won the Irish apprentice title two years in a row. They came close to Classic glory in their first season when Dimenticata was beaten a neck by Finsceal Beo in the Irish 1,000 Guineas and it had been a long wait to go one better.

"These are the days you dream of," Hayes said. "I'm delighted to have won a Group 1 for Lady O'Reilly. She has been very good to me. I've ridden winners for her as a 10lb claimer right down to today."

Hayes had ridden his first Group 1 winner just eight days earlier when he took the Matron Stakes on La Collina for Kevin Prendergast, another long-time supporter. That victory had reduced him to tears but he managed to keep his emotions in check after his Classic success. Perhaps, by then, he was becoming used to the feeling.

THE CLASSICS
in pictures

1 Jamie Spencer with his trophy after winning the Irish 1,000 Guineas on Just The Judge

2 Ruler Of The World wins the Derby, giving jockey Ryan Moore his second victory in the race and trainer Aidan O'Brien his fourth

3 Magician (Joseph O'Brien) wins the Irish 2,000 Guineas, leading a one-two for Ballydoyle from Gale Force Ten

4 Kevin Manning celebrates his first Irish Derby success after riding Trading Leather to victory by a length and three-quarters from Galileo Rock

5 Ralph Beckett greets Richard Hughes after Talent's victory in the Oaks. Talent, at 20-1, was Beckett's second string according to the betting but she beat her stablemate, the 3-1 second favourite Secret Gesture, by three and three-quarter lengths

6 Just The Judge (Jamie Spencer) wins the Irish 1,000 Guineas, giving trainer Charlie Hills his first Classic success

7 Richard Hughes clinches the first British Classic of his career on Sky Lantern in the 1,000 Guineas

8 Leading Light lands the St Leger for Aidan O'Brien and Joseph O'Brien

9 Dawn Approach, trained by Jim Bolger and ridden by Kevin Manning, streaks clear to win the 2,000 Guineas by five lengths

10 Johnny Murtagh returns in triumph on Chicquita after her Irish Oaks victory

11 A first Classic win for Chris Hayes as the Dermot Weld-trained Voleuse De Coeurs lands the Irish St Leger

STYLE AND SUBSTANCE

SIR HENRY CECIL 1943-2013

Sir Henry Richard Amherst Cecil, whose greatness as a trainer was matched only by his popularity, died on June 11, aged 70. His genius is remembered in these excerpts from the Racing Post's special tribute edition

By Alastair Down

BORN to the castle but beloved of the country cottage and council house, Sir Henry Cecil was the most cherished and totemic figure of his era, and beyond any doubt among the two or three finest and most instinctively gifted racehorse trainers of all time.

And there was an aura about Henry that made you feel that while the knight of Warren Place was still around the age of chivalry was not yet dead. There was always the whiff of glamour about Henry, but it was no superficial thing as his style was always backed by substance.

While his achievements were remarkable and almost without precedent, what made Cecil unique was the unshakeable bond he forged with the racing public. Nobody else in racing over the last 40 years has been held in such respect and affection. The public loved the man and it is devoutly to be hoped he fully understood what he meant to people and, in recent times, drew some spiritual sustenance from it.

Cecil started training in 1969 and won the Eclipse in his first season. Up to then all the years were BC – Before Cecil. But from that point in time everybody who follows the sport will have their own particular memories of the defining trainer of their age.

Successive generations have grown up and grown old with him, which is why the sadness in many a racing household is not at the death of some remote grandee but the loss of someone

regarded almost as a friend who had stitched many a moment of magic into the weave of our sporting lives.

In a way Henry died once before – professionally. Having ruled the heights, suddenly everything went adrift and between July 2000 and October 2006 he did not saddle a single Group 1 winner and many a mutter was that he had gone at the game. In 2005 there were just a dozen winners, Warren Place was haemorrhaging money as the stable strength dwindled from 200 horses to 50. The decline looked irreversible.

But running through every corpuscle in Cecil was an insatiably competitive streak and, crucially aided by the unswerving loyalty of Khalid Abdullah, he chiselled his way back inch by hard-fought inch. And how we all enjoyed and celebrated his return from a wilderness in which he spent much longer than the customary 40 days and 40 nights.

Most admirably, he brought his ferocious competitiveness to bear on the battle with cancer, which was first revealed in 2006. He refused to bow

▶ (Clockwise from top left) Sir Henry Cecil looks into the eyes of Frankel after his Queen Anne victory at Royal Ascot; with Steve Cauthen at Newbury in 1988; astride his hack on the Newmarket gallops; showing off his treasured roses at a garden party; on Warren Hill in Newmarket; after winning the Champion Stakes with Twice Over at Newmarket in 2010

to it and the courage with which he "fought the long defeat" made him the lion in summer. He never once burdened us with details of treatment, complaints about pain or the sheer medical drudgery of trying to stay alive – he just got on with it, doing his job in public, fighting his battle in private.

Of course we could all see the toll gradually increasing, the almost ludicrous good looks of his undoubtedly wild youth being overhauled by something more gaunt. You couldn't stop your heart going out to the man. When Frankel won last year's Juddmonte International at York, Henry, black-hatted, husky of voice and plenty frail, stood next to his equine masterpiece and you could all but feel the goodwill emanating from the crowd.

Many there that August afternoon knew full well that it was unlikely they would see him on his beloved Knavesmire again, but it was important for them to stand and applaud and be witness to a famous day made unforgettable by two indelible greats.

▶ **Continues page 142**

MEMORIES OF CECIL

"He was a great trainer but an even greater person. Everything he did in life was different class. His brilliant handling of Frankel, making the right call at every turn, underlined what a wonderful trainer he was" *Stable jockey Tom Queally*

"He was an amazing man and a truly exceptional trainer who could see something in a horse that nobody else would" *Assistant trainer Mike Marshall*

"I do not believe this country has ever produced a better trainer than Henry. I know there has never been one so loved" *Sir Michael Stoute*

"He was an incredible trainer and an incredible man. His training of Frankel was testament to his outstanding talent. He will never be forgotten" *Aidan O'Brien*

"Henry set the standard as the most instinctive and brilliant trainer of his generation" *John Gosden*

▶ Tom Queally (nearest) and other jockeys observe a minute's silence at Salisbury on the day Cecil died; (right) how the Racing Post reported his death

The respect there as usual, the affection as always.

To go and visit him in Newmarket was to enter something of an enchanted world, the heart of the wise wizard's kingdom. When last there the roses were not yet in full bloom but the famous mummy's peas were shooting and the recently discovered prehistoric tree growing steadily away.

The garden at Warren Place was where Henry took his mind when it needed rest and respite. Training a couple of hundred bluebloods was always pressure enough and one can only muse at what thoughts flickered across that brain during the barren years.

Once he was ill and the struggle far advanced there will have been days when, as flower, fruit and vegetable came to their peak, he knew he was seeing their seasonal splendour for the final time.

For all the Classic winners and the myriad Group 1s, it will be Frankel with whom he will forever be linked, the unbeatable trained by the inimitable.

Nobody who was on the Rowley Mile that afternoon when Frankel barnstormed the 2,000 Guineas will ever forget the palpable shock of his brilliance. Nobody had ever seen anything like it for the very simple reason nothing like it had ever happened before.

▶ Continues page 144

MEMORIES OF CECIL

Caught on a train

My story is of him sitting on a train from London to Epsom on Derby day when someone called out: "What are you doing here, Henry? Has your helicopter broken down?" To which he replied: "Yes, that is exactly what has happened."

When we got off at Tattenham Corner my counterpart walked up to him and asked: "Will Slip Anchor win the Derby, Mr Cecil?" Henry looked at him and said: "Yes, he will."

Richard Gurney
Fletching, East Sussex

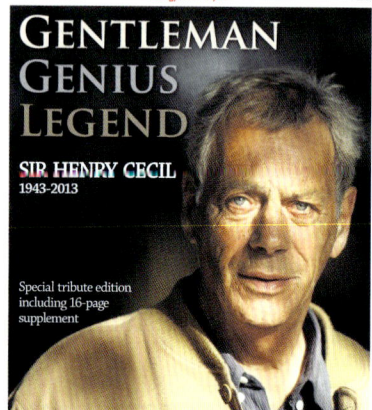

RACING POST

GENTLEMAN GENIUS LEGEND

SIR HENRY CECIL
1943-2013

Special tribute edition including 16-page supplement

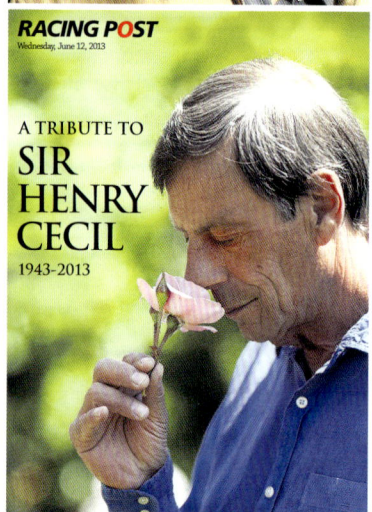

RACING POST
Wednesday, June 12, 2013

A TRIBUTE TO
SIR HENRY CECIL
1943-2013

GIANT OF THE TURF

Full name Sir Henry Richard Amherst Cecil (knighted 2011)

Born Aberdeen, 11 January 1943; elder of twin brothers

Parents Hon. Henry Cecil (brother of 3rd Baron Amherst of Hackney) and Rohays, daughter of Sir James Burnett, 13th Baronet of Leys

Educated Canford School, Dorset, and Royal Agricultural College, Cirencester

Assistant to his stepfather, champion trainer Sir Cecil Boyd-Rochfort, Newmarket 1964-68

Stables Freemason Lodge, Newmarket 1969; Marriott Stables, Newmarket 1970-76; Warren Place, Newmarket, from 1977

First winner Celestial Cloud, Ripon, 17 May 1969, ridden by Bill O'Gorman

First big winner Wolver Hollow (1969 Eclipse Stakes)

British Classic winners Bolkonski (1975 2,000 Guineas), Wollow (1976 2,000 Guineas), One In A Million (1979 1,000 Guineas), Light Cavalry (1980 St Leger), Fairy Footsteps (1981 1,000 Guineas), Oh So Sharp (1985 1,000 Guineas, Oaks, St Leger), Slip Anchor (1985 Derby), Reference Point (1987 Derby, St Leger), Diminuendo (1988 Oaks), Snow Bride (1989 Oaks), Michelozzo (1989 St Leger), Commander In Chief (1993 Derby), Bosra Sham (1996 1,000 Guineas), Lady Carla (1996 Oaks), Sleepytime (1997 1,000 Guineas), Reams Of Verse (1997 Oaks), Wince (1999 1,000 Guineas), Ramruma (1999 Oaks), Oath (1999 Derby), Love Divine (2000 Oaks), Light Shift (2007 Oaks), Frankel (2011 2,000 Guineas)

Other Classic winners Cloonagh (1973 Irish 1,000 Guineas), Ardross (1981 Prix Royal-Oak), El Cuite (1986 Prix Royal-Oak), Indian Skimmer (1987 Prix de Diane), Diminuendo (1988 Irish Oaks dead-heat), Old Vic (1989 Prix du Jockey-Club, Irish Derby), Alydaress (1989 Irish Oaks), Rafha (1990 Prix de Diane), Commander In Chief (1993 Irish Derby), Ramruma (1999 Irish Oaks)

Most prolific Group 1 winner Frankel (10 wins)

Most wins in a British season 180 in 1987

Champion trainer in Britain 1976, 78, 79, 82, 84, 85, 87, 88, 90 (1993 in win money only)

BARRY GERAGHTY

ON AT THE RACES

Get real insight in his exclusive blog every weekend and throughout the major National Hunt festivals.

attheraces.com/barry

AT THE RACES

SKY 415 | VIRGIN 534 | UPC 418

As Frankel's tale grew in the telling there was something spectacularly gratifying that he was in Henry's hands. The great man might indeed be suffering, but if Frankel was going to be his swansong then it was a glorious one that would echo down the centuries by way of a monument.

If Henry was increasingly frail, the sage in his loafers still had plenty of his old spark. He was, as ever, the very prince of politeness who could have written a textbook on manners. As the hacks gathered round after yet another spectacular Frankel triumph the customary happy pantomime would begin as Henry tilted that great head to one side and inquired of the assembled scribes: "What do you think?"

It was all you could do not to blurt out: "I think you are a bloody genius mate, and I wish you weren't ill."

Though he was by no means a saint, I can recall no whiff of scandal or suggestion of chicanery ever attaching itself to his horses or the way in which they ran. If he had occasional ups and downs in his personal life, the public saw his shortcomings as being like their own and thought none the worse of him.

For the next few days and weeks racing will be awash with tributes. But those closest to him and who loved him most dearly will simply be awash.

What is for certain is that racing's landscape will look very different no longer illuminated by the beacon of brilliance that was Cecil. Royal Ascot

▸▸**Continues page 146**

MEMORIES OF CECIL
Gentleman of the road

Travelling along the A14, tyre bursts on my caravan. Park on roadside to await AA. Many vehicles shuffle by. One stops and reverses back. Driver drops window and asks: "Are you all right?" (I was 75 at the time).

I reply: "I'm awaiting AA."

"I can't help, then?"

"No, but thanks for stopping."

Henry Cecil then continues on his journey.

D Lambert, Groby, Leics

▸▸ Sir Henry Cecil's memorial service at Ely Cathedral on September 16

YOUR £10,000 OPPORTUNITY!

The Racing Post Yearling Bonus Scheme would like to thank all vendors and purchasers that have supported this scheme and wish all participants the best of luck in the bonus maidens

'The foremost British Flat trainer of his time'

By John Randall

SIR HENRY CECIL was the greatest trainer of his generation and dominated British racing for half his four decades as a licence holder. Champion trainer ten times, he triumphed in each of the five domestic Classics at least twice and won 25 in all, more than any trainer since 1900. The last of them was with Frankel, the greatest horse of his career.

The Newmarket maestro achieved such a consistently high level of success that none of his colleagues could rival him for both quality and quantity of winners. His Classic tally included four in the Derby – Slip Anchor, Reference Point, Commander In Chief and Oath – and eight in the Oaks.

Until the advent of Frankel, Cecil's list of stars was headed by Reference Point, a champion two-year-old who went on to dominate European racing in 1987 with victories in the Derby, King George and St Leger. Not far behind in terms of merit were Slip Anchor, the runaway 1985 Derby victor; Old Vic, wide-margin winner of the French and Irish Derbys in 1989; and globetrotting celebrity Royal Anthem. His best fillies were 1985 Triple Crown heroine Oh So Sharp and multiple Group 1 winners Indian Skimmer and Bosra Sham.

The other Cecil champions included three outstanding stayers in Buckskin and dual Gold Cup winners Le Moss and Ardross; top milers Bolkonski, Wollow and Kris; King George winner King's Theatre; fillies One In A Million, Diminuendo and Ramruma; and two-year-olds Diesis, High Estate and Be My Chief.

His stable never fully recovered from a split with Sheikh Mohammed in 1995 and his fortunes, personally and professionally, slumped early in the new millennium. However, they revived dramatically through the exploits of Frankel and the award of a knighthood for his services to racing.

Frankel was an outstanding champion in each of his three seasons and the brilliance of his performances suggests he might be the best horse that any trainer, not just Cecil, has ever had.

Cecil was born with a silver spoon in his mouth but no-one could have made more of the opportunities given to him. Patience was his main virtue and, although he had champion two-year-olds, it was with Classic horses and mature stayers that he excelled. He never had a champion sprinter, nor was he notably keen to run his horses abroad, although his Group 1 winners in France alone included Ardross, Indian Skimmer and Old Vic. Not surprisingly, he seldom targeted handicaps.

He was the first to acknowledge the contribution of his team at Warren Place over the years, including head lads Paddy Rudkin and Frank Conlon, but only a master trainer could have delivered the goods consistently over several decades. His hard work, dedication, enthusiasm and shrewd assessment of the ability and potential of his vast string were phenomenal.

Despite his aristocratic background and bearing, he was always amiable and approachable, and came across as a man of the people. In interviews he habitually answered a question with one of his own, head self-deprecatingly on one side.

In the Directory of the Turf, he listed his hobbies as "Gardening, shooting and shopping". His casual, dandyish air sometimes suggested he was a dilettante less interested in his horses than in his rose garden, his stylish clothes, his Gucci shoes, his collection of tin soldiers and his latest Mercedes, but that masked a fierce desire to be the best in his profession.

Louis Freedman, the owner-breeder of Reference Point, once said: "You watch him carefully for a while and you realise that he's watching every move on the board. You shouldn't be fooled by his light-heartedness and facetiousness."

Lord Howard de Walden, Slip Anchor's owner-breeder, said more succinctly: "He has, in gardening terms, green fingers."

Cecil's owners regularly sent him the choicest yearlings from the world's studs and sales rings, and his skill at maximising their potential enabled him to succeed Fred Darling and Noel Murless as the foremost British Flat trainer of his time.

A man of unique achievement whom all young trainers dreamed of emulating, Cecil embodied British racing at its best, and was a giant of the Turf.

▸ Sir Henry and Lady Jane Cecil on Warren Hill in Newmarket on March 21 this year

was for many years his stamping ground and where he ruled supreme, season in, season out.

Next week's meeting will be the first of my working lifetime without that lofty presence immaculately attired. I can see him now at the Ascot of old, silk-topped, often blue of shirt and yellow of tie, with a saddle under his arm and striding towards the saddling boxes at the top of that beautiful paddock guarded by its phalanx of mighty trees, centuries in the making.

If Hollywood had tried to create the dashing, patrician English racehorse trainer they would never have dared come up with anything as splendid as Cecil.

When great men die they inevitably pass into the hands of obituary writers and historians and Henry will be no exception. Facts and figures will be piled high and his praises rightly sung.

But for those of us whose racing life coincided with his, there is a genuine pang at his passing because with him goes the strongest connection with so much of our own racing histories. Henry composed and orchestrated the sporting back catalogue of countless hundreds of thousands of us for more than four decades. No surprise then that it hurts a bit because part of our own past dies with him.

There is a sense of relief that his suffering has come to an end and, although he must have been bowstring-weary with the fight, nobody could have been more valiant.

He will be mourned in every corner of the racing village because his appeal was universal and enduring. But above all he should be celebrated because he had more life, vigour, courage, individuality and sheer, natural, rampant talent than can usually be found in a legion of folk.

Our bright spark of genius has been extinguished. Well may the trumpets sound for him on the other side.

MEMORIES OF CECIL

The flag will always fly

Back in the winter I wrote to Sir Henry Cecil thanking him for all the special racing memories he had given me over the decades and extending my very best wishes for the coming season. To tell the truth, I did not expect or require a reply. However, back came a handwritten letter thanking me and ending: "Hopefully we have some very nice horses and, you never know, the flag may fly again."

Sir Henry took this trouble with just an ordinary racegoer. The flag will always fly over Henry.

John Ellison
Plymouth

The Hotel Royal Barrière in Deauville, the place to be in France!

© Patrick McGann

3
DEAUVILLE

Book your next stay
on www.royal-barriere.com

Royal Barrière
Deauville

LHW LEADING HOTELS®

London – Deauville flights on www.cityjet.com

Kingdom and Joseph O'Brien lead the five-runner field round the first bend of the mile-and-a-half handicap at Tipperary on May 1. Kingdom was pipped at the post by the Dermot Weld-trained favourite Pay Day Kitten, who won by a head

PATRICK McCANN
(RACINGPOST.COM/PHOTOS)

RACING WITH A DIFFERENCE

The Arabian racing scene is growing fast and in 2013 the sport took more steps forward

By Stuart Riley

WHEN Nigel Jones arrived at Newbury on August 15 for the Dubai International Arabian raceday he did not think he would be leaving with a fiancée. He had made it 15 years into his relationship with Georgina Roberts without popping the question. But then those 15 years hadn't brought him into contact with the tour de force that is Derek Thompson.

That afternoon at Newbury, Thompson was the catalyst in changing his life in more ways than one. First, the irrepressible master of ceremonies drew his name as one of six winners of a trip to Dubai. Then he offered Nigel a deal: if he proposed to his partner, in front of a packed crowd, on camera, Thompson promised to persuade those in charge to throw in flights for their two children, Rebecca, 13, and Adam, 9.

Nigel agreed, Georgina said yes, and Tommo was as good as his word. And a family could not have been more deserving of a trip to Dubai, or a long

and happy life together. Two years ago they lost their youngest boy when, on the walk home from school, he stepped into the road and was hit by a bus right in front of them. "Not much has gone right for us," Nigel said. "Maybe today can be the turning point, maybe we can start to build a normal life again."

Not many race meetings have the ability to transform an entire family's fortunes, but 'transformation' could be a byword for the entire sport of Arabian racing in Britain.

Huge investment from the Middle East has raised the standard and profile of the sport, with the flourishing Dubai International raceday among the highlights of a growing calendar.

Hereford racecourse, which closed for jump racing in 2012, was back in action when it staged five legs of the 2013 Wathba Stud Farm Cup, an international series that also visited Newbury. The series is part of the Sheikh Mansoor Global Arabian Horse Racing Festival, which concluded with a glittering finals day in Abu Dhabi in November. Promoting Arabian horses and racing around the world is a key aim.

In 2014 Britain will host a leg of the Sheikh Zayed Bin Sultan Al Nahyan Cup, the flagship event of the global series, at Newbury in May. The race, worth £70,000, is being run in Britain for the first time and is joined on the card by a leg of the HH Sheikha Fatima Bint Mubarak Ladies World Championship, which has been given a 50 per cent increase in prize-money to £30,000.

Those events will be another step forward for a sport that has only around 150 pure-bred Arabians in training but has a growing presence and prestige.

In 2013 total prize-money for Arabian racing in Britain topped £530,000, almost double the figure from six years ago, and for the first time an Arabian race featured on a Classic card in Britain when the Group 1 Qatar Racing and Equestrian Club Harwood International Stakes – worth a cool £150,000 – was part of the supporting cast to the St Leger, Britain's oldest Classic.

"To feature on such an important day and attract the very best Arabian horses from around the world proves just how much the British scene has to offer

internationally," says Arabian Racing Organisation director Genny Haynes, who is both proud and a little taken aback at the rapid progress of the sport, which was launched in Britain in 1977.

"This country now has some of the best Arabian racing on offer and that's exciting. It's been the most amazing breakthrough year for us with everything that's happened. We've been going for more than 30 years but we've never had a year like this. I have to pinch myself sometimes when I see how far we've come.

"The sport is booming. I don't know how we'll top this next year but it's our job to take this impetus forward. I'm already working on 2014 and it's our job to make it an even better year."

In essence Arabian racing in Britain is much like point-to-pointing, a sport for the amateur enthusiast, but the international flavour of the sport was evident at Newbury. Alongside winners for Bill Smith and Gillian Duffield, two stalwarts of the British scene, runners trained in the Netherlands and France landed two of the Group 1 events on the eight-race card.

Some conventional racing fans may

▸▸Action and colour from Dubai International day (clockwise from top left): The presentation for the best painted horse; watching the field pass the winning line in the opener won by Ambrose and Simon Walker; Al Mouhannad and Roberto-Carlos Montenegro land the Group 1 Jebel Ali Racecourse Zaabeel International Stakes; a striking design in the best-dressed lady competition; a novel creation in the children's best hat contest; Djet Taouy gets plenty of attention in the winner's enclosure; the Jones family after winning a trip to Dubai; photographers focus on Sheikh Hamdan Al Maktoum, a great supporter of Arabian racing and owner of Aljawaaher, who won the finale

look down on the Arabian sport, but the two branches are not so different. Two of the three founding stallions of the thoroughbred breed, Godolphin and Darley, were Arabian and the differences with thoroughbreds are minimal. Arabian horses have shorter necks, dished faces and high tail carriages. They are generally smaller at around 15.2 hands and, as they were bred for stamina-sapping trips across deserts, they are slower.

Duffield, who has been involved in the sport for more than a quarter of a century and trains 35 horses in Newmarket, says Arabians have a special quality.

"They're very intelligent and they like people. They can become very attached to the people who look after them," she says. "They thrive on variety, rather than the monotony of doing the same thing every day, but they learn the wrong thing very quickly. They can be like a child's naughty pony."

The main difference in the racing is that Arabians are much slower than thoroughbreds. "Over the last 20 years they have been bred more and more for speed," Duffield says, "but the majority

don't have a turn of foot. Only the elite ones have that. Most of them keep going at the same pace."

Often that leads to close finishes, giving racegoers a familiar sense of excitement but in slower motion. On Newbury's big day five of the eight races were won by half a length or less and there was an upset in the day's Group 1 highlight as the fast-improving Dutch-trained Djet Taouy got the better of Mkeefa and Rathowan, the two highest-rated Arabian horses.

The whole vibe is different to mainstream racing. "This is miles better," said one Newbury racegoer, no doubt influenced by the rather 'bling' watch he had just won. It was not hard to see where he was coming from.

Entry was free and 39 other watches were given away, as well as six trips to Dubai and a car. There were competitions for the best-dressed lady, best children's hat and the model horse-painting talents of local schoolchildren.

Arabian racing offers a day at the races with a difference and it's a demonstration of just what can be achieved, and the value that can be given to racegoers, if money is no object.

THE SUMMER
in pictures

1 Racegoers watch the action from Trundle Hill on day four of Glorious Goodwood

2 Jazz Girl and Connor King lead up the home straight on their way to victory in the J & B O'Sullivan Builders Kingdom Gold Cup Premier Handicap at Killarney's August festival

3 Captain May, ridden by Wayne Lordan, wins the Gilna's Cottage Inn Maiden at Laytown in September

4 A splash of colour at Leopardstown on Irish Champion Stakes day

5 All the fun of the fair at Cartmel on August bank holiday Monday

6 Adelana and Declan McDonogh break from stall five before going on to win the Irish Stallion Farms EBF Fillies Median Auction Maiden at Killarney in August

7 Flashlight, the mount of Joe Fanning, wins the Terry Mills Handicap at Epsom's August bank holiday meeting

8 The Curragh is in full bloom as Pat Smullen leaves the weighing room

9 Stresa and William Buick lead the runners past the stewards' box in a 1m2f handicap at Lingfield

THE ANNUAL 20

Our selection of the horses and people – some established, some up-and-coming – who are likely to be making headlines in 2014

JAMES DOYLE AND KINGMAN

AL KAZEEM took Doyle to new heights in 2013 and the jockey will be aiming to climb even higher in his first full season as retained jockey for Khalid Abdullah, one of the most prized jobs in Flat racing.

Doyle made a perfect start after his appointment in August by winning the Group 3 Solario Stakes on Kingman *(right)*, his first ride in the famous green, pink and white silks, and the John Gosden-trained colt is his principal hope for a first Classic win.

The 25-year-old has become increasingly accustomed to the feel of a high-class horse and he was impressed by Kingman. "He's got a great attitude and showed all the credentials to be a top performer," he said. "He has a very good temperament, he's well balanced and he has a good turn of foot."

Significantly, there was a ringing endorsement of Kingman from

Simon Crisford, racing manager for Godolphin, after their runners had finished second and third. He described Kingman as "different class" and added: "He won exceptionally well and looks a fantastic horse for the future."

Kingman was 2,000 Guineas favourite after the Solario and held on to that status even after missing the Dewhurst, his intended late-season target. Abdullah's racing manager Teddy Grimthorpe explained: "He had a bit of a setback. We're assessing it but as far as we can tell he's going to be okay for next year."

Doyle, along with the rest of Kingman's connections, will be hoping the prognosis for a full recovery during the winter proves accurate.

Although the beauty of the Abdullah job for Doyle is that he will not be reliant on one horse for his big-race hopes, a flying start in the Classics with Kingman would be the ideal scenario.

CONNOR KING

AN incredible four-timer at Cork in early August, headed by his first Listed winner, catapulted Connor King *(above)* into the racing public's consciousness. He was a couple of weeks short of his 17th birthday at the time, with almost a year left at school, and had been an apprentice jockey only since October. By any standard, it was a meteoric rise but King did not stop there. Wherever he went, at the summer festivals and beyond, he was in demand and among the winners as he drove towards the apprentice title.

The talent of the boy from Kilbrin, County Cork, did not appear overnight. He was a star of the pony-racing circuit, having started at the age of 11, and was so ready for the step up to the racecourse that he won on his very first ride. That was for his boss David Wachman, who has given him every opportunity to learn the racing game but also advised him to stay on at school and complete his Leaving Cert.

King is likely to be down to a 3lb claim by the time he finishes school in June 2014, and that can be a testing time for young apprentices, but Wachman believes he can cope. "Connor has a big future," he says. "His year has been phenomenal. Horses run for him. He seems to have a lot of the attributes to be a jockey.

"He is quite tall, which is not a negative to his riding. It might make his weight harder to manage later on but he has a very good attitude and I don't see why he can't handle it."

Handling everything, from horses to the attention that comes with being a teenage sensation, has not been a problem for King so far.

MY TITANIA

TO SAY John Oxx had a difficult 2013 would be an understatement. Only four years after his brilliant campaign with Sea The Stars, the master of Currabeg was in the doldrums and in the autumn came the news that he would not be sent any yearlings by the Aga Khan, for whom he has trained for 24 years. Inevitably that will have a serious impact on Oxx's numbers and make a recovery that much harder.

Amid the gloom were two bright spots for Oxx: the outpouring of goodwill towards him after the Aga Khan's move and the smart two-year-old filly My Titania *(below)*, who is from the first crop of Oxx's old friend Sea The Stars and, like him, carries the colours of Christopher Tsui. My Titania won two of her three starts, rounding off with victory in the Group 3 CL Weld Park Stakes to leave Oxx dreaming of a Classic end to his nightmare.

"She's a bit like her sire in that she pulls up a bit in front," Oxx said after My Titania had become the first Group winner for Sea The Stars. "But she has great speed and should stay well. She has a lot of natural ability and is a nice prospect. The key to her is fast ground. If all goes well she'll be in the 1,000 Guineas and Oaks in Britain but that's a big step up. We'll see what the spring does."

My Titania went into winter quarters as a 16-1 shot for the 1,000 Guineas and 20-1 for the Oaks. If she does win a Classic for Oxx, the reception for the filly and her trainer will raise the roof.

AUSTRALIA

AS AN Aidan O'Brien-trained son of Galileo out of the brilliant racemare Ouija Board, Australia *(right)* came to the races saddled with huge expectation and at first it seemed the burden might be too great. He was beaten first time out at the Curragh, after a slow start, before returning there to break his maiden with a narrow win. Solid enough, but not exactly spectacular.

Then came his six-length victory over Free Eagle, the erstwhile Derby favourite, and that was spectacular. With his stablemate Kingfisher setting the pace in the Group 3 mile contest at Leopardstown, Australia tracked Free Eagle before being set alight by Joseph O'Brien with a furlong and a half to run. The race was quickly over as Australia sprinted clear before being eased close home.

After that Australia was 5-1 Derby favourite and Free Eagle drifted to 20-1, and Aidan O'Brien could hardly contain himself. "We've always thought the world of him, we always thought he was the best horse we've ever had. He was always doing things no two-year-old has ever done before," he said. "He's so laid-back he's almost asleep. He doesn't even know he's racing and that's what's so very special about him. When Joseph asked him to go, the gears were there. He has some pace."

In light of the boom at the top end of the 2013 yearling market, the 525,000 guineas Coolmore paid for Australia in October 2012 looks a relative bargain. Only time will tell, but Australia could be the next big thing.

LADY CECIL

IN every way, Lady Cecil *(right)* conducted herself with dignity and fortitude following the death of her husband, Sir Henry Cecil, and her decision to take up the reins at Warren Place. Even when grief intruded again, with the heart attack suffered by Thomas Chippendale shortly after winning the Hardwicke Stakes at Royal Ascot, she was emotional but unbowed.

Having announced in late September that she will carry on training in 2014, Cecil faces new challenges. Preparing the ground for a new campaign is different to taking over a stable mid-season and she will have to do so without Mike Marshall, assistant trainer at Warren Place for six years, who has left to work for Ismail Mohammed.

Warren Place will continue to attract press and public attention, but Cecil will rely on the rhythms and methods established by her late husband in 44 years as a trainer. "I have very good staff and it's not about me, it's about everyone here," she said. "We've kept the routine the same. Henry kept everything simple, happy horses and happy staff. Why would we change it?"

The simple approach brought results in the latter half of 2013. Cecil won with her first runner, Morpheus, at Nottingham two days after Sir Henry's death and that was just the start as she maintained a strike-rate well above 20 per cent. Thomas Chippendale was her second Royal Ascot winner, following Riposte's Ribblesdale victory, and she had a big handicap success when Tiger Cliff landed the Ebor.

The dream scenario in Cecil's first full season would be a Classic or other big-race victory for Joyeuse, Frankel's half-sister. Many will be hoping it comes true.

OUR CONOR

NOVICE hurdlers as dominant and impressive as Our Conor *(above)* are a rarity and Richard Hughes, the son of his trainer Dessie, had to go back deep into his own childhood to find what he considered a worthwhile comparison after the Triumph Hurdle. "I remember watching Golden Cygnet and that was very similar. To be that good and so far ahead of the others at such a young age is amazing," he said.

Golden Cygnet, of course, was the brilliant winner of the 1978 Supreme Novices' Hurdle by 15 lengths – the same distance by which Our Conor won the Triumph – and widely regarded as the best novice hurdler ever. To be mentioned in the same breath as Edward O'Grady's ill-fated star is high praise, especially as Our Conor was two years younger than Golden Cygnet when he took the Cheltenham Festival by storm.

Our Conor is certainly the best four-year-old hurdler in the history of Racing Post Ratings and normal improvement in the 2013-14 season will take him to Champion Hurdle-winning standard. As a comparison, his RPR on entry to the senior ranks of 164 is 6lb above where dual Champion Hurdle winner Hurricane Fly was at the end of his novice campaign.

Normal improvement is the least expected of Our Conor and, as his best run as a novice came the only time 'good' was in the going description, it is conceivable that quicker ground than we had last winter will suit him even more. With his slick hurdling and turn of foot, he will be suited by fast-run races.

Tragically, Golden Cygnet's life was cut short in his novice season following a fall in the Scottish Champion Hurdle and his immense promise was never fulfilled. Our Conor has the chance to achieve the greatness that was denied him.

KINGSTON HILL

ROGER VARIAN ensured a seamless transition when he took the reins at Kremlin House Stables from Michael Jarvis in 2011 and he has increased his tally each season, as well as nurturing high-class talent in the same quiet and careful way as his long-time mentor.

That approach could pay dividends with Kingston Hill *(right)*, who showed distinct promise in opening his career with a seven-furlong maiden win at Newbury followed by victory in the Group 3 Autumn Stakes over a mile at Newmarket. The son of Mastercraftsman was clearly still a work in progress at Newmarket, where he raced greenly and idled once he hit the front, but he did well to beat the more experienced Ballydoyle raider Oklahoma City. The runner-up had previously finished closer to his well-regarded stablemate Geoffrey Chaucer in a Group 2 at the Curragh.

The Autumn Stakes has quite an illustrious history, with past winners including Nashwan and Nayef, and Varian is hopeful Kingston Hill will be better as a three-year-old. "It's nice going into the winter with a horse who looks highly promising," he said. "He's not flashy, he's what you'd call hardy. He's very laid-back and he might well be up to competing over a mile. Equally he might get a bit further as well."

Both wins came with 'soft' in the going description but Varian does not believe that is a prerequisite for Kingston Hill. "He's a good mover and will be fine on better ground."

Varian, 34, has had a Group/ Grade 1 winner in each of his three seasons but has yet to have one on home soil or with a colt. Kingston Hill might just be the one to break both of those ducks.

CHAMPAGNE FEVER

WILLIE MULLINS has a better record over hurdles than fences at the Cheltenham Festival, and he has yet to turn one of his novice hurdle scorers into a festival chase winner, but Supreme Novices' Hurdle winner Champagne Fever (above) could help to rebalance the figures.

The Arkle Chase is the aim and, in fact, his Supreme victory was something of a bonus along the road

to a career over fences, which has always looked likely to be his forte. In the winner's enclosure after the Arkle, Mullins was already looking forward: "Next season will be all about chasing. We've schooled him and he already jumps fences better than hurdles. He is electric over a fence."

Trendspotters will point out that the Supreme winner rarely turns out to be a top-class chaser, but it is not all about the winners. Since 2000

Best Mate, Kicking King, War Of Attrition and Sprinter Sacre were all placed in the Supreme before going on to great things over fences, and Champagne Fever cannot be faulted for succeeding where they failed.

Having made the running in the Supreme, Champagne Fever had every excuse to throw in the towel when he was strongly challenged by the JP McManus pair My Tent Or Yours and Jezki but he toughed it out up the hill to reaffirm his love

for Cheltenham. Defeating a pair of high-class, speedy hurdlers was a tremendous achievement and the form of his 2012 Champion Bumper success stands up well too, as he had Jezki and The New One behind him that day.

If Champagne Fever's fencing stands up to the test of Cheltenham, as Mullins believes it will, he has an outstanding chance of completing a festival hat-trick in three different disciplines.

DARYL JACOB

TWO years ago Daryl Jacob (below) featured in the Annual as a rising star after he was appointed Paul Nicholls' number-two jockey and he has done so well that the Ditcheat trainer had no hesitation promoting him to the top job following Ruby Walsh's decision to base himself in Ireland full-time.

Jacob, 30, is now firmly in the top bracket, both in rank and achievement, after a second successive top-ten finish in the jockeys' title and he can look forward to a first century of winners as he takes the bulk of the rides for Nicholls.

Most of all, it is in the major races where Jacob will be judged. It is a different task entirely being entrusted with Nicholls' biggest hopes than his previous position of picking up the rides rejected by Walsh. And, from being an ally of Walsh where horses and tactics could be discussed between them, Jacob will now have to go head to head against him in the biggest contests.

Whenever he has had the chance, however, Jacob has always risen to the occasion and he will be spoiled for choice this season. Nicholls may be in a transitional phase, but he has established stars such as the returning Big Buck's, Silviniaco Conti, Zarkandar and Al Ferof, as well as the usual young hopefuls.

"I hope we're heading for exciting times but I'm all too aware I have some very big boots to fill, as Ruby set a very high standard," Jacob said on his appointment.

Trying to be the next Ruby will be an impossible task, but if Nicholls' new number one sticks to being Daryl Jacob he should do very well indeed.

OISIN MURPHY

HE HAS the family pedigree, he has the education and he has the natural talent. Oisin Murphy (right), at the age of 18, appears to have it all. For more than a year now, the nephew of Cheltenham Gold Cup-winning jockey Jim Culloty has been based at Andrew Balding's apprentice academy at Kingsclere, which has nurtured the likes of William Buick in the past, and he has passed every exam with flying colours.

The most eyecatching results came on Ayr Gold Cup day when the 5lb claimer took the big race on the Balding-trained Highland Colori and proceeded to mop up the rest of the card for a 9,260-1 four-timer. That came only three months after he gained his riding licence and took his tally to 28 winners at that stage.

The only difficulty for Balding has been to rein in Murphy's desire for more. Looking to the future, Balding restricted him to the bigger days rather than using up his claim at bread-and-butter meetings and both trainer and jockey should feel the benefit when he is let off the leash next year.

At Kingsclere they make no secret of their regard for Murphy, who hails from Killarney in County Kerry. "He is William Buick all over again," Ian Balding, the trainer's father, says. "Both William and Oisin are natural horsemen who know exactly what is going to happen in a race." On Ayr Gold Cup day, Richard Phillips, Balding's travelling head groom, said: "I've been there 25 years and I've seen all the good guys. Pound for pound he is up there, definitely."

Balding's focus in the apprentice title race in 2013 was Thomas Brown, another talented member of the academy. The aim is for 2014 to be Murphy's year.

SAM TWISTON-DAVIES

WHEN Paddy Brennan split from Nigel Twiston-Davies in 2011, leaving the trainer's son as the stable jockey, some might have wondered if family sentiment had held sway.

But any doubts about the ability of Twiston-Davies (right), now 21, have been swept away as he builds an increasingly impressive career as a top jump jockey. Ferdy Murphy, now based in France and one of the best judges around, is just one of a growing army of fans. "Sam is tremendous," Murphy said after Twiston-Davies had ridden a winner for him early this season. "Everyone is talking about Jason Maguire being champion jockey but it is only a matter of time before this guy is."

Twiston-Davies might have to wait a few years for a real shot at the title but he has youth on his side. Having set a personal-best of 87 winners last term, he looks likely to score his first century in the 2013-14 season and he might grab a top-three finish.

The most exciting aspect for Twiston-Davies, however, is his partnership with the Neptune Novices' Hurdle winner The New One, who gave him his first professional victory at the Cheltenham Festival to go with the Foxhunter he won on Baby Run as an amateur in 2010. Twiston-Davies was big enough to admit a mistake when he was beaten on The New One at Cheltenham in January and it was a mark of his growing maturity and skill that he put matters right in emphatic fashion in the Neptune.

Both The New One and Twiston-Davies seem set to go from strength to strength.

THE £5.25m FILLY

THREE days after Treve's runaway victory in the Prix de l'Arc de Triomphe, her owner Sheikh Joaan Al Thani had another sensation on his hands when he paid 5m guineas at Tattersalls for a yearling sister to Oaks winner Was by Derby hero Galileo. The price, which equates to £5.25m, was a world record for a yearling filly – in fact, it was double the previous record set by a daughter of Sadler's Wells in 2007, the year before the crash.

Only 24 hours earlier, the sale had produced a European record for a yearling at public auction when a brother to Oaks runner-up Secret Gesture, also by Galileo, fetched 3.6m guineas to the bid of Coolmore supremo John Magnier. The 5m guineas filly (below), on whom Magnier was underbidder, took that record as well.

Nicolas de Watrigant, Sheikh Joaan's principal buyer, explained the thinking behind the record purchase. "How can you quantify that beauty and that quality?" he said. "We didn't expect to have to go this far, but she has everything and we didn't want to miss her. She'll go into training with Andre Fabre – hopefully she's another Treve."

The filly's progress will be closely watched, although her breeding suggests her debut is likely to come towards the backend of 2014 with a view to the middle-distance Classics as a three-year-old. Of course, a high price is no guarantee of success and she might never appear at all. That was the fate of the previous filly to hold the record, who was named Liffey Dancer and put into training with Luca Cumani but never raced.

Another Treve, though? That would be exciting.

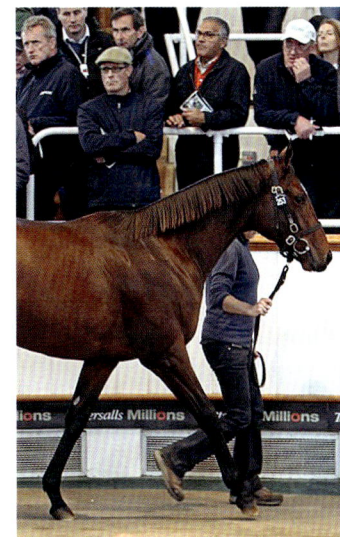

AT FISHERS CROSS

IN MOST other seasons At Fishers Cross *(right)* would have been hailed as an outstanding novice hurdler after an unbeaten six-race campaign in 2012-13 but, as part of a stellar crop, he perhaps did not get the credit he deserved.

By the end of the season, however, he had taken two Grade 1 wins as well as a number of notable scalps – including Neptune Novices' Hurdle winner The New One – and plans to send him novice chasing were being redrawn in favour of a tilt at the World Hurdle.

The Rebecca Curtis-trained six-year-old was a slow developer, mainly because he was not a natural hurdler, but on last winter's heavy ground he went from strength to strength in his jumping and in overall achievement.

His first standout piece of form was his neck victory over The New One at Cheltenham in January and he matched that standard with a clear-cut win in the Albert Bartlett Novices' Hurdle before an easy second Grade 1 success at Aintree.

Chasing was put on hold for At Fishers Cross, who could develop into the main danger to the returning Big Buck's in the staying hurdle division. "Rebecca has done unbelievably well to turn him around," jockey Tony McCoy said at Aintree. "He stays and he isn't slow. He's a proper little horse."

If there is any chink in Big Buck's after his long injury layoff, the tough and classy At Fishers Cross looks well placed to exploit it.

FRANKIE DETTORI AND TREVE

ASTAIRE and Rogers, Bogart and Bacall, Dettori and Treve. Some partnerships just click, especially when both parties are exceptional talents in their own right.

Dettori and Treve *(right)* have appeared together just once so far and it was a five-star performance from both of them. Dettori wanted to win the Prix Vermeille – of course he did, in his new job as Sheikh Joaan's retained jockey – but he was also mindful that the Prix de l'Arc de Triomphe was only three weeks away

and winning there was the priority with Treve.

The jockey somehow had to balance the two objectives and it didn't look possible to achieve both when he was trapped on the inside with a wall of rivals in front of him early in the straight. A couple of rehearsals with Treve on the gallops had given him great faith in his partner, however, and together they found a way out of trouble to win decisively in the end.

The true value of Dettori's gentle handling of the filly became clear in the Arc, when Treve peaked with a record-breaking performance, but

he wasn't there to partner her after breaking his ankle.

After the race trainer Criquette Head-Maarek's first thought was for Dettori. "I want to say thank you to him because he rode an amazing race in the Vermeille," she said. "I told him to think of the Arc and not to use the whip and he did. He really saved her for today. I thank him very much and I'm sorry he's not here."

The silver lining for Dettori was that Treve will still be around in 2014 and he can spend a winter dreaming of what they might achieve together. The resumption of their partnership will be hotly anticipated.

DANNY MULLINS

WHEN Barry Connell decided he needed a retained jockey for his growing string, the promising but inexperienced Danny Mullins (right) was the choice. The son of trainers Tony and Mags Mullins, and nephew of champion jumps trainer Willie Mullins, had long been regarded as a future star but instantly he was thrust into the full glare of the spotlight as he was handed the rides on potential Grade 1 performers such as Mount Benbulben and Connell's expensively purchased bumper horse Golantilla.

The pressure on Mullins would have been intense enough even without Connell's next big move in the transfer market: the purchase of Champion Hurdle favourite Our

Conor within days of his impressive Triumph Hurdle success in March. Taking the ride on Our Conor in his first full season with Connell ensures Mullins' every move will be scrutinised and he is bound to be compared with Bryan Cooper, the

partner of Our Conor before the switch.

Mullins, a champion pony racing rider before leaving school at 15 to serve an apprenticeship with Jim Bolger, had to wait almost a month for his first winner in his new job, when Mount Benbulben landed a Grade 2 chase at Thurles. But he settled in gradually and at the Punchestown festival he partnered the same horse to victory in the Champion Novice Chase. It was a first Grade 1 victory for Mullins, on his 21st birthday.

With Our Conor and Mount Benbulben, a possible for the King George VI Chase, Mullins has been handed the key to the door of further big-race success. How he fares will be one of the talking points of the new season.

FAUGHEEN

WHILE the usual host of young Willie Mullins-trained horses made their names last season, Faugheen (right) was not one of them. He was meant to have been, but he wasn't ready.

More than a year elapsed between his point-to-point win at Ballysteen and his first appearance on a racecourse, in a Punchestown bumper in May 2013, but it was worth waiting for. Ridden by Patrick Mullins, the five-year-old simply ran away from his rivals to score impressively by 22 lengths. After that, he was put away to wait for a winter over hurdles.

"He has been working well and was ready to run last year only for a problem to hold him up," the trainer

said at Punchestown. "He looks a nice prospect to go novice hurdling with."

Those associated with the Mullins yard were not surprised by the manner of Faugheen's victory, as he had long been touted as potentially

the best bumper horse in the stable. Now he is one of the most exciting novice hurdling prospects for Mullins and he went into the winter as a 20-1 shot for both the Supreme and Neptune Novices' Hurdles.

His optimum distance is still to be established – his bumper win was over two miles and his point-to-point success at three miles – but his credentials are not in dispute. He is by Germany, the sire of 2008 Supreme winner Captain Cee Bee, and was nurtured in the Andy Slattery point-to-point yard that produced Mullins' high-class chasers Cooldine and Quel Esprit.

Slattery described him as "a real good horse" in his point-to-point days. This season, at last, could be when Faugheen shows everyone just how good he is.

MISS FRANCE

FRANCE has her wonder filly in Treve and, while Miss France (right) may not be another, there is the prospect of a British Classic success with the Andre Fabre-trained filly.

Miss France is proven at Newmarket after her victory in the Group 3 Oh Sharp Stakes in September, which left her vying for 1,000 Guineas favouritism at around the 6-1 mark. In fact, it was no accident that she ended up having her first Group test at Newmarket, rather than Longchamp.

"The reason we came here rather

than running in Paris was we thought she would be suited by a stronger pace and better ground," Anthony Stroud, representing owner Diane Wildenstein, explained. "I think she will come back for the 1,000 Guineas but it is up to Diane and Andre. She has all the talent and is an extremely nice filly."

The pace was indeed quick in the Oh So Sharp and, although Miss France's margin of victory over Lightning Thunder was only a head, the first two pulled well clear. In another sign that minds were already turned towards the Guineas, jockey Mickael Barzalona was at pains not

to use his whip on Fabre's filly and she probably could have won by further.

The ground at Newmarket was good to firm and Miss France had previously won on good at Chantilly; what her connections clearly wanted to avoid was the kind of soft ground on which she had been beaten on her debut, albeit over six furlongs. The Chantilly win was over a mile, which suggests a combination of quick pace and quick ground would bring out the best in her in the Guineas.

Fabre, better known in Britain for his colts, might have his best chance yet of a first 1,000 Guineas success.

DAN SKELTON

WHEN Dan Skelton *(above)* took on the job as assistant trainer to Paul Nicholls while still a teenager, he was lucky enough to be there right at the start of the golden generation of Kauto Star, Denman and Big Buck's.

Nine years later Skelton, 28, has fulfilled his ambition of becoming a trainer in his own right and, while he hasn't exactly started at the bottom, that sort of quality remains a dream. But his background – not just with Nicholls but as the son of Olympic medal-winning showjumper Nick Skelton, who owns his purpose-built yard in Warwickshire – brings expectation, and he knows it.

Even before he had his first runner in August, Skelton was 14-1 to have a Cheltenham Festival winner in his first season. His response? "Do they know how hard it is to win one of those races? I'd say I'd be closer to 14-1 to have a runner."

He was also quoted at 5-6 to train 15 winners or more and he believes that is possible from his 38-horse string – well up on the dozen he budgeted for. "We have a nice mix of horses. The most expensive is Storm Of Swords, who won his bumper at Fairyhouse and cost €90,000."

Skelton has family support all around him. Grace, whom he married in 2012, is in charge of the office, his Irish Grand National-winning brother Harry is stable jockey and dad Nick, whose showjumping yard is nearby, has provided state-of-the-art facilities.

And he has brought with him a simple philosophy learned during his time with Nicholls. "Our job is to do what Paul always did: get them very fit, keep them healthy and run them in races where they have a chance."

Skelton's team may not be ready for Cheltenham just yet, but they are worth keeping an eye on.

JUST A PAR

"THIS is one for all your 'to follow' lists." That is how Paul Nicholls described Just A Par *(above)*, one of 81 horses paraded by the seven-time champion jumps trainer at his annual owners' day in early September.

Just A Par is rated the best prospect among Nicholls' staying novice chasers and the hope is that he will be worth following all the way to the big spring festivals. "He's a really lovely prospect for chasing," the trainer said.

That has always been the aim since Nicholls purchased him on behalf of Paul Barber and Graham Roach for £260,000 at the Brightwells Cheltenham sale in November 2012. In the month before the sale Just A Par had won a three-mile point-to-point and a maiden hurdle at Punchestown over two and a half miles, but Nicholls waited until February to bring him out in his new colours in a novice hurdle at Exeter, where he finished second to Oliver Sherwood's useful Many Clouds.

Just A Par's next assignment was a big step up to Grade 1 company to take on At Fishers Cross at Aintree. He acquitted himself well, finishing second to the Albert Bartlett Novices' Hurdle winner, and for Nicholls it was all with an eye on his novice chase season. "He's a really exciting horse and we're really pleased with him," he said at Aintree. "He jumps and gallops and stays – he's just a little bit green. We weren't coming here expecting anything, we just wanted a nice run and to get more experience."

Expectation levels are raised this season as Just A Par sets out to justify his high price tag in the arena that should suit him so well.

For Just A Par, the future starts now.

AKORAKOR

MUCH of the focus before and after the Racing Post Champion Point-To-Point Bumper at Fairyhouse is on Michael O'Leary's annual lucrative offer to buy the winner. This year was no different, except that O'Leary won the race himself with Akorakor *(right)* in the Gigginstown House Stud colours and he donated the €200,000 bounty to the fund for JT McNamara.

Inevitably, Akorakor was rather lost amid the headlines about O'Leary's generosity but the race has a good track record of unearthing stars and he could be another.

In the past the race has been won by subsequent top-level chasers Simonsig, Pandorama, Last

Instalment and Tofino Bay, which helps to explain O'Leary's interest each year. In one respect, Akorakor has already achieved more than those previous winners by landing the race as a four-year-old.

His only previous start had been a month earlier in a point-to-point, which he won, and he followed up with a brave and determined performance at Fairyhouse.

Gordon Elliott, who trained Akorakor then before passing him over to Mouse Morris for the new season, was sure there would be much better to come. "He's only a baby but he's massive and he'll be some horse with a summer's grass in him," he said.

Eddie Hales, trainer of third-placed Blow The Doors Off, gave a ringing endorsement of the form. "That is going to turn out to be a very good bumper," he said.

In which case, Akorakor may turn out to be another very good winner of the race.

Worth Every Penny and Terence White race through the water splash during the open lightweight mares' cross-country race at the Tattersalls Farm point-to-point, County Meath, in May

**PATRICK McCANN
(RACINGPOST.COM/PHOTOS)**

AND THE WINNERS ARE . . .
The Annual Awards 2013 **p168**

DREAM COMEBACK
Steve Drowne lands Nunthorpe on Jwala **p172**

GALWAY QUEEN
Busted Tycoon's historic hat-trick **p174**

final furlong
stories of the year – from the serious to the quirky

Prodigious sons make history
Records fall to Joseph O'Brien and Patrick Mullins

By David Jennings

IT'S no good being in a privileged position if you can't take full advantage of the privileges. Surely Calum Best would have got a trial with Manchester United if he could do a few keepy-uppies and Stella McCartney might well have got a record deal if she had a note in her head.

Being the son of Ireland's champion Flat trainer afforded Joseph O'Brien luxuries that his weighing-room colleagues craved, but he had to prove he was deserving of the opportunities available to him at father Aidan's Ballydoyle yard. And, with his 6ft frame likely to limit how long he would be able to ride on the Flat, time was short.

O'Brien hasn't hung about, accumulating five British and Irish Classic victories, an Irish Flat jockeys' championship and big-race successes at the Breeders' Cup and Dubai World Cup night, all before he turned 20. Within two days of leaving his teens behind, on May 23 this year, he took another Classic on Magician in the Irish 2,000 Guineas and later added the St Leger on Leading Light as well as enough winners to take a second title.

More than enough winners actually. On October 9 O'Brien rode a treble at Navan to surpass Mick Kinane's 115-winner record for most winners in an Irish Flat season. The record had stood since 1993, the year of O'Brien's birth.

O'Brien, who struggles to ride below 9st, said: "I'm not sure if it's any more difficult for me than any of the other lads trying to do weight, but I have been very lucky to have some really nice horses to ride. At the start of the season I was hoping to ride 100 winners and I'm delighted to break the record."

His father thanked the stable's owners. "We're in a very lucky position," he said. "He's been doing well and it's not easy for him as 9st is his minimum weight, so he has had to work hard. Long may it last."

▶▶ Joseph O'Brien (top) and Patrick Mullins both had record-breaking seasons capped by victories on the biggest stages

Over jumps Patrick Mullins is in a similar position as stable amateur for his father Willie and, like O'Brien, he has been making the most of his chances. In 2013 he scored his third career win at the Cheltenham Festival on Back In Focus in the National Hunt Chase and added three bumper winners for his father at the Punchestown festival.

Like O'Brien, the young Mullins, 23, is a record-breaker too. At the end of 2012 he beat Billy Parkinson's mark for the amount of winners in a calendar year by an Irish amateur. The record had stood for 97 years and Ruby Walsh couldn't get near it; nor could Nina Carberry. Even Mullins thought it was unattainable at one stage.

"I had it in my head around September time but then we had a bad spell and I gave up on it. But our luck changed in November and things started to click."

Parkinson's tally of 72 winners was equalled at Navan on December 16 when Mullins swooped late on Union Dues to land a bumper. But with the weather causing havoc and chances missed, he had to wait until the penultimate meeting of the season at Leopardstown to set a new mark.

If Mullins was feeling the heat on Zuzka, 11-10 favourite for the Grade 3 mares' hurdle, he certainly didn't show it as he cruised to a six-and a half length success. He'd done it.

And just in case any young whipper-snapper fancied snatching the record off him in years to come, he made it that bit harder for them by completing a double on Outlander in the last to take his final total to 74.

"Things for me can only go as well as my father's horses are going," he said. "There are lads in the weighing room who work twice as hard as me and are probably twice as good as me but they don't get the chance to ride the calibre of horses I do."

Famous fathers – they can be a hindrance or a help. For the O'Brien and Mullins boys, definitely the latter.

Alexander the great

Scottish rider becomes first female champion conditional

By Lee Mottershead

HER father feels she should think about racing a little less than she does. Her agent cannot think of a jockey who has ever thought about racing more. The father's daughter and the agent's client agrees she has tunnel vision, but a somewhat blinkered approach to life has so far done Lucy Alexander no harm whatsoever.

In April, Alexander became the first woman to be crowned jumping's champion conditional jockey. At the age of 22 she was a history-maker, her 38-strike haul for the campaign getting her home three wins clear of nearest rival Brendan Powell.

She had held the lead all season, despite being sidelined early in the year with a broken collarbone, and by maintaining clear water to the final day she emulated northern Flat colleague Amy Ryan, who five months earlier had become the first woman to take the apprentices' title outright.

Ryan had Hayley Turner, who had to settle for a share of the apprentices' championship, as an example. Alexander had nobody so dominant to use as a role model but has instead taken on the pioneering role herself.

While the likes of Gee Armytage and Lorna Vincent rode many winners over jumps, and some on the sport's biggest stages, they were not nearly as prolific as Alexander, who has proved herself one of the northern weighing room's most serious talents, regardless of gender. Although 21 of her 2012-13 victories came for father Nick – whose training business has grown alongside his pride and joy's riding career – others, like Donald McCain, Jim Goldie and Ferdy Murphy, have been keen to utilise the services of the Fife-based rider, who is delighted to have written her name into the record books.

"It meant a huge amount to me, especially as it got close towards the end," she says. "It was a big relief. Hopefully long term it will help my career, but whether it does or it doesn't, nobody can take it away from me.

"It doesn't mean I'm now going to be a success but I hope I can build on being champion conditional. I haven't set a specific target for the new season but I would like to do better than last season. I want to establish myself without my claim and to feel I'm doing a good job.

"What Hayley and Amy have done on the Flat has broken down barriers. I know that jumping is different but compared with 20 years ago, or even less than that, I don't think so many people would think twice about putting up a girl."

Richard Hale, whose jockeys' agency is dominant in the north, knows very well how hard it once was to persuade trainers to use a female rider – and how easy it now is when the rider in question is Alexander.

"I remember a time when I couldn't sell a girl for any money but Lucy and Amy are special," Hale says. "The great thing about Lucy is she is so dedicated. The only thing she wants is to be a successful jockey and she is open to constructive criticism. I don't think I've ever known a rider who has such dedication. She has tunnel vision."

Hale's comments are amusing to Alexander. "Richard just means I'm boring," she says – and then partially agrees. "I never go out," she admits. "I don't really do anything else and I don't really have a life outside racing, but I'd say a lot of jockeys are the same. I work very hard and Richard is right when he says I have tunnel vision.

"Dad thinks I should do more things outside of racing and he wants me to broaden my horizons. If I'm honest, racing is pretty much it. I'd even watch all-weather racing – up to a point."

Alexander's career has run in tandem with her father's and will continue to do so. But possibly not forever.

"Like me, Dad wants to build on what he has already done," she says. "We will never have many more than 35 horses but we are trying to get better horses. In the beginning it was a hobby for Dad and his other work paid to keep the horses. Now the racing operation is definitely a business and he puts a lot of time and effort into it.

"Hopefully he can keep going in the right direction, but I don't have to stay up here forever myself. If I was offered the right job in the south I would take it.

"Even so, I don't think I could get a big job, one that would provide me with the number of rides I would need to get right up the table. I'm also not expecting to get rides at Cheltenham. I don't know why I think that, but I do. I just don't think it could happen, even though I would like it to."

Not many, however, were predicting a woman would become champion conditional jockey. Alexander is modest, self-effacing and unassuming, but she is also extremely talented and widely admired. In the north, maybe one day in the south, and perhaps on many days at Cheltenham, we should expect her to do better than she seemingly expects to do herself.

'The only thing she wants is to be a successful jockey. I don't think I've ever known a rider with such dedication. She has tunnel vision'

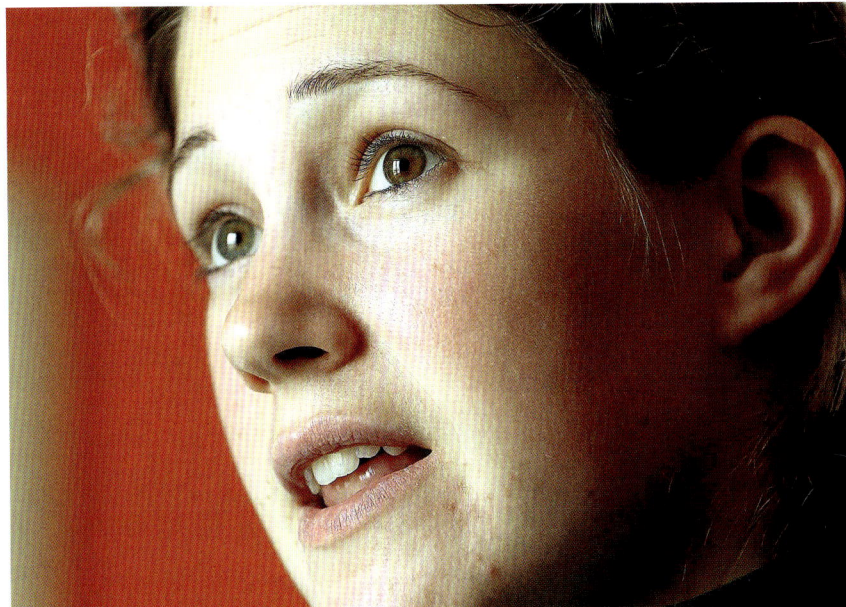

▶▶ Lucy Alexander is aiming to do better than last season's record-breaking 38-winner haul

The Annual Awards 2013
Our pick of the best of the year

Horse of the Year (Flat)
Treve

For most of the year it was a tough call but in the end Treve streaked to the front with her exhilarating five-length Arc triumph. Toronado, Dawn Approach, Al Kazeem, Novellist, Sky Lantern, Lethal Force and Moonlight Cloud all had strong claims, but none of them produced a performance as memorable as Treve's Longchamp romp.

Horse of the Year (jumps)
Sprinter Sacre

There was tangible 'Arkle fever' in the air at Punchestown in April when Sprinter Sacre closed his brilliant season with a show for the people. He has the X factor to go with his considerable ability and most of the jaw-dropping moments of the jumps season were provided by him.

Ride of the Year (Flat)
Richard Hughes on Sky Lantern

All seemed lost when Sky Lantern was drawn out wide in stall 16 in the 17-runner Coronation Stakes, as Richard Hannon jnr related afterwards: "I asked Hughesie if there was any point running her."

The challenge was like a red rag to Hughes, whose brilliance as a hold-up rider was never better demonstrated. Leaving the stalls, he tacked across to the back of the pack and was still virtually last as they entered Ascot's short straight. He quickened to join the leaders approaching the final furlong and then, in a moment of extreme coolness, he eased off the throttle slightly before hitting the gas again. From first to last for a four-length win: genius.

Ride of the Year (jumps)
Ruby Walsh on Champagne Fever

Tony McCoy, as usual, compiled a shortlist all of his own (actually, rather a long list) and Wayward Glance at Worcester in August was probably the pick, but winning on the big stage is what counts for most people and there was nothing better than Walsh's front-running ride in a top-class Supreme Novices' Hurdle.

"I asked Ruby before the race if he knew what he was going to do. He said he did and I left it to him. He ran a fantastic tactical race from the front," Willie Mullins said. In this form, Walsh is a man to rely on.

Race of the Year (Flat)
St James's Palace Stakes

The rivalry between Dawn Approach and Toronado was the most compelling of the year and this was a right royal battle.

First there was a bump when a concertina effect pushed Dawn Approach towards Toronado as they started to make their runs and that allowed Dawn Approach to get first run and grab the rail.

For more than a furlong there was never more than a neck between them as they cut and thrust at each other. But every time Toronado looked as if he would get his head in front, Dawn Approach bravely found a little more to repel him and win by a short head.

Comeback of the Year
Steve Drowne

Through no fault of his own, Drowne had to restart his career virtually from scratch at the age of 41 and the difficulty of that task in the competitive world of Flat racing cannot be overstated. He put in the hard yards, taking more than 400 rides, and got his reward in 57 glorious seconds at York in August. Victory on Jwala in the Nunthorpe was Drowne's sixth Group 1 success and by far the sweetest.

Unluckiest horse
Oscar Delta

A shot at winning the amateurs' Gold Cup can be a once-in-a-lifetime opportunity and for Oscar Delta and his rider Jane Mangan it was snatched away in the cruellest fashion.

Oscar Delta was showing no sign of stopping and Salsify, the favourite, was making no impression as the principals in the Foxhunter started up the Cheltenham hill. But then Mangan's mount jinked at the tape that had replaced the running rail and, with the line in sight, the 19-year-old was unable to stay on board. Unlucky hardly begins to describe it.

Most improved horse
Lethal Force

With a name like that, surely he was capable of better than the Group 2 win in blinkers at odds of 25-1 that was the height of his three-year-old season. As a four-year-old he was a lethal force all right – bigger, stronger, faster and utterly dominant in the top sprints when he had fast ground.

Disappointment of the Year
Camelot

After standing on the verge of history in September 2012, before his failed bid for the Triple Crown, Camelot managed to win only one Group 3 race between then and his retirement 13 months later. No doubt the colic that afflicted him late in 2012 didn't help, but still it was a letdown.

Race of the Year (jumps)
Cheltenham Gold Cup

Backers of all the principals would have gone through moments of hope and heartache in a race where victory hung in the balance until the final gruelling climb. Silviniaco Conti's fall three out left Long Run and Sir Des Champs with a five-length lead, but Bobs Worth doggedly reeled them in and led over the last. Still it was not over as Sir Des Champs rallied again but Bobs Worth was not to be denied. One of the golden greats.

THE ALTERNATIVE AWARDS

The HS2 'Is this rail really necessary?' Award
Cheltenham racecourse

Choosing tape instead of a rail to mark the run-in of the Foxhunter proved costly for 19-year-old rider Jane Mangan when her mount Oscar Delta jinked at the tape and lost a race they should have won.

The Lance Armstrong Award for finally backing down in the face of overwhelming evidence
Mahmood Al Zarooni

Having held up his hands to systematic doping, the former Godolphin trainer decided to appeal against the severity of his eight-year ban. He even appointed a top international barrister to fight the case. Then seven more horses were found to have tested positive and he withdrew the appeal.

The Clare Balding Award for asking a direct question
Clare Balding

She became possibly the first person to render Richard Hannon jnr speechless by asking whether he would be taking over from his father for next season. "Watch this space," he eventually managed, although it seemed as good as saying yes.

. . . and the runner-up
Clare Balding

To Sheikh Mohammed following Dawn Approach's victory in the 2,000 Guineas, less than a fortnight after the Godolphin scandal broke: "In terms of the BHA handling of the investigation, are you happy with that?" The Sheikh

The Clive Brittain Award for Racecourse Dancing
Clive Brittain

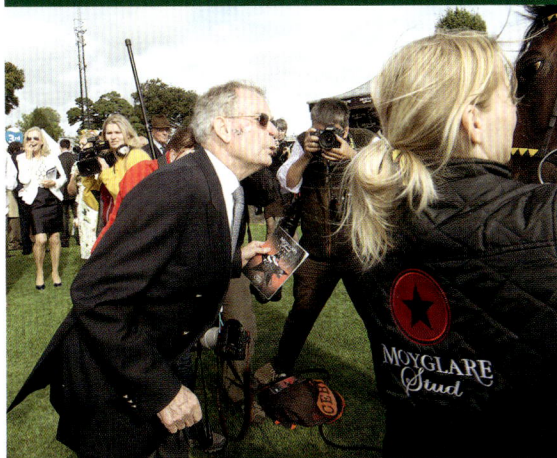

The trademark jig greeted Rizeena's victory in the Moyglare Stud Stakes, the 79-year-old trainer's first Group 1 winner in four years, and he might need his dancing shoes after the 1,000 Guineas if his hopes for the filly are fulfilled. Brittain took the award named in his honour from Sheikh Mohammed, the 2012 winner, who didn't feel like dancing this year.

quickly turned and walked away.

The 'Somebody Up There Doesn't Like Me' Award
Frankie Dettori

Treve was supposed to be Dettori's horse of destiny in Arc week but instead it was the 72-rated Eland Ally, who unseated him on the way to the start at Nottingham and put him out of the big race with a broken ankle.

The Gap Year Backpacker's Award for picking up something nasty in India
Martin Dwyer

Having been at the centre of a near riot after a losing ride at Mahalaxmi racecourse in February, he had to fight for eight months against a ban that would never have been imposed in Britain.

The 'Big Sigh of Relief' Award
Tracy Piggott

It was a shame for Peter Casey that his stable star Flemenstar was transferred to Tony Martin but at least Piggott will no longer have to conduct interviews with the risk of the kind of references not entirely appropriate for a daytime TV audience.

The Ultimate 'That's Racing' Award
Ryan Mania

Grand National-winning hero one day, Newcastle hospital in-patient the next. Fortunately, the fall at Hexham that brought him crashing down to earth resulted in only minor injuries and he was back riding the following week.

The Daily Mail 'Want to Rethink That Headline?' Award
Estimate

Riposte's tearjerking victory in the Ribblesdale Stakes, nine days after the death of Sir Henry Cecil, was a headline writer's dream. Forty minutes later sub-editors around the country were singing the National Anthem through gritted teeth as Estimate won the Gold Cup for the Queen and the news cycle moved on a notch.

The Marco Polo Intrepid Traveller Award
Darryll Holland

Holland made history by becoming the first British jockey to ride full-time in South Korea and then achieved another Far Eastern landmark when he was the first professional British jockey to ride in mainland China.

The Dylan Thomas 'Do Not Go Gentle' Award
John McCririck

The racing pundit's age discrimination claim against Channel 4 kept him in the spotlight and showed he was as combative and outspoken as ever.

The 'And I'd Like to Thank . . .' Award
Novellist's connections

They may have missed out on a shot at the Prix de l'Arc de Triomphe but they earned the sport's respect by taking out a full-page advert to thank British racing after their colt won the King George at Ascot with a record-breaking run.

◆◆◆◆

ONE OF the biggest turnarounds of the year came in a four-runner novice chase at Wincanton in January. At the second-last Valoroso and Ambion Wood were "miles clear", in the commentator's words, of the distant third, Milans Well, but everything changed at the last fence. Valoroso fell and an extremely tired Ambion Wood only just clambered over the fence, allowing Milans Well – matched at 1000 (999-1) in running – to claim an unlikely victory.

Brendan Powell, Milans Well's trainer, said: "I'm pretty sure I haven't trained a luckier winner. A winner is a winner, so I'm taking it."

◆◆◆◆

ADRIAN NICHOLLS became the first racing professional to be fined for a tweet after he was found guilty of behaviour prejudicial to the proper conduct or good reputation of racing over comments he made on Twitter in response to a whip ban.

After Nicholls won on Rocket Ronnie at Thirsk on August 12, he was given a two-day ban for misuse of the whip. In response, he tweeted: "F**k the 2 days I got great 2 bang 1 in!!"

Nicholls was fined £100 at a disciplinary hearing after he admitted using inappropriate language.

"I was pleased to get that winner and I wasn't being malicious," Nicholls said. "I think the BHA was unhappy with the swearing as much as anything."

Asked if it would change his attitude to Twitter, where he has around 5,400 followers, Nicholls said: "I'll monitor what I do a lot more closely now. I won't leave Twitter, though. I have too many followers."

Numbers crunched

Complaints after past greats are downgraded in ratings

WHEN the World Thoroughbred Rankings were released in January nobody had any argument with Frankel heading the list for the second year running, nor with the unbeaten and now-retired champion being rated the greatest in the history of the rankings on a mark of 140.

But there were howls of protest over what happened to the greats of previous eras. In drawing up the rankings, the handicappers took the opportunity to 'recalibrate' the rankings right back to their inaugural year in 1977. It was a long overdue task, as the early years of the rankings were increasingly viewed as being out of line with modern handicapping methods and, as a result, too many horses were rated too highly.

The problem was that some of the best-loved Flat horses had to be downgraded in order to accommodate Frankel at the top without pushing the ratings ever higher. Dancing Brave, the 1986 Arc winner who had been the best until Frankel came along, was dropped from a mark of 141 to 138. Shergar (down from 140 to 136), Alleged (140 to 134) and El Gran Senor (138 to 135) were other notables whose marks were reduced.

Walter Swinburn, the rider of 1981 Derby winner Shergar, was "baffled" by the revised ratings. "It's disappointing Frankel becomes a better horse by others becoming worse," he said. "I went to bed and Shergar was rated 140 and when I woke up he was 136."

Dancing Brave's trainer Guy Harwood was equally unhappy. "I think it's a load of nonsense," he said. "If they wanted to put Frankel top they should have given him an extra pound and let him be celebrated."

Former senior British handicapper Geoffrey Gibbs, one of the three-member panel who drew up the first international rankings in 1977, admitted the ratings needed to be revised.

"Between 1977 and 1986 the ratings were 5lb to 8lb too high," he said. "They have done the right thing and I'm pleased they sorted it out once and for all."

Steve Dennis, in his
Racing Post column,
put a novel twist on the
ratings controversy

IT WAS a quiet morning at the Upstairs Club, where good horses, not-so-good horses and horses who used to be good but have fallen victim to recalibration go when their time on Earth is done.

Sunlight slanted in at the high windows, illuminating a large dusty room full of large dusty armchairs occupied by large dusty horses, many of them dozing after a hearty breakfast. A man stood behind a bar, polishing glasses and whistling tunelessly. Suddenly the door creaked open and a chestnut horse with a flaxen mane and tail walked in and put down a suitcase.

"Why the long face?" said the barman. The horse turned towards him, a look of infinite pity in its deep, brown eyes.

"Very funny. I bet you say that to everyone," said the horse. "I'm dead – wouldn't you have a long face?

"My name's Generous – perhaps you've heard of me? Anyway, first thing this morning I was fine – ate up, licked the bowl, bit the groom, the usual. Then I fired up the iPad, saw the headlines, and that did for me. The shock, you see."

The barman leaned on the bar, fiddling with a beermat. "Shock of what, if you don't mind my asking? Fancy a drink? The water's very good."

"Thanks," said Generous. "No ice, thanks, the cubes get up my nose. Shock of the historic recalibration, of course. I've been 137 for

'How can they do this to me after 27 years? I've always been top-rated, ever since Longchamp. Is this because of Santa Anita? It wasn't my fault'

more than 20 years, then without so much as a notice in the Racing Calendar I'm busted down to 136. It's a diabolical liberty. I blame that bloody Frankel. Is this my chair?"

He trotted over to a vacant armchair and sat down. "Excuse me," he said, nudging the slumbering horse next to him, his chair bearing the legend 'Dancing Brave'. "Wake up, mate, and smell the haylage. Man, you aren't going to like this."

Dancing Brave opened an eye, stretched, yawned, stretched again. "Like what? Who are you? Oh,

hello Generous. Sorry you're dead."

"Never mind about all that," said Generous. "Have you heard the news?"

At that precise moment, an ancient teleprinter in one corner of the room began to rattle, and paper started to scroll through it. Dancing Brave ambled over and bent his nose low to the machine.

"Frankel top-rated horse ever on 140," he read, and then he looked again. "Can't be, I'm top-rated. 141. They've made a mistake, they've done their sums . . ."

His voice trailed away and he lifted his face towards

Generous, his eyes rolling in panic. "Have you seen this? I'm 138. I'm only 138. How can they do this to me after 27 years? I've always been top-rated, ever since Longchamp . . . is this . . . is this because of . . . Santa Anita? It wasn't my fault!"

He began to cry, his body shaking with sobs, the noise waking the other horses in the room. "What is it, DB old boy?" said one from underneath a cosy-looking General Accident 2,000 Guineas Winner blanket. Dancing Brave wiped his nose on his fetlock and indicated the teleprinter.

"Sorry to have to tell you, El Gran, but you've been historically recalibrated too. You're 135 now. The only one who hasn't been cut off way past his prime is Montjeu – he's still 135. As for the rest of us . . ."

The room fell quiet, the silence broken only by a jaunty "eh bien!" from the window. "Shut up Montjeu," said El Gran Senor, bitterly. "Anyone seen Shergar?"

Heads were shaken, shoulders shrugged. The barman discreetly busied himself with the dishwasher.

"Nothing new there," said El Gran Senor. "When he eventually turns up he won't be happy – he's down 4lb to 136."

A cry came from the teleprinter.

"Alleged's down too," said Generous. "He's on 134." There was a collective sharp intake of breath.

"Alleged down 6lb?" squeaked El Gran Senor.

"Mon Dieu!" rasped Montjeu, his voice hoarse with Gauloises.

"Is nothing sacred?" asked Dancing Brave. "I mean, don't two Arcs mean anything any more?"

He turned to the room, his eyes still bright with tears. "Okay, okay, so they wanted Frankel to be the best," he said. "I can handle that, times change, people forget. But couldn't they have left us all where we were and just bunged Frankel up a couple of pounds? Pity it wasn't anyone's leaving do. What will they change next?"

The teleprinter chugged into life again, stopping him in full flow.

Generous followed the stream of words with his hoof. "Hey Dancy, you'll never believe this," he said excitedly.

"There's been another historic recalibration – and I think you'll like it."

All the horses clustered eagerly around the teleprinter, their ears pricked. The print was faint, the ribbon old, but the message was still legible.

STOP PRESS . . .
BY ORDER OF THE RECALIBRATION COMMITTEE . . .
DANCING BRAVE WINS 1986 DERBY . . .

Published in Racing Post on January 17, 2013

THE winning feeling was worth the wait for Keith Griffin, who finally made it to the No.1 spot after 41 years as an owner.

"I can't stop smiling," Griffin said as he welcomed Dont Do Mondays to the winner's enclosure after his victory in a two-mile novice hurdle at Warwick in March.

During his 41 years as an owner Griffin has had 15 horses, including with winning trainer David Bridgwater's dad Ken, and he took matters into his own hands when it came to buying Dont Do Mondays.

Recalling the trip to Doncaster sales in May 2012, Griffin said: "I was meant to meet David but he couldn't make it, so I had a look at a few myself. I called David twice asking about different horses and he told me not to touch them. The third time I called I said, 'I've bought one', and this was it."

Asked if he had ever thought of giving up on ownership, Griffin said: "Never. National Hunt racing is my sport."

When Chris Shirran walked through the gates at Yarmouth, her local racecourse, on August 25 she was not an owner, but she left a winner thanks to a snap decision to join the Hoofbeats Racing Club.

Her £180 membership fee paid an instant dividend when the club's Honeymoon Express rattled home in the five-furlong handicap.

"My husband and I had been thinking about joining a club for some time and we just went for it when we saw their stall," Shirran said. "To be standing in the winner's enclosure just two hours later is unbelievable."

Drowne enjoys dream ending

Returning jockey lands Nunthorpe on Jwala

By Nick Pulford

WHEN Steve Drowne returned to the saddle in March after a year on the sidelines, he was realistic about his prospects. "It may take me six months to get going. I'm going to need a bit of luck to get on a really nice horse," he said.

Drowne, 41, had every right to feel pessimistic after a layoff that had cost him so much through no fault of his own, but he found that 'nice horse' quicker than he expected. Just over five months into his second coming, he was back in the big time when he scored a 40-1 upset on Jwala in the Group 1 Nunthorpe Stakes at York. Nobody deserved it more.

The previous year, Drowne had been forced to sit out the Nunthorpe – and every other race – owing to the intransigence of officialdom. In March 2012 Drowne passed out in his garden. Doctors initially put it down to an "undiagnosed seizure", which resulted in

Drowne's driving licence being withdrawn. Even when medical opinion was quickly revised, identifying the problem as an enlarged heart caused by a virus, the DVLA would not relent. Under the terms of a jockey's public liability insurance, no driving licence means no riding licence. For months the DVLA refused to budge, until Drowne's local MP, Claire Perry, took up his case.

Finally, 12 months after the fainting incident, Drowne got his licence back. By then, however, he had lost the top rides at Roger Charlton's stable to James Doyle and only the support of the Injured Jockeys Fund had prevented him having to sell his home. The one bright spot was that he got to spend more time with his five-year-old twin girls.

"Everyone knows the problems I had and I'm just glad to be back," Drowne said after the Nunthorpe. "It was so frustrating. What I had should have kept me out for only a fortnight, but when the DVLA got my report it took them five

months just to look at it. That was horrendous.

"When you miss a month you probably miss 30 per cent of your horses running. When you miss a year you

miss 100 per cent of your horses. If good people have ridden them they keep the ride. All you're left with is the ones who can't win."

But then he found Jwala.

"I've had to start again but luckily this filly came along," he said. She was one who could win and, after all his problems, Drowne made sure she did.

SIX OF THE BEST
Comebacks

Steve Drowne Group 1 winner after being forced to start all over again

Gary Stevens Aged 50 and on his second comeback, he rode his ninth winner in a Triple Crown race

Solwhit After almost two years off, he came back as a stayer and won two Grade 1s

Al Kazeem Returned from serious pelvic injury to land a Group 1 hat-trick in six weeks

Clive Brittain Back in the Group 1 spotlight with Rizeena after four years away

Farhh Missing from May to October but came back better than ever

▸ Steve Drowne wins the Nunthorpe on Jwala

BRITTAIN'S GOT TALENT IN RIZEENA

CLIVE BRITTAIN enjoys nothing better than defying the odds. He has done it with countless horses in his 41-year training career and he did it again in 2013 when, at the age of 79, he was back on the Group 1 roll of honour and back in the Royal Ascot winner's enclosure with Rizeena.

Royal Ascot had not seen Brittain's trademark victory jig for three years

and his last Group 1 winner had been Hibaayeb in the 2009 Fillies' Mile but the always optimistic, ever hard-working trainer never lost hope.

"We've trained about 50 Group 1 winners around the world over 40 years but you have to have years where you don't have those horses," he said, shortly after Rizeena's victory in the Queen Mary Stakes at the royal meeting. "When they come along, though, horses like Rizeena make a tremendous difference to the yard and give everyone a little bit of pride after a quiet time."

Rizeena ran in three Group 1 races, winning the Moyglare Stud Stakes and finishing second in the Fillies' Mile and third in the Prix Morny. Brittain had won the Moyglare before, with Sayyedati in 1992, and she went on to win the 1,000 Guineas. He has the ambition to do the same with Rizeena in 2014, by which time he will be 80.

"That's the way I feel about her and have done for some time," he said in midsummer. "She's got that bit of size and scope and she looks very much a Guineas horse for next year."

After the Moyglare he was even more

convinced. "I've trained some good horses over the years, great fillies, and one day she may not be far behind."

Rizeena is owned by Sheikh Rashid Dalmook Al Maktoum, a relative of Sheikh Mohammed, and after the Moyglare it was suggested the filly might go to Godolphin, as Hibaayeb did at the end of her juvenile year. That was downplayed by connections and Brittain said: "What I can't control, I can't control, but I would love to have her again next year."

The next triumphal jig, Brittain hopes, is not too far away.

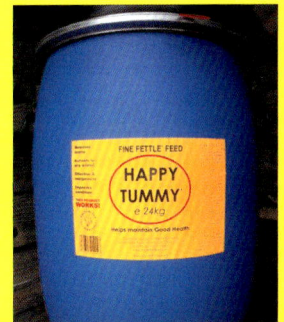

Tycoon hits rich vein of form

The Tony Martin-trained filly takes Galway by storm

IRISH owner John Breslin made his home and his fortune in the United States but he and his wife Debbie love nothing more than coming home to the Galway festival in the hope of a winner or two. This year it was four and, extraordinarily, three of them came from the history-making Busted Tycoon.

Even before Galway, it was a year to remember for Breslin after Ted Veale had won the County Handicap Hurdle at the Cheltenham Festival.

Ted Veale was the big hope at Galway too, and by the time he ran Breslin had already enjoyed victories with Busted Tycoon and Blackmail. Disappointment followed when Ted Veale was beaten favourite in the Galway Hurdle but it did not last long because Busted Tycoon was far from finished yet.

Following her victory in a two-mile Flat handicap, the four-year-old filly turned out again four days later to win another under a 5lb penalty. That was remarkable in itself, although by no means unusual at the Galway

▶▶ Trainer Tony Martin (left) and owner John Breslin celebrate Busted Tycoon's third win of Galway week

festival, but what followed was extraordinary.

Less than 22 hours after her second success, Busted Tycoon was back on the track but this time it was over hurdles in a two-mile handicap for mares. Under firm driving from Ruby Walsh, and amid mounting excitement in the stands, she got up close home for a famous victory.

Famous and unique. Busted Tycoon became the first triple winner at the Galway festival in its storied history and the only comparable feat was reckoned to be Don Mobile's hat-trick – in a hurdle race, a chase and a Flat race – for Edward O'Grady at the 1978 Tramore festival.

"What can I say? It's just unbelievable. That was the

icing on the cake, absolutely fantastic. I've never witnessed anything like this before," said Breslin, whose building supplies company has provided the hoisting and scaffolding for the rebuilding of Ground Zero in New York.

Tony Martin, who trains Breslin's string, had eight winners at Galway but there was no doubt Busted

Tycoon's hat-trick was the highlight.

"It's magic," he said. "It's nice to be part of history. John and Debbie are great owners and they give me a free hand to do what I want, so it's nice it's worked out. To be honest, at the start of the week I was hoping to get two runs into her. I never dreamed she could win three in a week."

YOUNG PIGGOTT MAKES DEBUT

FEW jockeys attract as much attention for their first ride as Jamie Piggott did at Killarney in July, but then not many have such a famous father.

The 19-year-old son of the legendary Lester made his debut on Pivotal Rock in the Killarney Grand Live Music Handicap over a mile and there

seemed a 'Piggott factor' at play in the betting, as Pivotal Rock was sent off 6-1 favourite even though he was winless in more than a year. In the end Piggott and his mount finished seventh.

"It was a good experience," said Piggott (right), a 10lb claimer who is attached to Pivotal Rock's trainer Tommy Stack. "I completed my A-levels in maths and three sciences before giving riding a go. I've only been riding properly for eight months.

Hopefully I can make a career of being a jockey now."

His father watched the race on TV at home in England while sister Tracy, an RTE Sport presenter, was a bundle of nerves at the track. "I'm so proud of him and it's something he really wanted to do," she said. "I'm just so glad it's all over."

Fozzy Stack, assistant to father Tommy, said: "He happens to have an unfortunate surname as nobody will ever beat his father."

Landmark victory for Dwyer

Jockey clears his name after long fight against Indian ban

FORGET Toronado versus Dawn Approach; the longest-running battle of the year was away from the track as jockey Martin Dwyer fought to clear his name after being banned for a ride in India. Finally, after eight months, he was successful.

"I'm relieved it's all over, it has felt like I've served months of mental torture," Dwyer said at the conclusion of the controversial case in October. "I couldn't take it lying down and kept fighting to clear my name."

The saga began when Dwyer was third on 6-4 favourite Ice Age in a six-furlong handicap at Mahalaxmi racecourse, Mumbai, in February. Amid a near-riot Dwyer was forced to shelter in the weighing room for two hours and said he had feared for his life. Dwyer was adamant the filly had bled during the race – and the head-on camera showed her veering markedly right in the closing stages – but the Royal Western India Turf Club (RWITC) found

▶ Martin Dwyer "couldn't take it lying down" after receiving ban in India

him guilty of not permitting Ice Age to run on her merits and handed him an eight-week ban.

When Dwyer appealed, and lost, the ban was increased to eight months. A further appeal hearing resulted in the original suspension being reinstated, but Dwyer was determined to fight the case all the way.

Riding bans are normally enforced worldwide but in October the BHA disciplinary panel decided not to reciprocate the suspension on the grounds that it was unjust.

Jamie Stier, director of raceday operations and regulation for the BHA, said: "It was the BHA's view that there were a number of areas during the process which fell short of being demonstrably fair and were not in accordance with the principles of natural justice.

"One such example was the decision of the RWITC stewards to make a finding that Ice Age had not been run on her merits and declare her a non-runner, before conducting an inquiry and hearing from Martin Dwyer."

The landmark ruling was vindication for Dwyer, who had wondered at times whether he was right to continue the battle. "I'm delighted at the result and that I can walk away with my reputation intact. I feel like a weight has been lifted off my shoulders," he said.

"It's been difficult because it has been hanging over me for so long, but the support from everyone kept me going.

"I remember walking into Warwick one wet Monday for a couple of rides and a racegoer came up to me and said he hoped I would win. It was quite humbling."

TARTAN STUNNER FOR SCOTLAND

TARTAN SNOW was a fairytale winner in the Aintree Fox Hunters – for his trainer Stuart Coltherd, a sheep farmer, for his 18-year-old rider Jamie Hamilton and for punters, including his owner-breeder Rory Westwood, who backed the 100-1 winner.

Coltherd was up at 2am on raceday, lambing on his farm in the Scottish Borders, and he hardly had time to dream of victory at Aintree. When it came, it felt good.

"It's a bit of a fairytale," he said. "We hardly thought we would come down and win the race, but he's done it. We always had faith in Tartan Snow (right). He's won seven times now. We didn't know how he would adapt to these fences but he pulled out everything and won."

Tartan Snow's thrilling neck victory owed plenty to the skill of Hamilton, who only a fortnight earlier had won the Gentleman Amateur Riders' Handicap at Doncaster for his boss Richard Fahey. That was a first winner

on the Flat for the son of clerk of the scales Michael Hamilton and it was an impressive achievement to switch codes and win on his debut at Aintree, especially after surviving a blunder at Becher's Brook. "Jamie was great on him," Coltherd said. "He's got a fantastic record on him and he's a great little jockey."

Westwood, another sheep farmer, had a £5 each-way bet on Tartan Snow on the Tote, which paid £845. "The owner always backs him hoping that the dream will come true," Coltherd said. On that glorious day in April, it did.

Nature takes its course

Even all-weather racing has to stop sometimes

EVEN an all-weather track can't cope with flooding. Racing at Southwell, usually a staple of the winter season, was out of action for more than two months after the River Greet burst its banks and swamped the course and public areas.

The track lost 21 meetings on the Flat and five over jumps – almost 40 per cent of its annual quota of fixtures – before re-opening for business on February 5.

Both the home and back straights had to be completely relaid owing to the damage caused by the flooding and water rose as high as nine inches inside some of the buildings.

The course, which is owned by Arena Racing Company, had been flooded in 2007, which at the time was regarded as a rare event.

"I know it's ironic for some people that we can't race, but we're under water," Nathan Corden,

▸ Southwell racecourse lost almost 40 per cent of its fixtures because of flooding

an Arena spokesman, said when the floods returned last winter. "Back in 2007 the Environment Agency said it was something that happened once every 50 years, but unfortunately it's only been five years."

◆ ◆ ◆ ◆

SEDGEFIELD had to make a change of course at its mid-May meeting after a nesting mallard and her six eggs were discovered in the fence after the grandstand.

It is illegal to disturb the nest of a wild bird during the breeding season and, although the meeting went ahead, the runners and riders were diverted around the fence.

"One of our staff was going round repairing the fences after the last raceday and he noticed there was a duck sitting in one of them," said clerk of the course Phil Tuck.

"She became quite agitated when he went near

but eventually flew off and he saw she had laid five eggs. By the time we went back later that day there were six eggs.

"All the fences on the course are able to be bypassed, but I don't think there can be many other sports where an animal forces everything to change."

◆ ◆ ◆ ◆

RACING at Chantilly on July 8 was delayed by half

an hour while a swarm of bees was safely moved out of harm's way.

The bees arrived from a neighbouring field less than an hour before racing was due to start and took up residence close to the winning post.

"It's the first time we've had them so close to the track, although it is something that happens from time to time," said clerk of the course Mathieu Vincent.

"It was just past the winning post and there was a danger a horse or jockey could have swallowed a bee. We had to put racing back by half an hour but what can you do? It's nature."

Two firefighters in beekeeping suits gingerly tended to the problem. "They have a product that enabled them to subdue the bees before they placed them in a bag and relocated them to another field," Vincent said.

BATTLE GROUP AT THE DOUBLE

Springtime at Aintree brings out the best in Battle Group and in 2013 that was the case not once but twice.

On two previous visits to the Grand National meeting, Battle Group had won the opening day's Grade 3 handicap hurdle in 2011 and finished a close second in the Listed handicap chase on National day in 2012. This time, however, he ran in both races and, remarkably, he won both.

First came the handicap hurdle and, ridden by Brendan Powell, he won by ten lengths – his first success since

landing the same race two years earlier. Forty-six hours later he turned out again for the handicap chase and won even more decisively, by 16 lengths, under Daryl Jacob.

His previous wins had been for David Pipe but the amazing Aintree double was achieved for the Kevin Bishop yard following his transfer in February. Johnny Farrelly, a former Pipe rider who had become Bishop's assistant, oversaw Battle Group's preparation and was confident the eight-year-old could perform equally well second time round.

"Some horses can't do it and some can," Farrelly said after the second win. "He hadn't run since Cheltenham in January, so we knew he was fresh

and well. He won well on Thursday, we got him home that evening and I took him out for a walk on Friday. He was his normal self, jumping around, so that was the decision made."

Battle Group had a day's rest between his two victories – unlike Solfen, who, at the 1960 Cheltenham Festival, won the race that is now the RSA Chase and, the very next day, landed the Spa (now World) Hurdle. Feroda won chases on consecutive days at the Grand National meeting in 1989.

But Battle Group wasn't finished there. Just over a month after his Aintree double, the tough campaigner went back to handicap hurdling at Haydock, having gone up 15lb in the

ratings, and completed a hat-trick. Aintree runner-up Jetson got closer this time, three-quarters of a length, but could not turn the tables on Battle Group even on 12lb better terms.

That success took Battle Group's winning prize-money to £81,000 in little more than five weeks and Farrelly is hoping there is still more to come in the new season.

Now training in his own name next door to Bishop in Bridgwater, Somerset, Farrelly has Battle Group among his string. "There are a couple of nice pots he can go for," he said. "We might mix fences with hurdles. We'll just see what comes up."

The chances are a return trip, or two, to Aintree will be in the plans.

Everybody's Favourite

blüegrass

Fuelled by Bluegrass

With a range of feeds designed for racehorses in light, medium and hard work, we are sure to have a feed to suit your needs.

We use Stamm 30 balancer in many of our products as it is one of the most flexible balancers on the market.

It is an equine-specific highly concentrated source of vitimans and minerals designed for all horses.

Economical to buy and easy for your horse to digest.

Tel: +44 (0)28 3754 8276 • E: info@bluegrasshorsefeed.com • www.bluegrasshorsefeed.com

A-Z of 2013

The year digested into 26 bite-size chunks

DREAM RIDE FOR OWNER

LIFE in the saddle began at 40 for owner John Reddington when his first racecourse ride gave him a fairytale triumph at Navan in January.

Reddington, the boss of a north London-based construction company, won a bumper on the Charlie Swan-trained newcomer Agent James, who carries his red and green quartered silks.

"It was an absolutely fabulous day. All the pain and torture you go through, you would take it ten times over to experience a feeling like that," said Reddington, whose fitness regime involves riding out every morning at the pre-training yard of his friend Thomas Gallagher in Radlett, Hertfordshire, before heading to the office.

The father of two, who tips the scales at 11st 3lb, added: "I've never really had time before to do anything like this, I've been too busy working, but fortunately I've had a lot of luck in life and I thought it would be fun to give race-riding a go. I'm only sorry I waited until 40 to take out an amateur licence."

Reddington's victory on the 16-1 shot will live long in his memory. "When we went past the post I can't explain how exciting it was."

A is for **Al Zarooni**. Godolphin trainer Mahmood Al Zarooni brought disgrace on himself, his employers and British racing in a doping scandal of shocking proportions.

B is for **Busted Tycoon**, the Tony Martin-trained filly who scored an unprecedented hat-trick in six heady days at the Galway festival.

C is for **Champions Day**. Without Frankel, the crowd was smaller but Farhh and his fellow combatants in the Champion Stakes gave them a day to remember.

D is for **Dawn Approach**. He was one of the few bright spots in a dark year for Godolphin and, more importantly, his season-long battle for supremacy with Toronado was one of the highlights on the track.

E is for **Estimate**, who fortunately cannot read and was therefore unaware of all the expectation riding on her when she carried the Queen's colours in the Gold Cup. Even more fortunately, she can run a bit.

F is for **fourteen**. Ireland had a record number of winners at the Cheltenham Festival, leading to plenty of sore heads and bulging pockets by the end of the four days.

G is for **Great British Racing**. The new name for Racing For Change is catchier, that's for sure, but still their thinking can be difficult to fathom. The latest big idea is a Champions Weekend in 2014 – held on different racecourses 80 miles apart. And the weekend, apparently, starts around 2pm on Friday afternoon – tell that to the boss!

H is for **Henderson**. Like fine wine, Nicky Henderson gets better with age and 2013 was his greatest vintage yet as Sprinter Sacre, Bobs Worth and Simonsig carried all before them in their respective divisions and he won his first trainers' title in 26 years.

I is for **India**. After Richard Hughes's problems on the sub-continent in 2012, this year it was the turn of Martin Dwyer to fall foul of the Indian racing authorities' rather strange version of justice. Will anyone dare take the risk of being third time unlucky this winter?

J is for **Japanese jinx**. There was no hard-luck story in this year's Arc, as Orfevre was beaten fair and square by Treve, but Japanese trainers must wonder whether they are fated to be the eternal second in Europe's richest race.

K is for **King**. Ireland's apprentice sensation Connor King looks impossibly young to be a jockey but inside he has the determination to be a winner.

L is for **Lasix**. Having prohibited the anti-bleeding drug in its two-year-old races and pledged to extend the ban to its other events, the Breeders' Cup went back to square one in a move that drove a wedge between horsemen in the United States and Europe.

M is for **Moonlight Cloud**, flagbearer for the older fillies and mares as they proved more than a match for their male counterparts in the top open races.

N is for **Nottingham**, the place where Frankie Dettori's Arc dreams were dashed as a broken ankle ended his stuttering season just when he was on the verge of something spectacular.

O is for **Our Conor**. He was the best four-year-old hurdler in the history of Racing Post Ratings and surely will only get better with age. And his earnings this season will go to help JT McNamara and Jonjo Bright.

P is for **perfection**. The best horses don't seem to get beat anymore, do they? First there was Frankel, and then this year Sprinter Sacre, Hurricane Fly and Treve were among those who completed perfect seasons. It wasn't because they had ducked any of the big challenges; it was just that they were brilliant.

Q is for **Quevega**. Willie Mullins' remarkable mare became only the second horse to win five times at the Cheltenham Festival with another victory in the Mares' Hurdle. She joined the great Golden Miller, who won the Cheltenham Gold Cup every year from 1932 to 1936. Illustrious company indeed.

R is for **relief**. After two years of negative headlines, the Grand National was run without a hitch. It was the best result jump racing has had in years.

S is for **Stevens**. Top American jockey Gary Stevens made a second comeback, after seven years out of the saddle, and within months he was a Classic winner at the age of 50 on Oxbow in the Preakness.

T is for **Treve**, whose wondrous performance in the Arc was a joy to

behold – unless your name is Frankie Dettori.

U is for **underwater**. That was the fate of Southwell, one of Britain's two original all-weather tracks, as flooding kept it out of action for two months over the winter. Perhaps it's time to call it a 'most-weather' track.

V is for **viewing figures**. Channel 4's first year as racing's sole terrestrial broadcaster was widely expected to see a fall in the audience for the Grand National but, in fact, the peak figure of 8.9 million was higher than in three of the last four years on the BBC.

W is for '**what recession**?' In three days at Tattersalls sales in October, racing's super-rich created their own bubble as they splashed out a European auction record of £74m on a total of just 339

yearlings and the record for a yearling sold at public auction was broken twice. How the other 0.01 per cent live, eh?

X is for **X factor**. Frankel had it and in 2013 the baton was passed to Sprinter Sacre, whose star appeal was most apparent in front of a worshipping crowd at Punchestown.

Y is for **you're fired**. Racecourse judge Dave Smith was sacked by the BHA after calling a dead-heat at Kempton in June that later had to be amended, with evens favourite Extra Noble ruled to have won by a nose from 16-1 shot Fire Fighting.

Z is for **zebra racing**. Fair Grounds, in New Orleans, had 'exotic' racing, featuring zebras and ostriches, alongside the more traditional fare at a January fixture. The Zebra Zip was run over 140 yards.

◆◆◆◆

OSTEOPATHIC REMEDY achieved a remarkable feat in August when he won the historic Ripon Rowels Handicap for a record fourth time.

Making his sixth appearance in the race, the Michael Dods-trained nine-year-old added to his successes in 2008, 2010 and 2012 with a two-length victory under Connor Beasley, who was the fourth rider to win the race on him.

"He must be a legend locally and this race was the toughest of his four wins," Kevin Kirkup, his owner, said. "He's probably improving with age and his record here is untouchable."

Kirkup is an osteopath from Chester-le-Street, Durham, which explains the horse's name, and he is already eyeing a fifth success in 2014.

◆◆◆◆

COUNTY DOWN trainer Aaron Stronge has had plenty of success on the point-to-point circuit with his small string but he had to wait ten years for his first winner on the racecourse.

The breakthrough finally came at Fairyhouse in January with Carsonstown Bridge and Stronge, who combines training with running Daft Eddy's restaurant on Strangford Lough, was celebrating in more ways than one.

"It's my birthday as well, so everything's rolled into one," he said. "We've hit the bar that many times I thought we'd knocked it over. It's just nice to get it out of the way."

Stronge soon added to his tally with General Maccreevy and Shershewill. Clearly the restaurateur had made a note of the winning recipe.

Cartmel under Magic spell

Seven up for remarkable course specialist

CARTMEL in midsummer is one of the quaint delights of British racing and no-one loves it more than Soul Magic, the 11-year-old handicap chaser who can't win anywhere else but is almost unbeatable around the idiosyncratic Lake District track.

This year Soul Magic won twice at Cartmel to take his tally to seven victories from ten starts. He now shares the record for number of wins at Cartmel with Deep Mystery, whose seven victories were recorded over nine seasons from 1976 to 1984. Soul Magic, by contrast, took two years and three months to achieve the feat, which is remarkable even with the increased number of meetings at Cartmel nowadays.

Harriet Graham, who trains Soul Magic at Jedburgh in the Scottish Borders, believes the gelding is 10lb better at Cartmel than anywhere else.

"It's hard to pinpoint the exact reason but it's probably because Cartmel is such a unique course

and everything plays to his liking," she says. "The minute he gets there he starts enjoying himself, strutting his stuff. He loves looking at the fairground and the picnics.

"He's quite a slow horse at home and the fences are quite close together at Cartmel in two groups, so maybe it just suits his stride pattern. He will take three or four lengths out of the field at every fence. He loves it when there's a big crowd and he goes up the middle and they're all shouting. He must think it's all for him. The last time he won there, he looked like finishing third until he heard the crowd."

Soul Magic was winless in 12 starts when he first went to Cartmel in June 2011, at the age of nine. "I actually got fed up with him at one time and gave him away as a riding horse," Graham says. "But he's a biter, so he came back to us. I didn't really know what to do with him but I was getting him wrong. I thought he was a stayer but he isn't. We took him to Cartmel and ran him over two miles five furlongs on the Saturday and he

got beaten, then he ran on Monday over two miles and won. So I just thought, he seems to like it there, we might as well go back."

If Graham had not taken him there in the first place, Soul Magic would have sunk into obscurity but instead he is a local hero in the Lake District. He will be back

there at the age of 12 in May, July and August, when he will have the chance to claim the outright record.

"If we're careful we're hoping we can get another couple of years out of him there," Graham says.

The Cartmel crowds who have grown to love Soul Magic will hope so too.

▶▶ Soul Magic's seven wins at Cartmel give him a share of the record at the Lake District track

SIX OF THE BEST
Course specialists

Soul Magic Two more wins at Cartmel in 2013 took him to a record seven in all

Jonnie Skull Loves to be beside the seaside, winning five times at Yarmouth in 2013

Hopes N Dreams Won four out of five at Hamilton in 2013, taking his course tally to six

Beacon Lady The Brighton belle, with four wins in 2013 including a hat-trick in the space of 16 days

Scotch Warrior All six wins have been at Perth, including three from five runs in 2013

That's Rhythm Still going strong at 13, winning all three starts at Bangor in 2013 to take his course tally to seven

ANNECDOTE QUITE A STORY FOR OWNER

TOM EDWARDS, a 92-year-old Second World War veteran, had a memorable first visit to Royal Ascot when Annecdote gave him victory in a blanket finish to the Sandringham Handicap.

And, having turned down a host of offers for the Jonny Portman-trained

filly both before and after Ascot, Edwards enjoyed further success at Glorious Goodwood when Annecdote followed up in the Group 3 Oak Tree Stakes.

Edwards, a former builder from Melksham, Wiltshire, savoured his moment in the hallowed Ascot winner's enclosure. "That was very good, especially as the Americans wanted to buy her and we decided not to sell," he said. "I've been interested in horses all my life but I've only been involved in ownership

for the last 30 years. I've been to Ascot before but I hadn't ever come to Royal Ascot until today. The big crowds always put me off, but I've enjoyed today immensely."

As for the offers, Edwards said after the Goodwood win: "If I'd been younger I'd have seriously thought about selling, but what would I do with the money now?"

Only one day before the Ascot win, Edwards had received confirmation in the post that he would be given a

medal for his role taking supplies to Russia during the Arctic Convoys, the maritime missions that Winston Churchill described as the most dangerous of the war. Of the 70,000 British Navy sailors or Merchant Navy seamen who were involved, more than 3,000 lost their lives.

Edwards was presented with his medal in September at a ceremony in Trowbridge, which honoured the 29 surviving veterans of the Arctic Convoys. A fitting conclusion to a special year.

◆◆◆◆

SIR ALEX FERGUSON was used to winning the biggest prizes in football but the now retired Manchester United manager was still happy with victory in one of the least heralded versions of the Champion Hurdle.

Ferguson's If I Had Him, trained by George Baker, scored a narrow win in Jersey's Champion Hurdle in July and the owner's delight was measured in typical football terminology.

"Sir Alex is absolutely over the moon," Baker said. "I believe it is Sir Alex's first Champion Hurdle, so it's great.

"If I Had Him, Champion Hurdle and Sir Alex Ferguson are words I never thought I would be able to mention in the same sentence."

◆◆◆◆

FLATFOOT BOOGIE was bought as a yearling by Noel Glynn, who produced him to win on two of his first three starts over hurdles. It sounds a familiar tale, except that the gap between the sale and his first run was almost seven years.

Now an eight-year-old, Flatfoot Boogie made his racecourse debut in June 2013 at Uttoxeter, where he finished a promising fourth in a maiden hurdle. Five weeks later he built on that promise with a maiden hurdle win at Cork, followed quickly by a novice hurdle success at Killarney.

Glynn, a larger-than-life character, summed up the remarkable story in his own inimitable style. "My mother is in a nursing home and this fella has more problems than her," the County Clare trainer said. "I've been nursing him for seven years but it's worth it now."

Over and out for Mangan

Cheltenham fall from Oscar Delta brings despair

▸▸ The agony of the fall from Oscar Delta (above) and the aftermath (right) for teenage rider Jane Mangan

By Jessica Lamb

THE moment Jane Mangan most wants to consign to history lingers like the smell of old milk. In a split-second she went from leading the Foxhunter Chase at the Cheltenham Festival to sitting on the grass watching her mount Oscar Delta gallop riderless to the line behind Salsify, the fortunate winner.

Oscar Delta was in front and seemingly set for victory when he saw flapping white tape, rather than the solid rail that had been there up to that point. He was alarmed and jinked, taking his 19-year-old rider completely by surprise and leaving her on the ground.

The shock, the crowds and the bruising from the fall brought Mangan to tears, but father Jimmy, trainer of Oscar Delta, quickly reached her out on the course and on the walk back to the weighing room his words and her thoughts altered her outlook.

"It kind of put a lot of things in perspective and made me grow up a little bit," she says. "The whole thing did; being over at Cheltenham and riding in front of such a big crowd was brilliant. I was very fortunate to be in that position.

"Mentally it was quite challenging. I remember his owner [Karen O'Driscoll] was very good about it. I remember walking into the parade ring and seeing her. She didn't even have to say anything."

For many in Britain that will be their first memory of Mangan, but back at home in Ireland respect for her ability was already high and the way she handled that incident only bettered her reputation.

She continued her successful partnership with Gordon Elliott and Gigginstown House Stud, one that shows no signs of weakening, and through that earned the ride on the David Pipe-trained The Liquidator. Together they won the Grade 1 Champion Bumper at the Punchestown festival.

"That was pretty huge," she says. "Amateurs only get a couple of chances every year even to ride in a Grade 1, never mind win one."

Elliott, formerly based with Pipe's father Martin, recommended Mangan for the mount, further showing how highly she is regarded. Her lightweight frame means that becoming a professional jump jockey would not hinder her health, but that is not on the cards and she is already planning for the day when riding takes a back seat.

"I'm studying marketing at Cork University," she says. "I enjoy it and I hope there's a future in that."

The workload is a chore to juggle and for now racing comes first, but her days out of the saddle and at the desk are welcomed. "Racing can consume your life and is definitely on your mind all the time. I try to go in to college and switch off. I'm not saying I do, but I try."

It is perhaps a testament to the mindset she works on in those days that when asked about last season she describes herself as "delighted" with the way it went, choosing to focus on the Grade 1 and the other positives rather than the blip.

Cheltenham will see her and Oscar Delta again, stronger and more determined.

COOLAGOWN STUD 2014

CARLOTAMIX
Grey 2003 by Linamix
Group 1 Winner Grade 1 Sire
Sire of Gemix from his 1st crop

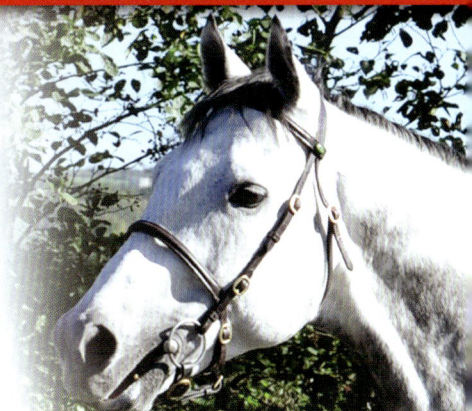

DAYLAMI
Grey 1993 by Doyoun
7 time Group 1 winner
Proven Gr1 Flat & NH Sire

FROZEN FIRE
Bay 2005 By Montjeu
1st Irish Derby Winner to retire direct to NH
"Siring very attractive , good walking foals "

PAPAL BULL
Bay 2003 By Montjeu
Multiple Group winner 7f to 13f
Proven Sire from 2 crops of racing age

SHANTARAM
Bay 2009 By Galileo
Group Winner of Bahrain Trophy over 13F
Bred on the Classic Galileo/Darshaan Cross

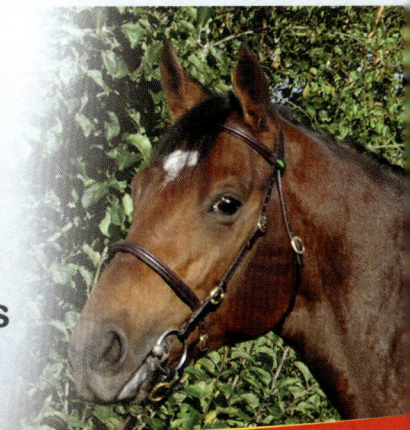

Coolagown Stud Coolagown Fermoy Co.Cork Ireland.
Tel: +353 25 36642 Fax: +353 25 36901 Web: www.coolagown.ie

DAVID STACK Mobile: +353 86 2314066 email: info@coolagown.ie
EAMON CULLEN Mobile: +44 7587 930622 email: eamonn@ecbloodstock.com
PETE HICKEY Mobile: +44 7966 705147 email: fosseracing@googlemail.com

THE
BIGGER
PICTURE

Every vantage point is taken on the third day
of Chester's May meeting as the runners in
the seven-furlong handicap won by Captain
Bertie race down the home straight
**EDWARD WHITAKER
(RACINGPOST.COM/PHOTOS)**

BURGER & FRIES

LEADING FLAT HORSES 2013

Older horse

FARHH

Trainer **Saeed Bin Suroor**
Owner **Godolphin**

NOVELLIST

Trainer **Andreas Wohler**
Owner **Christoph Berglar**

RACING POST RATINGS

Farhh	128
Novellist	128
Cirrus Des Aigles	127
Al Kazeem	126
Orfevre	126
St Nicholas Abbey	126

Farhh grabbed a share of top honours in the final major European race in this division with his thrilling Champion Stakes victory over Cirrus Des Aigles and Ruler Of The World. That was a career-best and a deserved reward for his consistency

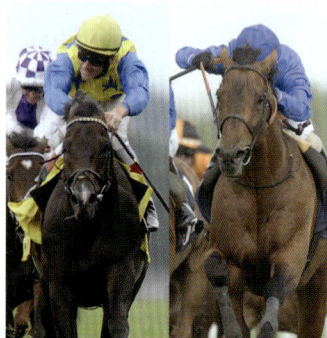

as it was the fifth time he had posted an RPR of 126 or more. Novellist's record-breaking King George had set the standard in a close and exciting division, although the three-year-old filly Treve came out best of the middle-distance horses with her stunning Arc win.

Three-year-old colt

TORONADO

Trainer **Richard Hannon**
Owner **Sheikh Joaan Al Thani**

RACING POST RATINGS

Toronado	129
Dawn Approach	128
Olympic Glory	127
Ruler Of The World	126
Intello	125

Toronado finally overtook his great rival Dawn Approach with a half-length win in the Sussex Stakes, the best race

in this division. Dawn Approach was a consistently high-class performer – recording RPRs of 127 in the 2,000 Guineas, 126 in the St James's Palace Stakes and 128 in the Sussex – but it was the defeat, rather than his earlier wins, that decided the spoils. Olympic Glory, Toronado's stablemate, was another high-class miler, while Derby winner Ruler Of The World achieved his best mark with his gallant third in the Champion Stakes.

Three-year-old filly

TREVE

Trainer **Criquette Head-Maarek**
Owner **Sheikh Joaan Al Thani**

RACING POST RATINGS

Treve	131
Sky Lantern	120
Integral	116
Tasaday	116
Winsili	116

Sheikh Joaan ended up with both three-year-old champions after his mid-season purchase of Treve from the Head family, who bred the filly. At the time she was full of promise after recording an RPR of 120 with a runaway win in the Prix de Diane and she delivered on that promise in no uncertain fashion with an even more decisive victory in the Arc against a high-class field. That made her clearly the best performer in any division in the European season and there might be better to come in 2014. Sky Lantern was a distant second despite three Group 1 wins.

Sprinter

LETHAL FORCE

Trainer **Clive Cox**
Owner **Alan Craddock**

RACING POST RATINGS

Lethal Force	124
Moonlight Cloud	122
Society Rock	122
Gordon Lord Byron	121
Sole Power	120

Lethal Force improved 8lb from 2012 to land two Group 1 wins. He recorded an RPR of 123 with a two-length victory over Society Rock in the Diamond Jubilee Stakes at Royal Ascot and then beat that same rival again in the July Cup at Newmarket with a record-breaking run that took him slightly higher to a mark of 124. He wasn't as good as Black Caviar (RPR 128 in 2013) but he was the sprint king of Europe. Moonlight Cloud rated next-best with her Prix Maurice de Gheest victory, although she did better (RPR 125) in winning the Prix Jacques le Marois at a mile.

Stayer

LEADING LIGHT

Trainer **Aidan O'Brien**
Owner **Derrick Smith, Sue Magnier and Michael Tabor**

LES BEAUFS

Trainer **Valerie Seignoux**
Owner **Stephane Seignoux**

RACING POST RATINGS

Leading Light	118
Les Beaufs	118
Ahzeemah	117
Brown Panther	117
Altano	116
Camborne	116
Simenon	116

Estimate had the most memorable victory in this division when she took the Gold Cup for the Queen but her RPR of 113 was bettered by several others. Leading Light (below), having won the Queen's Vase at Royal Ascot, stepped up to a mark of 118 with his victory in the St Leger. Les Beaufs twice ran to 118 with a Listed win and second place, giving weight, in the Group 2 Prix Vicomtesse Vigier.

Two-year-old colt

TOORMORE

Trainer **Richard Hannon**
Owner **Middleham Park Racing IX and James Pak**

RACING POST RATINGS

Toormore	121
War Command	118
Karakontie	117
No Nay Never	117
Astaire	116

Toormore improved with each of his first three runs until setting the standard in this division with a decisive victory over Sudirman by two and three-quarter lengths in the National Stakes at the Curragh.

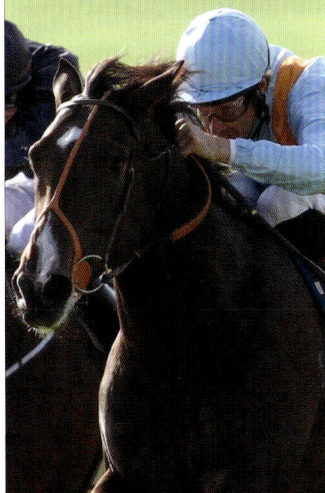

Sudirman had previously won the Group 1 Phoenix and Giovanni Boldini went on from his National third to a smart Listed win, so the form was solid, and Richard Hannon is hopeful Toormore will be even better at three. "He's a big shell of a horse and is not a precocious two-year-old by any means," he said. Dewhurst winner War Command was next, just ahead of Karakontie and No Nay Never.

Two-year-old filly

CHRISELLIAM

Trainer **Charlie Hills**
Owner **Willie Carson, Emily Asprey and Chris Wright**

RACING POST RATINGS

Chriselliam	114
Rizeena	113
Vorda	113
Miss France	112
Indonesienne	111
Kiyoshi	111
Tapestry	111

Victory in the Fillies' Mile at Newmarket gave Chriselliam a narrow edge over fellow Group 1 winners Rizeena and Vorda, as well as Andre Fabre's Group 2 Newmarket scorer Miss France, in a division with promising but not yet dominant performers. Rizeena, having previously won the Moyglare Stud Stakes, was beaten a length by Chriselliam, who stepped up markedly on earlier beaten efforts in Group 3 and Listed company. France has several good prospects: Vorda, Miss France and Prix Marcel Boussac winner Indonesienne.

FLAT WINNERS 2013

British Group 1 Winners in 2013

Winner	Race	Course (Distance, Month)
Dawn Approach	2,000 Guineas	Newmarket (1m, May)
Sky Lantern	1,000 Guineas	Newmarket (1m, May)
Farhh	Lockinge	Newbury (1m, May)
Talent	Oaks	Epsom (1m4f, May)
St Nicholas Abbey	Coronation Cup	Epsom (1m4f, June)
Ruler Of The World	Derby	Epsom (1m4f, June)
Sole Power	King's Stand	Ascot (5f, June)
Dawn Approach	St James's Palace	Ascot (1m, June)
Declaration Of War	Queen Anne	Ascot (1m, June)
Al Kazeem	Prince of Wales's	Ascot (1m2f, June)
Estimate	Gold Cup	Ascot (2m4f, June)
Sky Lantern	Coronation	Ascot (1m, June)
Lethal Force	Diamond Jubilee	Ascot (6f, June)
Al Kazeem	Eclipse	Sandown (1m2f, July)
Elusive Kate	Falmouth	Newmarket (1m, July)
Lethal Force	July Cup	Newmarket (6f, July)
Novellist	King George	Ascot (1m4f, July)
Toronado	Sussex	Goodwood (1m, July)
Winsili	Nassau	Goodwood (1m2f, Aug)
Declaration Of War	International	York (1m2f, Aug)
The Fugue	Yorkshire Oaks	York (1m4f, Aug)
Jwala	Nunthorpe	York (5f, Aug)
Gordon Lord Byron	Sprint Cup	Haydock (6f, Sep)
Leading Light	St Leger	Doncaster (1m7f, Sep)
Chriselliam	Fillies' Mile	Newmarket (1m, Sep)
Sky Lantern	Sun Chariot	Newmarket (1m, Sep)
Vorda	Cheveley Park	Newmarket (6f, Sep)
War Command	Dewhurst	Newmarket (7f, Oct)
Astaire	Middle Park	Newmarket (6f, Oct)
Seal Of Approval	Fillies and Mares	Ascot (1m4f, Oct)
Olympic Glory	Queen Elizabeth II	Ascot (1m, Oct)
Farhh	Champion Stakes	Ascot (1m2f, Oct)

TALENT IN THE FAMILY There was a long family story, both equine and human, behind the surprise Oaks success of Talent and her joint owner-breeder Mark Dixon had been there all the way through. Talent was the fourth successive generation of her family to run in the Oaks and the second to win, following her great granddam Bireme's victory in 1980. In between, her granddam Yawl was 12th in 1993 and her dam Prowess was ninth in 2009.

Bireme was bred and owned by Dixon's uncle, the late Dick Hollingsworth, and family history is important to the current custodian. "I was here 33 years ago for Bireme and I did have a feeling today," Dixon said after the Oaks. "Bireme didn't do much as a mare and Yawl has been pretty useless. Prowess is really the only one of any use I've had. I know nothing about horses and I'm only in it to try and keep the family going."

Winning the Oaks was not a bad way to go about it.

Irish Group 1 Winners in 2013

Winner	Course	(Distance, Month)
Magician	Irish 2,000 Guineas	Curragh (1m, May)
Al Kazeem	Tattersalls Gold Cup	Curragh (1m3f, May)
Just The Judge	Irish 1,000 Guineas	Curragh (1m, May)
Trading Leather	Irish Derby	Curragh (1m4f, June)
Ambivalent	Pretty Polly	Curragh (1m2f, June)
Chicquita	Irish Oaks	Curragh (1m4f, July)
Sudirman	Phoenix	Curragh (6f, Aug)
Rizeena	Moyglare	Curragh (7f, Sep)
La Collina	Matron	Leopardstown (1m, Sep)
The Fugue	Irish Champion	Leopardstown (1m2f, Sep)
Toormore	National	Curragh (7f, Sep)
Voleuse De Coeurs	Irish St Leger	Curragh (1m6f, Sep)

GOLDEN OLDIES Clive Brittain, 79, struck in the Moyglare with Rizeena, his first Group 1 winner in four years. When he was congratulated by Aidan O'Brien, trainer of runner-up Tapestry, Brittain told him: "If I can beat you I can beat anybody."

Six days later Kevin Prendergast, 81, took the Matron with La Collina, who had been the trainer's last Group 1 winner, as a two-year-old in 2011. "I'm like Clive Brittain," Prendergast said. "I'm getting better with age."

French Group 1 Winners in 2013

Winner	Race	Course (Distance, Month)
Pastorius	Prix Ganay	Longchamp (1m3f, Apr)
Flotilla	Poule d'Essai des Pouliches	Longchamp (1m, May)
Style Vendome	Poule d'Essai des Poulains	Longchamp (1m, May)
Maxios	Prix d'Ispahan	Longchamp (1m1f, May)
Silasol	Prix Saint-Alary	Longchamp (1m2f, May)
Intello	Prix du Jockey Club	Chantilly (1m3f, June)
Treve	Prix de Diane	Chantilly (1m3f, June)
Novellist	Grand Prix de Saint-Cloud	Saint-Cloud (1m4f, June)
Havana Gold	Prix Jean Prat	Chantilly (1m, June)
Flintshire	Grand Prix de Paris	Longchamp (1m4f, July)
Elusive Kate	Prix Rothschild	Deauville (1m, July)
Moonlight Cloud	Prix Maurice de Gheest	Deauville (7f, Aug)
Moonlight Cloud	Prix Jacques Le Marois	Deauville (1m, Aug)
Romantica	Prix Jean Romanet	Deauville (1m2f, Aug)
No Nay Never	Prix Morny	Deauville (6f, Aug)
Maxios	Prix du Moulin	Longchamp (1m, Sep)
Treve	Prix Vermeille	Longchamp (1m4f, Sep)
Maarek	Prix de l'Abbaye	Longchamp (5f, Oct)
Indonesienne	Prix Marcel Boussac	Longchamp (1m, Oct)
Karakontie	Prix Jean-Luc Lagardere	Longchamp (7f, Oct)
Dalkala	Prix de l'Opera	Longchamp (1m2f, Oct)
Treve	Prix de l'Arc de Triomphe	Longchamp (1m4f, Oct)
Moonlight Cloud	Prix de la Foret	Longchamp (7f, Oct)
Altano	Prix du Cadran	Longchamp (2m4f, Oct)

What happened to the winter Classics favourites?

Certify 1,000 Guineas

Unbeaten in four starts as a juvenile, she was 8-1 in the winter but was ruled out after being named as one of the most high-profile horses given steroids by Mahmood Al Zarooni in the Godolphin scandal. Sky Lantern, who had been beaten a length by Certify when they met in 2012, stepped up to give Richard Hughes his first British Classic. A general 20-1 shot in the winter, she won at 9-1

Dawn Approach 2,000 Guineas

After rounding off his six-race unbeaten campaign as a juvenile with victory in the Dewhurst, he was a best-priced 7-2 in the winter and his odds shortened as trainer Jim Bolger issued bullish reports and potential rivals fell by the wayside. He was 11-8 favourite on the day and won by five lengths from 150-1 outsider Glory Awaits. After finishing last in the Derby, he went back to a mile to win the St James's Palace

Kingsbarns Derby

The 2012 Racing Post Trophy winner was seen as Aidan O'Brien's number one Classic hope over the winter at 5-1 favourite for the Derby and 7-1 second favourite for the 2,000 Guineas. He missed all the Classics after suffering a foot infection, however, and was last of six in the Irish Champion when he finally appeared in September. O'Brien still won the Derby with Ruler Of The World, a general 25-1 shot in the winter

4 FAB FOURS

Four-year-olds were the dominant group in the all-age Group 1 races in Britain, Ireland and France, winning almost half of the 29 held by British Champions Day. Lethal Force and The Fugue led the way for the four-year-olds with two wins apiece, although the five-year-old mare Moonlight Cloud went one better with three. Toronado, in the Sussex, was the first three-year-old to win in all-age company, followed by Winsili (Nassau), Treve (Prix Vermeille), Sky Lantern (Sun Chariot), Treve, again, in the Arc and Olympic Glory (Queen Elizabeth II). The oldest winners were the six-year-old sprinters Sole Power (King's Stand) and Maarek (Prix de l'Abbaye).

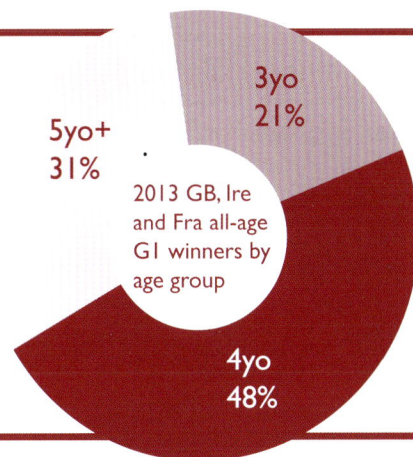

3yo 21%

5yo+ 31%

2013 GB, Ire and Fra all-age G1 winners by age group

4yo 48%

THE LIST

Classic firsts in 2013

Richard Hughes (Sky Lantern, 1,000 Guineas) First British Classic
Richard Hannon (Sky Lantern, 1,000 Guineas) First 1,000 Guineas
Kevin Manning (Dawn Approach, 2,000 Guineas) First 2,000 Guineas
Jim Bolger (Dawn Approach, 2,000 Guineas) First 2,000 Guineas
Richard Hughes (Talent, Oaks) First Oaks
Joseph O'Brien (Leading Light, St Leger) First St Leger
Charlie Hills (Just The Judge, left, Irish 1,000 Guineas) First British or Irish Classic
Kevin Manning (Trading Leather, Irish Derby) First Irish Derby
Chris Hayes (Voleuse De Coeurs, Irish St Leger) First British or Irish Classic

FLAT WINNERS 2013

Major British Handicap Winners in 2013

Winner	Race	Course (Distance, Month)	Value
Tiger Cliff	Ebor	York (1m6f, Aug)	£156k
Educate	Cambridgeshire	Newmarket (1m1f, Sep)	£100k
Excellent Result	Ladbrokes Mobile	Ascot (1m4f, Sep)	£97k
Highland Colori	Ayr Gold Cup	Ayr (6f, Sep)	£96k
Belgian Bill	Royal Hunt Cup	Ascot (1m, June)	£93k
York Glory	Wokingham	Ascot (6f, June)	£93k
Danchai	John Smith's Cup	York (1m2f, July)	£93k
Heaven's Guest	Challenge Cup	Ascot (7f, Oct)	£93k
Tominator	Northumberland Plate	Newcastle (2m, June)	£93k
Wentworth	Betfred Mile	Goodwood (1m, Aug)	£81k
Address Unknown	Chester Cup	Chester (2m3f, May)	£75k
Roca Tumu	Britannia	Ascot (1m, June)	£75k
Star Lahib	Old Newton Cup	Haydock (1m4f, July)	£62k
Field Of Dream	Bunbury Cup	Newmarket (7f, July)	£62k
Masamah	Betfred Mobile Sports	Ascot (5f, July)	£62k
Heaven's Guest	Betfred 'The Bonus King'	Newmarket (6f, July)	£62k
Magic City	Betfair Cash Out Stakes	Goodwood (7f, Aug)	£62k
Levitate	Lincoln	Doncaster (1m, Mar)	£62k
Body And Soul	Sprint Trophy	York (6f, June)	£62k
Rex Imperator	Stewards' Cup	Goodwood (6f, Aug)	£62k
Duke Of Firenze	'Dash'	Epsom (5f, June)	£62k
Galician	International	Ascot (7f, July)	£62k
Excellent Guest	Victoria Cup	Ascot (7f, May)	£53k
Redvers Fly	London Southend Airport	Ascot (7f, Sep)	£52k
Harris Tweed	Summer	Goodwood (1m6f, July)	£47k
Mont Ras	Clipper Logistics	York (1m, Aug)	£47k
Opinion	Duke of Edinburgh	Ascot (1m4f, June)	£47k
Prince Of Johanne	Challenge	Sandown (1m, July)	£47k
Elidor	King George V	Ascot (1m4f, June)	£47k
Lightning Cloud	Buckingham Palace	Ascot (7f, June)	£47k
Haafaguinea	Dubai Duty Free	Newbury (1m2f, Sep)	£47k
Dark Crusader	Melrose Stakes	York (1m6f, Aug)	£47k
Maputo	Boylesports.Com Download	Newmarket (1m2f, July)	£44k
Kingsgate Choice	Scottish Sprint Cup	Musselburgh (5f, June)	£44k
Baccarat	Great St Wilfrid	Ripon (6f, Aug)	£44k
Shebebi	Silver Bowl	Haydock (1m, May)	£40k

Major Irish Handicap Winners in 2013

Winner	Race	Course (Distance, Month)	Value
Brendan Brackan	Topaz Mile	Galway (1m, July)	£56k
Curley Bill	Guinness	Galway (1m4f, Aug)	£55k
Sweet Lightning	Irish Lincolnshire	Curragh (1m, Mar)	£49k
Northern Rocked	'Ahonoora'	Galway (7f, Aug)	£49k
Tandem	'Nasrullah'	Leopardstown (1m2f, July)	£49k
Moran Gra	Irish Cambridgeshire	Curragh (1m, Sep)	£49k
Sir Ector	Ulster Derby	Down Royal (1m5f, June)	£49k
Burn The Boats	Sprint	Curragh (6f, June)	£49k
Whozthecat	Rockingham	Curragh (5f, July)	£49k
Tobann	'Sovereign Path'	Leopardstown (7f, Aug)	£49k

HANDICAP STAR
Address Unknown

In the year that the Queen became the first reigning monarch to win the Gold Cup at Royal Ascot, Marwan Koukash reckoned he had something better with Address Unknown's Chester Cup triumph.

"Winning this race means everything to me," Koukash said. "Some people may take this as a surprise but for me winning this cup is better than winning the Gold Cup at Ascot, or any other race in Britain."

Address Unknown was the second Chester Cup winner for the Kuwaiti-born businessman, who has built up a big string in the past five years and in 2013 extended his sporting interests with his purchase of rugby league club Salford Reds.

Ian Williams, who gave Koukash his first Chester Cup success in 2008 with Bulwark, had trained Address Unknown up to the end of 2012 before the six-year-old was transferred to Richard Fahey – a switch that led to some confusion for his new trainer.

Address Unknown was having his first run for Fahey in the Chester Cup and was declared without his usual headgear. "I genuinely forgot," Fahey admitted. "I never even looked and had no reason to think he needed headgear. It was only when I looked at his form in the evening that I saw he usually wears a tongue-tie and visor. Marwan was as good as gold about it."

It didn't matter, as Address Unknown was always prominent under Jamie Spencer and, having struck for home early in the home straight, was able to fend off stablemate Ingleby Spirit by half a length.

The significance of winning for Koukash was not lost on Fahey, who joked: "It means I don't have to have another winner for him this week."

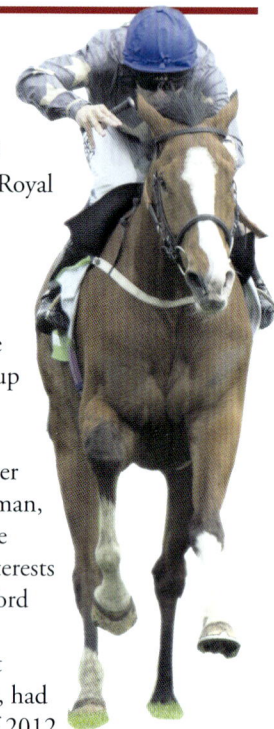

HANDICAP STAR
Maundy Money

Maundy Money is the gift that keeps on giving for trainer David Marnane and the Push The Button Syndicate and in 2013 he bounced back to top form to land his third win at the Galway festival – five years on from his previous two triumphs.

The ten-year-old, who cost just 4,500gns as a twice-raced juvenile, took his earnings past €177,000 (£150,000) with victory in the Guinness Time Handicap. It was his sixth successive year at Galway, having won twice in three days on his first visit in 2008. "He's a legend," Marnane said. "He's ten years of age and he's as fresh as paint."

GLOBETROTTER **ANIMAL KINGDOM**

"It has been up, down and up and down with this horse," Barry Irwin, co-owner of Animal Kingdom, said after the five-year-old's win in the Dubai World Cup in March.

Victory in the world's richest race was one of the ups, along with his Kentucky Derby success, but Animal Kingdom's career finished on a downbeat note when he was a well-beaten favourite in the Queen Anne Stakes at Royal Ascot.

The first part of the ambitious double bid went well. Animal Kingdom, who is trained by Maryland-based Englishman Graham Motion, became the ninth American winner of the Dubai World Cup and the first since Meydan's Tapeta replaced the dirt surface those before him enjoyed at Nad Al Sheba. He went clear early in the straight and was never threatened, scoring by two lengths from Red Cadeaux.

Animal Kingdom had been earmarked for Dubai in 2012 but was ruled out by a fracture in his left hind leg, the second he had suffered in the same leg. After all the problems, the World Cup was only his fourth run since June 2011 and credit was due to Motion for getting him back to his peak.

"This horse has been some kind of saga," Irwin said. "But we always knew he had a race like this in him. Graham did an incredible job and I'd never seen him look fitter."

Animal Kingdom's final stop before heading off to stud in Australia was Royal Ascot, where he was the year's star overseas attraction. He pulled hard early in the race, however, and finished 11th behind Declaration Of War.

It was a bitterly disappointing end and, after the excitement of Black Caviar in 2012, it was a shame for Royal Ascot and British fans that Animal Kingdom saved the worst run of his career for last. But still he retired with a record of five wins and five seconds from 12 starts, two Group/Grade 1 wins and earnings of £5.2m. Not bad for such an up-and-down horse.

UAE Group 1 Winners in 2013

Winner	Race	Course (Distance, Month)
Sajjhaa	Jebel Hatta	Meydan (1m1f, Mar)
Hunter's Light	Al Maktoum Challenge	Meydan (1m2f, Mar)
St Nicholas Abbey	Dubai Sheema Classic	Meydan (1m4f, Mar)
Reynaldothewizard	Dubai Golden Shaheen	Meydan (6f, Mar)
Sajjhaa	Dubai Duty Free	Meydan (1m1f, Mar)
Animal Kingdom	Dubai World Cup	Meydan (1m2f, Mar)
Shea Shea	Al Quoz Sprint	Meydan (5f, Mar)
Sahara Sky	Metropolitan H'cap	Belmont (1m, May)

Major US Grade 1 Winners in 2013

Winner	Race	Course (Distance, Month)
Game On Dude	Santa Anita H'cap	Santa Anita (1m2f, Mar)
Orb	Florida Derby	Gulfstream (1m1f, Mar)
Verrazano	Wood Memorial	Aqueduct (1m1f, Apr)
Java's War	Blue Grass	Keeneland (1m1f, Apr)
Princess Of Sylmar	Kentucky Oaks	Churchill Downs (1m1f, May)
Orb	Kentucky Derby	Churchill Downs (1m2f, May)
Oxbow	Preakness	Pimlico (1m2f, May)
Sahara Sky	Metropolitan H'cap	Belmont (1m, May)
Palace Malice	Belmont	Belmont (1m4f, June)
Verrazano	Haskell Invitational	Monmouth (1m1f, July)
Cross Traffic	Whitney Invitational H'cap	Saratoga (1m1f, Aug)
Dank	Beverly D	Arlington (1m2f, Aug)
Real Solution	Arlington Million	Arlington (1m2f, Aug)
Will Take Charge	Travers	Saratoga (1m2f, Aug)
Game On Dude	Pacific Classic	Del Mar (1m2f, Aug)
Alpha	Woodward	Saratoga (1m1f, Aug)
Ron The Greek	Jockey Club Gold Cup	Belmont (1m2f, Sep)

SON AND HERR History was made at Hoppegarten in July when Dennis Schiergen became the first amateur rider to win a Group 1 race in Europe.

Schiergen, 18, made all the running on Nymphea, the lesser fancied of two runners trained by his father Peter, to take the Grosser Preis von Berlin by three lengths. He stole the mile-and-a-half race from the front, building a huge lead by halfway and never looking likely to be caught.

His father, who was multiple champion jockey in Germany before finding fame as a trainer, notably with Arc and King George winner Danedream, described the ride as "perfect".

Schiergen, who was Germany's champion amateur in 2011 and 2012, has already registered more than 100 wins. He is a great talent but is already 5ft 8in and 8st 11lb, which casts doubt over whether he will be able to pursue a professional career.

"I hope I do not grow anymore," he said.

German Group 1 Winners in 2013

Winner	Race	Course (Distance, Month)
Lucky Speed	Deutsches Derby	Hamburg (1m4f, July)
Nymphea	Grosser Preis Von Berlin	Hoppegarten (1m4f, July)
Neatico	Grosser Dallmayr-Preis	Munich (1m2f, July)
Penelopa	Preis Der Diana	Dusseldorf (1m3f, Aug)
Seismos	Grosser Preis Von Bayern	Munich (1m4f, Aug)
Novellist	Grosser Preis Von Baden	Baden-Baden (1m4f, Sep)
Vif Monsieur	Preis Von Europa	Cologne (1m4f, Sep)

FLAT TRAINERS 2013

Top 20 Flat Trainers in Britain in 2013

	Wins-runs	Strike rate	Win and place prize-money £
1 Richard Hannon	222-1296	17%	3,778,256
2 Aidan O'Brien	13-73	18%	3,477,675
3 Mark Johnston	200-1395	14%	2,574,637
4 Richard Fahey	154-1211	13%	2,348,691
5 John Gosden	95-444	21%	1,836,263
6 Saeed Bin Suroor	98-473	21%	1,814,050
7 William Haggas	91-452	20%	1,670,626
8 Sir Michael Stoute	83-374	22%	1,647,407
9 Kevin Ryan	92-737	12%	1,576,673
10 Andrew Balding	93-682	14%	1,247,476
11 Charles Hills	67-506	13%	1,228,898
12 Roger Varian	78-361	22%	1,139,917
13 Roger Charlton	40-225	18%	1,084,273
14 David O'Meara	129-806	16%	1,076,281
15 Ralph Beckett	67-373	18%	1,006,028
16 Clive Cox	35-314	11%	1,003,704
17 Marco Botti	80-494	16%	971,166
18 Luca Cumani	61-305	20%	971,047
19 Jim Bolger	2-16	13%	939,089
20 Charlie Appleby	46-252	18%	852,878

Top 20 Flat Trainers in Ireland in 2013

	Wins-runs	Strike rate	Win and place prize-money €
1 Aidan O'Brien	124-458	27%	3,653,427
2 Jim Bolger	62-426	15%	2,119,985
3 Dermot Weld	57-369	15%	1,269,495
4 David Wachman	36-275	13%	1,053,115
5 Michael Halford	35-278	13%	688,280
6 Ger Lyons	29-218	13%	655,850
7 Edward Lynam	25-132	19%	513,315
8 Willie McCreery	23-199	12%	457,656
9 Kevin Prendergast	19-210	9%	454,922
10 John Gosden	1-1	100%	442,500
11 Paul Deegan	20-155	13%	401,470
12 Johnny Murtagh	14-128	11%	388,055
13 John Oxx	17-133	13%	334,557
14 Tommy Stack	17-147	12%	315,315
15 Roger Charlton	1-2	50%	282,300
16 Jessica Harrington	18-180	10%	280,520
17 David Marnane	15-161	9%	237,761
18 Andrew Oliver	18-238	8%	237,405
19 Alain de Royer-Dupre	1-1	100%	236,000
20 John Joseph Murphy	15-179	8%	230,200

BACK IN THE BIG TIME Sir Michael Stoute was the only different name in the British top ten of 2013 and it was a welcome return after a couple of years in the doldrums. The ten-times champion was away from the racecourse in the early part of the season owing to a gall bladder infection but he was back in time for Estimate's famous win in the Gold Cup at Royal Ascot, his first Group 1 triumph since Workforce's Arc in 2010. Classic success seemed possible for a while with Telescope and Liber Nauticus but in the end they were just solid Group 2 winners and Stoute's best performer on RPR was Hillstar, also a Group 2 winner in the King Edward VII Stakes.

The trainers who won most Group 1s in Britain and Ireland in 2013

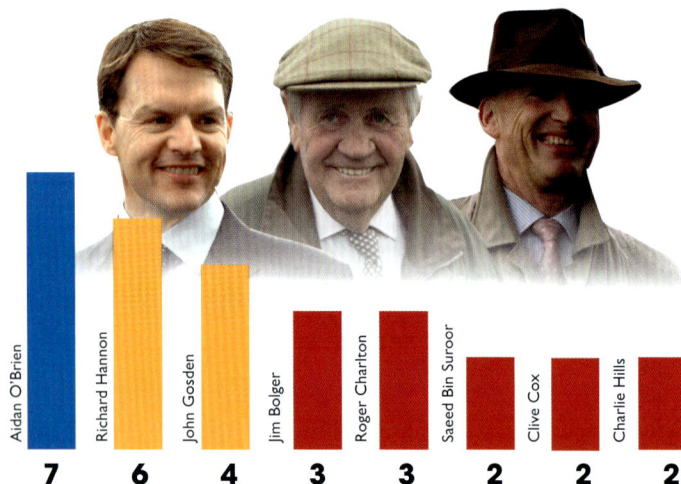

Aidan O'Brien	Richard Hannon	John Gosden	Jim Bolger	Roger Charlton	Saeed Bin Suroor	Clive Cox	Charlie Hills
7	6	4	3	3	2	2	2

HOME AND AWAY Aidan O'Brien took his usual prominent position in the Group 1 winners list but there was an unusual aspect in that only one of his victories – Magician in the Irish 2,000 Guineas –- was achieved on home soil. In Britain, meanwhile, he won Classics with Ruler Of The World (Derby) and Leading Light (St Leger) and scored other Group 1 victories with the two-year-old War Command (Dewhurst) and older horses Declaration Of War (Queen Anne, International) and St Nicholas Abbey (Coronation Cup).

FLAT JOCKEYS 2013

Top 20 Flat Jockeys in Britain in 2013

	Wins-rides	Strike rate	Win and place prize-money £
1 Richard Hughes	191-925	21%	3,403,774
2 Ryan Moore	174-826	21%	4,203,402
3 Silvestre de Sousa	127-676	19%	1,744,518
4 William Buick	109-592	18%	2,441,833
5 Neil Callan	105-629	17%	1,207,720
6 Joe Fanning	104-747	14%	1,322,964
7 Luke Morris	98-823	12%	685,460
8 Paul Hanagan	93-633	15%	1,733,531
9 Graham Lee	91-805	11%	1,145,048
10 Jim Crowley	89-594	15%	1,090,026
11 Jamie Spencer	80-529	15%	1,889,032
12 Daniel Tudhope	79-460	17%	727,875
13 James Doyle	75-538	14%	1,687,597
14 Andrea Atzeni	73-545	13%	1,146,374
15 Adam Kirby	72-565	13%	1,239,722
16 Franny Norton	70-466	15%	702,213
Dane O'Neill	70-470	15%	654,972
18 Mickael Barzalona	69-329	21%	1,029,518
Tom Queally	69-554	12%	1,366,677
20 Graham Gibbons	68-460	15%	625,255

Covers period from March 22 to October 13, 2013

Top 20 Flat Jockeys in Ireland in 2013

	Wins-rides	Strike rate	Win and place prize-money €
1 Joseph O'Brien	119-421	28%	2,916,077
2 Pat Smullen	77-555	14%	1,569,773
3 Chris Hayes	52-475	11%	1,115,921
4 Kevin Manning	47-380	12%	1,766,910
Shane Foley	47-447	11%	847,926
6 Wayne Lordan	41-417	10%	1,223,047
7 Fran Berry	7-380	10%	573,307
8 Declan McDonogh	36-292	12%	655,737
Connor King	36-314	11%	459,264
10 Colin Keane	29-206	14%	386,361
11 Billy Lee	28-300	9%	510,730
12 Johnny Murtagh	27-115	23%	1,112,670
Gary Carroll	27-326	8%	570,260
14 Seamie Heffernan	25-293	9%	1,020,850
15 Ronan Whelan	21-265	8%	505,267
16 Fergal Lynch	14-150	9%	246,536
Rory Cleary	14-280	5%	329,259
18 Emmet McNamara	13-163	8%	157,002
Niall McCullagh	13-217	6%	189,181
20 Danny Grant	12-1	46 8%	175,415

Covers period from March 24 to October 13, 2013

The jockeys who won most Group 1s in Britain and Ireland in 2013

Richard Hughes	Joseph O'Brien	Johnny Murtagh	William Buick	James Doyle	Kevin Manning	Silvestre de Sousa	Chris Hayes	Adam Kirby
8	7	5	4	4	3	2	2	2

LEADERS OF THE PACK Not so long ago this list would have looked very different but, with Godolphin and Sir Michael Stoute not the powerful forces they were and other factors playing a part, there was no place for Frankie Dettori, Ryan Moore, Paul Hanagan or Kieren Fallon.

New names appeared in 2014, as James Doyle, Chris Hayes and Adam Kirby all made the breakthrough at Group 1 level in Britain and/or Ireland, but there was room for the fortysomethings too. British Classic-winning life began at 40 for Richard Hughes, while Johnny Murtagh's five Group 1 wins came for different yards and Kevin Manning's partnership with father-in-law Jim Bolger brought him a first Irish Derby success on Trading Leather at the age of 46.

Top Five Apprentices in Britain in 2013

	Wins-rides	Strike rate	Win and place prize-money £
1 Jason Hart	43-328	13%	261,991
2 Thomas Brown	39-219	18%	238,042
3 Oisin Murphy	32-210	15%	295,156
4 Connor Beasley	31-265	12%	240,595
5 George Chaloner	29-203	14%	270,008
Robert Tart	29-309	9%	282,697

Top Five Apprentices in Ireland in 2013

	Wins-rides	Strike rate	Win and place prize-money €
1 Connor King	36-314	11%	459,264
2 Colin Keane	29-206	14%	386,361
3 Gary Carroll	27-326	8%	570,260
4 Ronan Whelan	21-265	8%	505,267
5 Emmet McNamara	13-163	8%	157,002

FLAT OWNERS 2013

SKY HIGH Ben Keswick is a one-horse owner but it is not through lack of finance and his one horse, Sky Lantern, has been something special for the Hong Kong-based businessman.

Keswick is the fifth generation of his family to be a 'taipan' of Jardine Matheson, the Hong Kong conglomerate where he is chairman and managing director. He limits himself to only one yearling purchase each year and his colours were little known in Britain until Sky Lantern, who cost €75,000, became his first horse in training with Richard Hannon.

After four Group 1 wins, Keswick's investment has been repaid more than ten times over and the grey filly's achievements include Classic victory in the 1,000 Guineas and a thrilling Royal Ascot success in the Coronation Stakes.

"I have lost my voice and it's incredibly exciting," Keswick said after the Coronation. "It's just the most amazing feeling and well done to the Hannons. It's very special for us."

Top 20 Flat Owners in Britain in 2013

	Wins-runs	Strike rate	Win and place prize-money £
1 Godolphin	149-741	20%	2,934,615
2 Hamdan Al Maktoum	99-581	17%	1,577,764
3 Mrs John Magnier	23-130	18%	1,260,836
4 Sheikh Hamdan Bin Mohammed Al Maktoum	93-607	15%	1,167,269
5 M Tabor	22-122	18%	1,163,751
6 K Abdullah	77-325	24%	1,090,855
7 Dr Marwan Koukash	77-575	13%	934,860
8 Derrick Smith	20-97	21%	921,958
9 Qatar Racing Limited	33-224	15%	786,700
10 Cheveley Park Stud	48-229	21%	720,284
11 Mrs J S Bolger	2-13	15%	679,785
12 D J Deer	8-55	15%	679,382
13 B Keswick	3-6	50%	625,044
14 Dr Christoph Berglar	1-1	100%	603,962
15 Alan Craddock	4-13	31%	599,892
16 Sheikh Joaan Al Thani	6-27	22%	493,353
17 Sheikh Mohammed Obaid Al Maktoum	20-74	27%	485,791
18 Saeed Manana	42-282	15%	478,768
19 Saleh Al Homaizi & Imad Al Sagar	19-97	20%	447,537
20 Hubert John Strecker	3-12	25%	401,379

Covers period from November 14, 2012 to October 13, 2013

Top 20 Flat Owners in Ireland in 2013

	Wins-runs	Strike rate	Win and place prize-money €
1 Mrs J S Bolger	37-322	11%	1,735,517
2 Michael Tabor & Derrick Smith & Mrs John Magnier	30-110	27%	1,108,485
3 Mrs John Magnier & Michael Tabor & Derrick Smith	37-144	26%	1,102,195
4 Derrick Smith & Mrs John Magnier & Michael Tabor	38-149	26%	918,610
5 Andrew Tinkler	17-128	13%	457,165
6 Lord Lloyd-Webber	1-1	100%	442,500
7 Lady O'Reilly	6-74	8%	282,485
8 D J Deer	1-2	50%	282,300
9 K Abdullah	9-42	21%	273,195
10 Michael O'Flynn	0-9	0%	272,585
11 Hamdan Al Maktoum	14-92	15%	252,030
12 Paul Makin	1-1	100%	236,000
13 Mrs Fitri Hay/Mrs John Magnier	3-6	50%	231,950
14 H H Aga Khan	11-100	11%	207,397
15 J Vasicek	3-14	21%	200,090
16 Sean Jones	0-59	17%	179,630
17 Qatar Racing Limited & Sangster Family	1-1	100%	177,000
18 K Leavy/L Cribben/ Mrs A McCreery	4-6	67%	162,500
19 Anamoine Limited	5-38	13%	162,175
20 Jaber Abdullah	11-51	22%	149,435

Covers period from March 24 to October 13, 2013

SHOP WINDOW No sooner had Chicquita won the Irish Oaks for Paul Makin than the Australian owner decided it was time to sell her, as part of a high-quality dispersal sale at Goffs in November.

"This is just another chapter in the Paul Makin story," Goffs' Australasian representative Mark Player said. "He enjoys building up a strong collection of racing and breeding stock, but he also enjoys the challenge of beginning the process all over again."

Makin certainly made the right choice in entrusting Chicquita to Alain de Royer-Dupre (left, with the filly). The trainer personally supervised the filly throughout her journey from Chantilly and for 48 hours once she was at the racecourse stables, walking her for an hour on the morning of the race. Royer-Dupre's care led to both Classic success and a higher value for Chicquita.

The 2008 Ryanair Chase winner Our Vic leads the string at the British Racing School in Newmarket in September. Now aged 15, the 13-time winning chaser is one of 68 former racehorses who help the school's aspiring jockeys to hone their riding skills

Two-mile chaser

SPRINTER SACRE

Trainer **Nicky Henderson**
Owner **Caroline Mould**

RACING POST RATINGS

Sprinter Sacre	190
Sizing Europe	173
Sanctuaire	171
Cue Card	170
Rubi Light	168

Sprinter Sacre, with a Racing Post Rating of 176, was champion two-miler even as a novice in 2011-12 and it was no surprise that he took a stranglehold on the division in his first season in the senior ranks. He improved fully a stone on RPR to 190, which he recorded in the Queen Mother Champion Chase with a 19-length defeat of

the 2011 winner Sizing Europe, his nearest rival among the two-milers. Such was Sprinter Sacre's dominance of the division that even his lowest RPR in 2012-13 was 5lb higher than Sizing Europe's best.

Two-and-a-half-mile chaser

SPRINTER SACRE

Trainer **Nicky Henderson**
Owner **Caroline Mould**

RACING POST RATINGS

Sprinter Sacre	190
Cue Card	178
Al Ferof	172
Sizing Europe	172
Menorah	172

Sprinter Sacre, having easily beaten all-comers over two miles, did the same over an extra half-mile when he won the

Melling Chase at Aintree by four and a half lengths from Cue Card. That performance was given a Racing Post Rating of 190, the same as his Queen Mother Champion Chase win at Cheltenham, and made him a dual champion. The admirable Cue Card had won the Ryanair Chase by nine lengths from First Lieutenant but was no match for Sprinter Sacre despite improving again at Aintree.

Three-mile-plus chaser

BOBS WORTH

Trainer **Nicky Henderson**
Owner **The Not Afraid Partnership**

RACING POST RATINGS

Bobs Worth	181
Silviniaco Conti	175
Long Run	174
Sir Des Champs	174
Tidal Bay	174

Like his stablemate Sprinter Sacre, Bobs Worth improved a stone as he stepped up from the novice ranks to secure senior honours despite having only two races. He could not match the heights of Sprinter Sacre but his fighting spirit and love of Cheltenham saw him record a Racing Post Rating of 181 as he took the Cheltenham Gold Cup by seven lengths from Sir Des Champs. The second-best performance in the division came in the Denman Chase from Silviniaco Conti, subsequently a faller in the Gold Cup and beaten favourite in the Betfred Bowl.

Novice chaser

SIMONSIG

Trainer **Nicky Henderson**
Owner **Ronnie Bartlett**

RACING POST RATINGS

Simonsig	167
Dynaste	165
Arvika Ligeonniere	164
Overturn	162
Sire De Grugy	162

Simonsig, champion novice hurdler in 2011-12, stepped up to take the novice chaser title with an unbeaten campaign that numbered just three runs. His most prestigious victory came in the Arkle Chase at Cheltenham with a Racing Post Rating of 163, but his best performance on RPR was the 167 he recorded at Kempton's Christmas meeting. The same meeting saw the next-best performance when Dynaste won the Feltham Novices' Chase with an RPR of 165 – a mark he almost matched at Aintree in the spring after being defeated by Benefficient in the Jewson at Cheltenham.

Two-mile hurdler

HURRICANE FLY

Trainer **Willie Mullins**
Owner **George Creighton and Rose Boyd**

RACING POST RATINGS

Hurricane Fly	173
Rock On Ruby	170
Countrywide Flame	169
Go Native	168
Darlan	167

Hurricane Fly was the best two-mile hurdler for the third season in a row after becoming only the second horse to regain the Champion Hurdle crown. He recorded a Racing Post Rating of 173 at Cheltenham – his best mark at the course and only the third time in his career he has reached that

level. A perfect season of five top-level victories took his total of Grade 1 wins to a remarkable 16. The second-best RPR was also recorded in the Champion Hurdle by Rock On Ruby, who was only 1lb below his 2012 winning mark as he finished runner-up to Hurricane Fly.

Two-and-a-half mile-plus hurdler

BIG BUCK'S

Trainer **Paul Nicholls**
Owner **The Stewart family**

RACING POST RATINGS

Big Buck's	175
Oscar Whisky	170
Reve De Sivola	166
Solwhit	165
Quevega	164

Big Buck's appeared only once in the 2012-13 season but his nine-length victory over Reve De Sivola at Newbury was enough to keep him comfortably on top of the stayers' division.

This was the fifth consecutive season that Big Buck's was the top staying hurdler and either the best or joint-best overall hurdler – on this occasion he was 2lb ahead of Hurricane Fly overall. Once Big Buck's was ruled out for the season with a leg injury, Solwhit was the big winner among the stayers with victories at Cheltenham and Aintree, but nevertheless he was well below the standard set by the absent champion.

Novice hurdler

CHAMPAGNE FEVER

Trainer **Willie Mullins**
Owner **Susannah Ricci**

OUR CONOR

Trainer **Dessie Hughes**
Owner **Barry Connell**

THE NEW ONE

Trainer **Nigel Twiston-Davies**
Owner **Sarah Such**

RACING POST RATINGS

Champagne Fever	164
Our Conor	164
The New One	164
My Tent Or Yours	163
Jezki	162

There was little to choose between an exceptionally talented group of novice hurdlers all season and in the end Racing Post Ratings could not split Champagne Fever, Our Conor and The New One. Champagne Fever was first to record an RPR of 164 in winning the Supreme Novices' Hurdle at Cheltenham, followed three days later by Our Conor in the Triumph Hurdle. The New One was also a Cheltenham winner, in the Neptune Novices' Hurdle, but recorded his best mark in finishing second to Zarkandar in the Aintree Hurdle.

JUMPS WINNERS 2012-13

British Grade 1 Winners in 2012-13

Winner	Race	Course (Distance, Month)
Silviniaco Conti	Betfair Chase	Haydock (3m, Nov)
Countrywide Flame	Fighting Fifth Hurdle	Newcastle (2m, Dec)
Captain Conan	Henry VIII Nov Chase	Sandown (2m, Dec)
Sprinter Sacre	Tingle Creek Chase	Sandown (2m, Dec)
Reve De Sivola	Long Walk Hurdle	Ascot (3m1f, Dec)
Long Run	King George VI Chase	Kempton (3m, Dec)
Darlan	Christmas Hurdle	Kempton (2m, Dec)
Dynaste	Feltham Nov Chase	Kempton (3m, Dec)
Taquin Du Seuil	Challow Nov Hurdle	Newbury (2m5f, Dec)
Melodic Rendezvous	32red Nov Hurdle	Sandown (2m1f, Jan)
Ruacana	Finale Juv Hurdle	Chepstow (2m1f, Jan)
Sprinter Sacre	Victor Chandler Chase	Cheltenham (2m1f, Jan)
Captain Conan	Challengers Nov Chase	Sandown (2m5f, Feb)
Cue Card	Ascot Chase	Ascot (2m6f, Feb)
Hurricane Fly	Champion Hurdle	Cheltenham (2m1f, Mar)
Champagne Fever	Supreme Nov Hurdle	Cheltenham (2m1f, Mar)
Simonsig	Arkle Chase	Cheltenham (2m, Mar)
Lord Windermere	RSA Chase	Cheltenham (3m1f, Mar)
Sprinter Sacre	Queen Mother Champion Ch	Cheltenham (2m, Mar)
Briar Hill	Champion Bumper	Cheltenham (2m1f, Mar)
The New One	Neptune Nov Hurdle	Cheltenham (2m5f, Mar)
Cue Card	Ryanair Chase	Cheltenham (2m5f, Mar)
Solwhit	World Hurdle	Cheltenham (3m, Mar)
Our Conor	Triumph Hurdle	Cheltenham (2m1f, Mar)
Bobs Worth	Gold Cup Chase	Cheltenham (3m3f, Mar)
At Fishers Cross	Albert Bartlett Nov Hurdle	Cheltenham (3m, Mar)
L'Unique	Anniversary 4yo Juv Hurdle	Aintree (2m1f, Apr)
Zarkandar	Aintree Hurdle	Aintree (2m4f, Apr)
Captain Conan	Manifesto Nov Chase	Aintree (2m4f, Apr)
First Lieutenant	Betfred Bowl Chase	Aintree (3m1f, Apr)
Sprinter Sacre	Melling Chase	Aintree (2m4f, Apr)
At Fishers Cross	Sefton Nov Hurdle	Aintree (3m1f, Apr)
Solwhit	Liverpool Hurdle	Aintree (3m1f, Apr)
Special Tiara	Maghull Nov Chase	Aintree (2m, Apr)

Irish Grade 1 Winners in 2012-13

Winner	Course	(Distance, Month)
Kauto Stone	Champion Chase	Down Royal (3m, Nov)
Hurricane Fly	Morgiana Hurdle	Punchestown (2m, Nov)
Arvika Ligeonniere	Drinmore Nov Chase	Fairyhouse (2m4f, Dec)
Jezki	Royal Bond Nov Hurdle	Fairyhouse (2m, Dec)
Zaidpour	Hatton's Grace Hurdle	Fairyhouse (2m4f, Dec)
Flemenstar	John Durkan Memorial Chase	Punchestown (2m4f, Dec)
Pont Alexandre	Navan Nov Hurdle	Navan (2m4f, Dec)
Arvika Ligeonniere	Racing Post Nov Chase	Leopardstown (2m1f, Dec)
Sizing Europe	Paddy Power Dial-A-Bet Chase	Leopardstown (2m1f, Dec)
Jezki	Future Champions Nov Hurdle	Leopardstown (2m, Dec)
Tidal Bay	Lexus Chase	Leopardstown (3m, Dec)
Back In Focus	Topaz Nov Chase	Leopardstown (3m, Dec)
Hurricane Fly	Festival Hurdle	Leopardstown (2m, Dec)
Benefficient	Arkle Nov Chase	Leopardstown (2m1f, Jan)
Hurricane Fly	Irish Champion Hurdle	Leopardstown (2m, Jan)
Boston Bob	Dr P J Moriarty Nov Chase	Leopardstown (2m5f, Feb)
Our Conor	Spring Juvenile Hurdle	Leopardstown (2m, Feb)
Champagne Fever	Deloitte Nov Hurdle	Leopardstown (2m2f, Feb)
Sir Des Champs	Hennessy Gold Cup	Leopardstown (3m, Feb)
Annie Power	Mares Nov Hurdle Championship	Fairyhouse (2m4f, Mar)
Realt Mor	Powers Gold Cup	Fairyhouse (2m4f, Mar)
Jezki	Champion Nov Hurdle	Punchestown (2m, Apr)
Mount Benbulben	Champion Nov Chase	Punchestown (3m1f, Apr)
Sprinter Sacre	Champion Chase	Punchestown (2m, Apr)
Morning Assembly	Irish Daily Mirror Nov Hurdle	Punchestown (3m, Apr)
Sir Des Champs	Punchestown Gold Cup	Punchestown (3m1f, Apr)
The Liquidator	Champion INH Flat Race	Punchestown (2m, Apr)
Arvika Ligeonniere	Ryanair Nov Chase	Punchestown (2m, Apr)
Quevega	Ladbrokes World Series Hurdle	Punchestown (3m, Apr)
Un Atout	Champion Nov Hurdle	Punchestown (2m4f, Apr)
Hurricane Fly	Rabobank Champion Hurdle	Punchestown (2m, Apr)
Diakali	AES Champion 4yo Hurdle	Punchestown (2m, Apr)
Glens Melody	ITBA Mares Hurdle	Punchestown (2m2f, Apr)

The horses who won most Grade 1s in Britain and Ireland in 2012-13

Hurricane Fly	Sprinter Sacre	Captain Conan	Arvika Ligeonniere	Jezki	At Fishers Cross	Cue Card	Champagne Fever	Our Conor	Sir Des Champs	Solwhit
5	5	3	3	3	2	2	2	2	2	2

Simonsig   Bobs Worth   Sprinter Sacre   Hurricane Fly   Our Conor   At Fishers Cross

THE UNTOUCHABLES
The Cheltenham stars who completed perfect seasons in 2012-13

Sprinter Sacre Five races, five wins (all G1) *Highlight* Hitting an RPR of 190 at both Cheltenham and Aintree *Best RPR* 190

Hurricane Fly Five races, five wins (all G1) *Highlight* Regaining his Champion Hurdle crown *Best RPR* 173

Bobs Worth Two races, two wins (one G1, one G3) *Highlight* Justifying favouritism in the Cheltenham Gold Cup *Best RPR* 181

Simonsig Three races, three wins (one G1, two G2) *Highlight* Winning the G1 Arkle Chase from Baily Green *Best RPR* 167

Our Conor Four races, four wins (two G1, one G3) *Highlight* Runaway 15l success in the Triumph Hurdle *Best RPR* 164

At Fishers Cross Six races, six wins (two G1, one G2) *Highlight* Cheltenham-Aintree G1 double *Best RPR* 156

The trainers and jockeys who won most Grade 1s in Britain and Ireland in 2012-13

Trainers

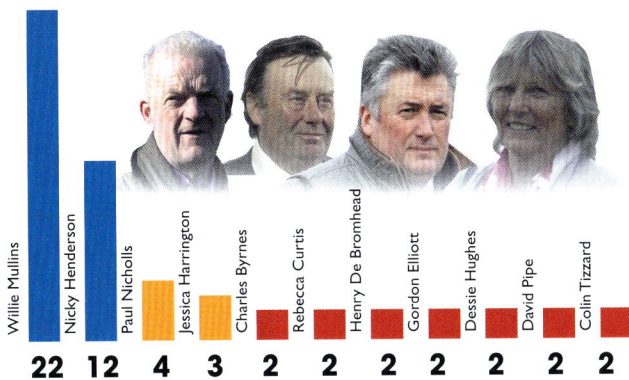

Willie Mullins	Nicky Henderson	Paul Nicholls	Jessica Harrington	Charles Byrnes	Rebecca Curtis	Henry De Bromhead	Gordon Elliott	Dessie Hughes	David Pipe	Colin Tizzard
22	12	4	3	2	2	2	2	2	2	2

Jockeys

Ruby Walsh	Barry Geraghty	Bryan Cooper	Tony McCoy	Davy Russell	Paul Townend	Paul Carberry	Davy Condon	Andrew Lynch	Denis O'Regan	Joe Tizzard
19	12	5	4	4	3	2	2	2	2	2

THE LIST

Cheltenham Festival first-timers in 2013

Jockeys

Brendan Powell Golden Chieftain (JLT Specialty Handicap Chase)

Bryan Cooper Benefficient (Jewson Novices' Chase), Our Conor (JCB Triumph Hurdle), Ted Veale (Vincent O'Brien County Hurdle)

Liam Treadwell Carrickboy (Byrne Group Plate)

Ryan Hatch Same Difference (Fulke Walwyn Kim Muir Handicap Chase)

Harry Derham Salubrious (Martin Pipe Conditional Jockeys' Handicap Hurdle)

Trainers

Jim Culloty Lord Windermere (RSA Chase)

Peter Maher Big Shu (Glenfarclas Cross Country Handicap Chase)

JUMPS WINNERS 2012-13

Big Handicap Chase Winners in Britain 2012-13

Winner	Race	Course (Distance, Month)	Value
Auroras Encore	Grand National	Aintree (4m4f, Apr)	£547k
Godsmejudge	Scottish Grand National	Ayr (4m1f, Apr)	£103k
Al Ferof	Paddy Power Gold Cup	Cheltenham (2m5f, Nov)	£91k
Quentin Collonges	Bet365 Gold Cup	Sandown (3m6f, Apr)	£85k
Bobs Worth	Hennessy Gold Cup	Newbury (3m3f, Dec)	£85k
Triolo D'Alene	Topham	Aintree (2m6f, Apr)	£68k
Hello Bud	Becher	Aintree (3m2f, Dec)	£62k
Unioniste	P Stewart Ironspine Gold Cup	Cheltenham (2m5f, Dec)	£60k
Opening Batsman	Racing Plus	Kempton (3m, Feb)	£57k
Roberto Goldback	United House Gold Cup	Ascot (3m, Nov)	£56k
Carrickboy	Byrne Group Plate	Cheltenham (2m5f, Mar)	£51k
Golden Chieftain	JLT Specialty	Cheltenham (3m1f, Mar)	£51k
Monbeg Dude	Coral Welsh National	Cheltenham (3m6f, Jan)	£51k
Alderwood	Grand Annual	Cheltenham (2m1f, Mar)	£51k
Big Occasion	Midlands National	Uttoxeter (4m2f, Mar)	£46k
Oiseau De Nuit	Red Rum	Aintree (2m, Apr)	£46k
Well Refreshed	Grand National Trial	Haydock (3m4f, Feb)	£43k

Big Handicap Hurdle Winners in Britain 2012-13

Winner	Race	Course (Distance, Month)	Value
My Tent Or Yours	Betfair	Newbury (2m1f, Feb)	£87k
Cause Of Causes	The Ladbroke	Ascot (2m, Dec)	£84k
Olofi	Racing Post	Cheltenham (2m1f, Nov)	£57k
Holywell	Pertemps Final	Cheltenham (3m, Mar)	£46k
Trustan Times	"Fixed Brush"	Haydock (3m, Nov)	£46k
Ted Veale	County	Cheltenham (2m1f, Mar)	£46k
Medinas	Coral Cup	Cheltenham (2m5f, Mar)	£46k
Flaxen Flare	Fred Winter	Cheltenham (2m1f, Mar)	£42k
First Avenue	Imperial Cup	Sandown (2m1f, Mar)	£40k

Big Handicap Chase Winners in Ireland 2012-13

Winner	Race	Course (Distance, Month)	Value
Liberty Counsel	Irish Grand National	Fairyhouse (3m5f, Apr)	£114k
Bob Lingo	Galway Plate	Galway (2m6f, Aug)	£100k
Colbert Station	Paddy Power	Leopardstown (3m, Dec)	£89k
Faltering Fullback	Kerry National	Listowel (3m, Sep)	£80k
Tofino Bay	Troytown	Navan (3m, Nov)	£43k
Jadanli	Thyestes	Gowran Park (3m1f, Jan)	£42k
Madam Bovary	Aon Nov	Punchestown (2m5f, Apr)	£40k
Klepht	Guinness	Punchestown (2m4f, Apr)	£40k
Raz De Maree	Munster National	Limerick (3m, Oct)	£40k
Lastoftheleaders	Dan Moore Memorial	Punchestown (2m, Feb)	£40k
Farrells Fancy	Leopardstown	Leopardstown (2m5f, Jan)	£39k
Like Your Style	Aon	Punchestown (2m5f, May)	£39k

Big Handicap Hurdle Winners in Ireland 2012-13

Winner	Race	Course (Distance, Month)	Value
Rebel Fitz	Galway	Galway (2m, Aug)	£131k
Abbey Lane	Boylesports.com	Leopardstown (2m, Jan)	£49k
The Paparrazi Kid	Setanta Sports	Punchestown (2m4f, Apr)	£40k

HANDICAP STAR Jupiter Rex

Venetia Williams set a personal-best of 90 winners in 2012-13 and nothing illustrated her mastery of training and placing horses better than Jupiter Rex's handicap seven-timer in the first three months of the year. Joint-owner Julia Young's husband Tim said: "Venetia spends hours studying form and has all sorts of different marks over her Racing Post," he said. "I don't understand what they all mean but her strategy clearly works and we're very grateful to her."

Ireland 14, Britain 13

The 27th and final race of the 2013 Cheltenham Festival, the Johnny Henderson Grand Annual Chase, came down to this: two JP McManus-owned horses, Alderwood and Kid Cassidy, one representing Ireland, the other Britain. The Nicky Henderson-trained Kid Cassidy led over the final obstacle but on the extended run-in (owing to the last fence being omitted) Alderwood, the 3-1 favourite from Tom Mullins' yard, forged ahead. Victory was Ireland's, not just in the race but also in the annual battle with Britain at the festival. Alderwood was the 14th winner for Ireland, a record score and the first time the raiders had beaten the home team.

Ireland also had the top trainer (Willie Mullins with five wins) and top jockey (Ruby Walsh, four wins) at their most successful festival, which beat the previous-best score of 13 in 2011.

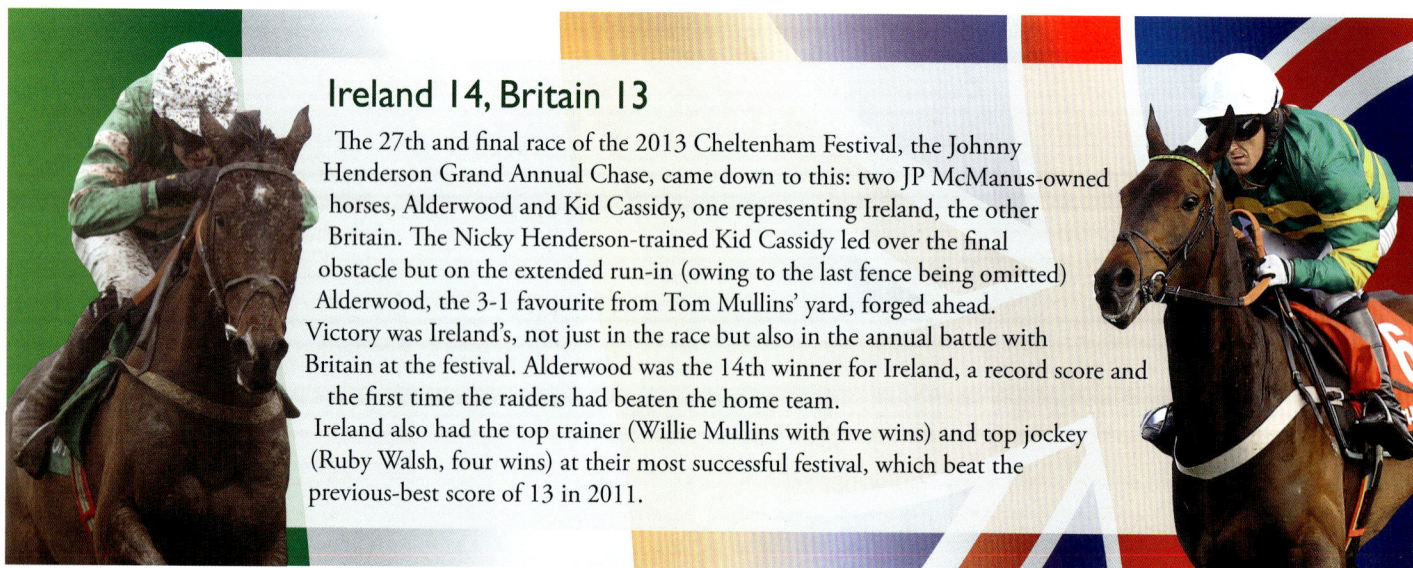

Top ten earning horses in Britain and Ireland in 2012-13

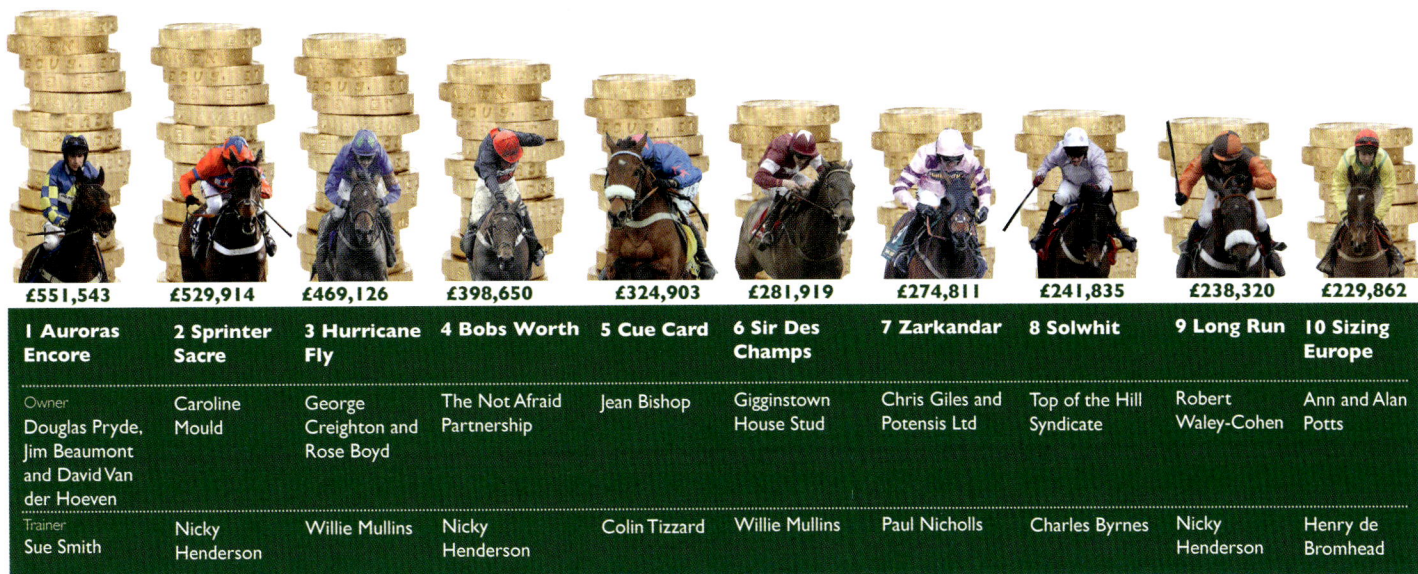

	1 Auroras Encore	2 Sprinter Sacre	3 Hurricane Fly	4 Bobs Worth	5 Cue Card	6 Sir Des Champs	7 Zarkandar	8 Solwhit	9 Long Run	10 Sizing Europe
	£551,543	£529,914	£469,126	£398,650	£324,903	£281,919	£274,811	£241,835	£238,320	£229,862
Owner	Douglas Pryde, Jim Beaumont and David Van der Hoeven	Caroline Mould	George Creighton and Rose Boyd	The Not Afraid Partnership	Jean Bishop	Gigginstown House Stud	Chris Giles and Potensis Ltd	Top of the Hill Syndicate	Robert Waley-Cohen	Ann and Alan Potts
Trainer	Sue Smith	Nicky Henderson	Willie Mullins	Nicky Henderson	Colin Tizzard	Willie Mullins	Paul Nicholls	Charles Byrnes	Nicky Henderson	Henry de Bromhead

HANDICAP STAR
Well Refreshed

The Gary Moore-trained gelding made an inauspicious chasing debut on his first start of 2012-13 when he unseated Josh Moore at the second fence of a Class 4 beginners' chase at Fontwell, but within a few months he had become one of the most improved chasers in training and a Grade 3 winner in the Grand National Trial at Haydock.

Well Refreshed started his rise off a mark of 100 when he returned to Fontwell three weeks after his mishap and won a Class 5 handicap chase easily. That was the first of four successes culminating in his marathon victory at Haydock, punctuated only by a fall at Lingfield (the winner that day, Pete The Feat, was also on a rapid rise up the ratings).

After his ten-length Haydock victory, trainer and jockey reflected on his journey. "He'd be unbeaten over fences but for those falls and even there he split the last almost in half, which was his fault as Josh asked him and he put down," said Gary Moore. Josh added: "We like to switch him off at the back and pick through a race because he's not a natural jumper but if you get him into a rhythm he is all right. He has done better than we imagined this season."

Unfortunately, a crack at the bet365 Gold Cup on the final day of the season proved a step too far – at least for now – when he was pulled up, but still he finished the season a remarkable 41lb higher than he started.

Trainers with most win prize-money in British and Irish handicaps worth at least £30,000 in 2012-13

£547,268	£395,688	£244,586	£191,913	£179,350	£135,983	£132,409	£130,500	£127,118	£117,915	£116,705	£114,634	£113,719
1 win	7 wins	5 wins	3 wins	3 wins	3 wins	3 wins	1 win	2 wins	2 wins	3 wins	1 win	3 wins
Sue Smith	Nicky Henderson	Paul Nicholls	Thomas Mullins	Alan King	Nigel Twiston-Davies	Colin Tizzard	Michael Winters	Gordon Elliott	Henry Daly	Venetia Williams	Dot Love	Dessie Hughes

JUMPS TRAINERS 2012-13

Top 20 Jumps Trainers in Britain in 2012-13

	Wins-runs	Strike rate	Win and place prize-money £
1 Nicky Henderson	125-509	25%	2,924,916
2 Paul Nicholls	131-565	23%	2,375,584
3 David Pipe	104-624	17%	1,142,417
4 Alan King	60-419	14%	1,066,685
5 Nigel Twiston-Davies	74-542	14%	1,026,313
6 Donald McCain	141-734	19%	992,457
7 Venetia Williams	90-533	17%	967,578
8 Philip Hobbs	68-504	13%	902,487
9 Sue Smith	31-276	11%	822,155
10 Colin Tizzard	43-311	14%	812,834
11 Evan Williams	57-506	11%	703,297
12 Jonjo O'Neill	90-705	13%	692,664
13 Willie Mullins	6-51	12%	688,530
14 Rebecca Curtis	49-210	23%	562,662
15 Tom George	39-243	16%	478,434
16 Tim Vaughan	85-646	13%	477,422
17 Lucinda Russell	59-478	12%	408,617
18 Gary Moore	33-282	12%	397,606
19 Peter Bowen	48-365	13%	378,662
20 Charlie Longsdon	54-404	13%	343,229

Top 20 Jumps Trainers in Ireland in 2012-13

	Wins-runs	Strike rate	Win and place prize-money €
1 Willie Mullins	193-595	32%	3,908,059
2 Gordon Elliott	54-329	16%	1,042,995
3 Dessie Hughes	51-366	14%	918,475
4 Noel Meade	47-344	14%	713,922
5 Henry de Bromhead	32-220	15%	665,450
6 Jessica Harrington	28-252	11%	603,833
7 Tony Martin	34-248	14%	543,822
8 Mouse Morris	21-142	15%	423,095
9 Thomas Mullins	10-97	10%	349,270
10 Paul Nolan	14-167	8%	307,947
11 Michael Winters	8-55	15%	295,750
12 Eddie Harty	10-77	13%	282,685
13 Michael Hourigan	15-240	6%	275,985
14 Edward O'Grady	16-193	8%	265,950
15 Eoin Doyle	21-182	12%	249,807
16 Oliver McKiernan	14-119	12%	242,355
17 Philip Rothwell	19-351	5%	239,990
18 Colm Murphy	16-121	13%	239,003
19 Dot Love	7-45	16%	230,482
20 Ted Walsh	11-37	30%	227,470

A LONG WAIT Nicky Henderson finally overhauled Paul Nicholls to become British champion jumps trainer for the third time, regaining the crown after a gap of 26 years. Having finished runner-up to Nicholls in the previous four seasons, Henderson put together the strongest squad of his 35-year career to beat Nicholls by almost £560,000.

"It's been a long time since this last happened," Henderson said. "A comeback is a bit weird but we've been knocking on the door and it's nice to finish back on top."

In the years since Henderson landed back-to-back titles in 1985-86 and 1986-87, only four trainers had been crowned champion – David Elsworth (once), Martin Pipe (15 times), David Nicholson (twice) and Nicholls (seven times).

When Henderson was last champion …

Margaret Thatcher was Prime Minister

Madonna was No.1 with La Isla Bonita

The average price of a pint of lager was 92p

Bobby Robson was England manager

JUMP JOCKEYS 2012-13

Top 20 Jump Jockeys in Britain in 2012-13

	Wins-rides	Strike rate	Win and place prize-money £
1 Tony McCoy	185-848	22%	1,734,591
2 Jason Maguire	144-747	19%	1,033,534
3 Richard Johnson	133-830	16%	1,241,996
4 Aidan Coleman	89-575	15%	795,143
5 Sam Twiston-Davies	87-615	14%	1,020,575
6 Tom Scudamore	85-546	16%	849,379
7 Daryl Jacob	73-419	17%	816,162
8 Tom O'Brien	70-457	15%	519,269
9 Nick Scholfield	66-505	13%	550,645
10 Noel Fehily	64-389	16%	675,758
11 Paddy Brennan	63-457	14%	623,381
12 Paul Moloney	60-517	12%	674,544
13 Ruby Walsh	57-211	27%	1,769,831
Barry Geraghty	57-225	25%	1,916,082
15 Dougie Costello	53-471	11%	445,788
16 Denis O'Regan	50-397	13%	531,552
17 Jamie Moore	47-477	10%	514,410
18 James Reveley	46-322	14%	282,454
19 Brian Hughes	44-455	10%	296,000
20 Wayne Hutchinson	38-304	13%	735,317
Lucy Alexander	38-383	10%	215,482

Top 20 Jump Jockeys in Ireland in 2012-13

	Wins-rides	Strike rate	Win and place prize-money €
1 Davy Russell	103-549	19%	2,099,277
2 Ruby Walsh	101-340	30%	2,174,790
3 Paul Townend	71-411	17%	1,437,665
4 Mr Patrick Mullins	63-189	33%	576,274
5 Bryan Cooper	61-489	12%	1,120,471
6 Paul Carberry	46-391	12%	773,425
7 Barry Geraghty	41-309	13%	845,137
8 Andrew Lynch	36-344	10%	915,220
9 Mark Enright	35-316	11%	518,925
10 Mark Walsh	32-357	9%	728,430
Davy Condon	32-369	9%	655,245
12 Andrew McNamara	31-377	8%	446,582
13 Robbie Power	30-253	12%	563,416
14 Phillip Enright	25-367	7%	354,980
15 Adrian Heskin	24-322	7%	317,207
16 Ms Nina Carberry	23-121	19%	226,697
17 Brian O'Connell	21-341	6%	290,812
18 David Casey	20-263	8%	384,280
Niall Madden	20-267	7%	270,055
20 Danny Mullins	19-187	10%	400,297

Tony McCoy was top dog in Britain on number of winners but in other significant respects his figures were bettered by two of his biggest rivals, Ruby Walsh and Barry Geraghty

McCoy ■ Walsh ■ Geraghty ■

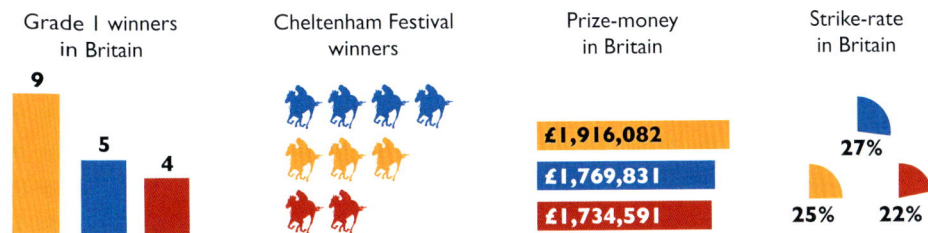

Grade 1 winners in Britain
9
5
4

Cheltenham Festival winners

Prize-money in Britain
£1,916,082
£1,769,831
£1,734,591

Strike-rate in Britain
27%
25% 22%

15 JANUARY The date McCoy could have called time on his season and still been crowned British champion jump jockey for the 18th year in a row. At Ffos Las that day he rode his 145th winner of the 2012-13 season and it was a mark none of his rivals could reach over the remaining three and a half months of the campaign, while McCoy moved serenely on to 185

How the champions compare

Tony McCoy		Davy Russell
39	Age	34
18	Titles	2
(Britain) 185	Winners	103 (Ireland)
41	Winning margin	2
22%	Strike-rate	19%
-104.90	Profit/loss	-107.34
Jonjo O'Neill	Trainer giving most winners	Gordon Elliott
4	Grade 1 wins in 2012-13	4
2	Cheltenham Festival wins in 2013	1

JUMPS OWNERS 2012-13

Top 20 Jumps Owners in Britain in 2012-13

		Wins-runs	Strike rate	Win and place prize-money £
1	John P McManus	95-585	16%	1,143,289
2	Mrs Caroline Mould	4-20	20%	466,840
3	The Not Afraid Partnership	2-2	100%	398,650
4	Gigginstown House Stud	2-38	5%	376,226
5	Chris Giles	18-66	27%	362,922
6	Mrs Jean Bishop	5-19	26%	350,429
7	Potensis Limited	13-50	26%	348,800
8	Mrs Diane Whateley	12-55	22%	347,658
9	Robert Waley-Cohen	6-29	21%	341,117
10	Simon Munir	15-67	22%	301,431
11	Mr and Mrs William Rucker	10-57	18%	286,475
12	D G Pryde	1-10	10%	277,165
13	Trevor Hemmings	25-179	14%	276,035
14	Andrea and Graham Wylie	10-42	24%	264,017
15	Top of the Hill Syndicate	2-2	100%	224,137
16	David Johnson	18-79	23%	209,774
17	Walters Plant Hire Limited	22-97	23%	197,996
18	McNeill Family	3-28	11%	182,561
19	Tim Leslie	22-108	20%	180,362
20	Favourites Racing	5-55	9%	168,537

Top 20 Jumps Owners in Ireland in 2012-13

		Wins-runs	Strike rate	Win and place prize-money €
1	Gigginstown House Stud	101-504	20%	2,025,420
2	John P McManus	81-781	10%	1,610,210
3	Mrs S Ricci	43-118	36%	1,047,340
4	Ann & Alan Potts Partnership	23-81	28%	440,120
5	Barry Connell	26-136	19%	343,787
6	George Creighton & Mrs Rose Boyd	4-4	100%	299,000
7	Andrea & Graham Wylie	9-15	60%	278,640
8	Redgap Partnership	14-115	12%	242,355
9	Brian Sweetnam	3-6	50%	234,870
10	Supreme Horse Racing Club	18-52	35%	227,910
11	Hammer & Trowel Syndicate	2-9	22%	195,450
12	Neale/Murtagh Partnership	3-11	27%	166,530
13	Ms Fiona McStay	6-10	60%	144,000
14	G McGrath	5-9	56%	136,470
15	Mrs Patricia Hunt	7-35	20%	134,135
16	R A Scott	7-16	44%	131,910
17	Mrs P Sloan	6-48	13%	131,110
18	Mrs Caroline Mould	1-1	100%	126,000
19	Stephen Curran	2-6	33%	125,150
20	John Patrick Ryan	6-71	8%	118,900

POWER BROKERS The big three owners in Irish jump racing may be about to become the big four and, as well as dominating in Ireland, they look likely to stretch their influence even wider into the top British races in 2013-14.

The powerhouses are Geneva-based businessman JP McManus (depicted above left), who retained his British title, and the Gigginstown House Stud team of Ryanair boss Michael O'Leary (second left), who finished fourth in Britain but pushed McManus down to second in Ireland.

Rich Ricci (right), the former Barclays banker, was third in Ireland with the high-quality string he owns with his wife Susannah. He had a remarkable eight Grade 1 wins in Britain and Ireland in 2012-13 and with his trainer Willie Mullins

he is likely to target more of the British prizes this season.

The new challenger is Barry Connell (second right), the high-rolling investment fund manager who was fifth in Ireland and has spent big on top prospects Our Conor and Golantilla. His credo is simple: "You are paying the same to keep a good horse in training as a bad one, so it makes financial sense to buy better horses."

Between them, the quartet raked in more than €5m in prize-money in Ireland alone in the 2012-13 season and they now own ten of last season's 25 individual Grade 1 winners in Ireland as well as Cheltenham Festival Grade 1 winners Champagne Fever, At Fishers Cross and Our Conor.

The stage is set for a titanic battle.